GREAT

AMERICAN

ADVENTURE

STORIES

GREAT
AMERICAN
ADVENTURE
STORIES

EDITED BY
TOM McCARTHY

GUILFORD
CONNECTICUT

An imprint of Globe Pequot

Distributed by NATIONAL BOOK NETWORK

Copyright © 2017 by Thomas P. McCarthy

British Library Cataloguing in Publication Information Available

Library of Congress Cataloging-in-Publication Data

Name: McCarthy, Tom, 1953–, editor of compilation.
Title: Great American adventure stories / edited by Tom McCarthy.
Description: Guilford, Connecticut : Lyons Press Classics, [2017] | Includes
bibliographical references.
Identifiers: LCCN 2017009072 (print) | LCCN 2017019341 (ebook) | ISBN
9781493030002 (electronic) | ISBN 9781493029990 (pbk. : alk. paper)
Subjects: LCSH: United States—History—Anecdotes.
Classification: LCC E179 (ebook) | LCC E179 .G755 2017 (print) | DDC
973—dc23 LC record available at https://lccn.loc.gov/2017009072

∞™ The paper used in this publication meets the minimum requirements
of American National Standard for Information Sciences—Permanence of
Paper for Printed Library Materials, ANSI/NISO Z39.48-1992.

Printed in the United States of America

For Maggie and Britta,
just starting their own American adventures

CONTENTS

ABOUT THIS BOOK

BY TOM MCCARTHY

Americans love adventure. It is what this country was built on. This collection will give you an unvarnished look back at the events that forged America's reputation for calm resolve, courage, and an undiluted can-do spirit in the face of unrelenting challenges. In fact, it will reinforce that well-deserved reputation in spades.

Americans have also long loved reading, sitting back, and enjoying their rich and vibrant history from the comfort of their favorite chair. I am certain you'll love reading *Great American Adventure Stories*, but I can't promise it will be relaxing.

As the stories in this collection will show, facing death and overcoming fear were just another day at the office for the people featured. None wanted to be heroes, though they were. None wanted attention, and for the most part, they received very little. Until now, perhaps. Modesty suited every single person featured here. After all, that is another American trait. Perhaps the stories here will finally deliver a bit of much-deserved attention.

There has never been a more exciting collection of stories selected specifically to celebrate the uniqueness of the American character and the indomitable spirit forged as our country came of age.

Great American Adventure Stories is guaranteed to inform, entertain, and keep you turning the pages—even if it at times it will have you on the edge of your seat. These fifteen tales are a testament to courage, bravery, and the almost-innate ability of Americans to carry on in the face of tremendous challenge.

These true stories will all show that the unquenchable American thirst for excitement and adventure has remained intact throughout the years. *Great American Adventure Stories* presents long-hidden gems, stunning both in their accounts and in their skillful, almost-magnetic ways of weaving a story that is guaranteed to get the adrenaline flowing.

And along the way, you'll learn some interesting facts that have eluded many history books.

How did residents of the quiet town of Northfield, Minnesota, react to a robbery of the only bank in town by the notorious James and Younger brothers? Not well, you will learn. Perhaps you might like to imagine yourself among the frightened but resilient group of 109 Union Army officers who dug themselves out of the notoriously brutal Libby Prison—and the fate of the forty-eight who were recaptured. Many disinterested scholars have written of John Brown's historic raid on Harpers Ferry, West Virginia, but few actually saw it. Samuel Vanderlip Leech did, and you will find here his contemporaneous account, unvarnished and unfiltered. Along the way, you might be surprised to learn that that among the minor participants in this event were Robert E. Lee, J. E. B. Stuart, and John Wilkes Booth.

What happened to the last American pirate in the North Atlantic? You'll read how Mogul McKenzie met his fate. Looking for a good detective story from the Old West? D. J. Cook, chief of the Rocky Mountain Detective Agency, describes a troubling Colorado murder and how it was solved. Residents of Golden, Colorado, might be interested in trying to find the graves of two desperadoes buried by angry citizens.

Maybe you might want to spend a few weeks with the doomed Donner Party, frozen and famished in the high Sierras? Want a taste of the American frontier? Here is how Daniel Boone saw it as he looked for more elbow room. And how the famed scout Kit Carson viewed it as the young country expanded and blossomed in the West.

Here also is an eyewitness account of the Johnstown flood and the heroics it sparked from normal citizens trapped by the cataclysm. Another story captures the heat and chaos of the Alaska gold rush, written by a preacher who was directed by a friend who knew the rowdy crowds in Nome, "You were never needed more." Yet another story will take you nervously onto the deck of a ship trying to run a Civil War blockade.

That is the magic and magnetism of this collection. These stories offer fresh, firsthand perspectives that are free of the often more gentle versions written and filtered years later by historians. You will be surprised by Daniel Boone's reflections and grudging admiration for the Native Americans who held him captive. You will be stunned by the chilling observations of eyewitnesses of the aftermath of the Galveston hurricane, as they watched as "people realized that with every passing moment souls were being hurried into eternity."

These tales all have one thing in common: the real spit, grit, and spirit of people who made this country what it is today. It is good reading, indeed. But will it be relaxing? That is up to you.

1

THE TUNNEL AT LIBBY PRISON

A Civil War Escape

BY FRANK E. MORAN

Richmond's Libby Prison was dank, miserable, and foreboding. The rats and the cold and the scarcity of food were just minor inconveniences. To the undaunted Union soldiers crammed into it, there was only one thing to do—escape. There were a few obstacles to overcome first.

Among all the thrilling incidents in the history of Libby Prison, none exceeds in interest the celebrated tunnel escape which occurred on the night of February 9, 1864. I was one of the 109 Union officers who passed through the tunnel and one of the ill-fated 48 that were retaken. I and two companions—Lieutenant Charles H. Morgan of the 21st Wisconsin regiment, who has since served several terms in Congress from Missouri, and Lieutenant William L. Watson of the same company and regiment—when recaptured by the Confederate cavalry were in sight of the Union picket posts. Strange as it may appear, no accurate and complete account has ever been given to the public of this, the most ingenious and daring escape made on either side during the Civil War. Twelve of the party of fifteen who dug the tunnel are still living, including their leader.

Thomas E. Rose, colonel of the 77th Pennsylvania Volunteers, the engineer and leader in the plot throughout—now a captain in the 16th United States Infantry—was taken prisoner at the battle of Chickamauga, September 20, 1863. On his way to Richmond, he escaped from his guards at Weldon, North Carolina, but, after a day's wandering about the pine forests with a broken foot, was retaken by a detachment of Confederate cavalry and sent to Libby Prison, Richmond, where he arrived October 1, 1863.

Libby Prison fronts on Carey Street, Richmond, and stands upon a hill which descends abruptly to the canal, from which its southern wall is divided only by a street, and having a vacant lot on the east. The building was wholly detached, making it a comparatively easy matter to guard the prison securely with a small force and keep every door and window in full view from without. As an additional measure of safety, prisoners were not allowed on the ground floor, except that in the daytime they were permitted to use the first floor of the middle section for a cook room. The interior embraced nine large warehouse rooms 105 × 45, with eight feet from each floor to ceiling, except the upper floor, which gave more room, owing to the pitch of the gable roof. The abrupt slant of the hill gives the building an additional story on the south side. The whole building really embraces three sections, and these were originally separated by heavy blank walls. The Confederates cut doors through the walls of the two upper floors, which comprised the prisoners' quarters, and they were thus permitted to mingle freely with each other, but there was no communication whatever between the three large rooms on the first floor. Beneath these floors were three cellars of the same dimensions as the rooms above them, and, like them, divided from each other by massive blank walls. For ready comprehension, let these be designated the east, middle, and west cellars. Except in the lofts known as "Streight's room" and "Milroy's room," which were occupied by the earliest inmates of Libby in 1863, there was no furniture in the building, and only a few of the early comers possessed such a luxury as an old army blanket or a knife, cup, and tin plate. As a rule, the prisoner, by the time he reached Libby, found himself devoid of earthly goods, save the meager and dust-begrimed summer garb in which he had made his unlucky campaign.

At night the six large lofts presented strange war pictures, over which a single tallow candle wept copious and greasy tears that ran down over the petrified loaf of cornbread, Borden's condensed-milk can, or bottle in which it was set. The candle flickered on until "Taps," when the guards, with unconscious irony, shouted, "Lights out!"—at which signal it usually disappeared amid a shower of boots and such other missiles as were at hand. The sleepers covered the six floors, lying in ranks, head to head and foot to foot, like prostrate lines of battle. For the general good, and to preserve something like military precision, these ranks (especially when cold weather compelled them to lie close for better warmth) were subdivided into convenient squads under charge of a "captain," who was invested with authority to see that every man lay "spoon fashion."

No consideration of personal convenience was permitted to interfere with the general comfort of the "squad." Thus, when the hard floor could no longer be endured on the right side—especially by the thin men—the captain gave the command, "Attention, Squad Number

Four! Prepare to spoon! One—two—spoon!" And the whole squad flopped over on the left side.

The first floor on the west of the building was used by the Confederates as an office and for sleeping quarters for the prison officials, and a stairway guarded by sentinels led from this to Milroy's room just above it. As before explained, the middle room was shut off from the office by a heavy blank wall. This room, known as the "kitchen," had two stoves in it, one of which stood about ten feet from the heavy door that opened on the Carey Street sidewalk, and behind the door was a fireplace. The room contained also several long pine tables with permanent seats attached, such as may be commonly seen at picnic grounds. The floor was constantly inundated here by several defective and overworked water faucets and a leaky trough.

A stairway without banisters led up on the southwest end of the floor, above which was a room known as the "Chickamauga room," being chiefly occupied by Chickamauga prisoners. The sentinel who had formerly been placed at this stairway at night to prevent the prisoners from entering the kitchen had been withdrawn when, in the fall of 1863, the horrible condition of the floor made it untenable for sleeping purposes.

The uses to which the large ground-floor room east of the kitchen was put varied during the first two years of the war, but early in October of 1863 and thereafter, it was permanently used and known as the hospital, and it contained a large number of cots, which were never unoccupied. An apartment had been made at the north or front of the room, which served as a doctor's office and laboratory. Like those adjoining it on the west, this room had a large door opening on Carey Street, which was heavily bolted and guarded on the outside.

The arrival of the Chickamauga prisoners greatly crowded the upper floors and compelled the Confederates to board up a small portion of the east cellar at its southeast corner as an additional cook room, several large caldrons having been set in a rudely built furnace; so, for a short period, the prisoners were allowed down there in the daytime to cook. A stairway led from this cellar to the room above, which subsequently became the hospital.

Such, in brief, was the condition of things when Colonel Rose arrived at the prison. From the hour of his coming, a means of escape became his constant and eager study, and with this purpose in view, he made a careful and minute survey of the entire premises.

From the windows of the upper east or "Gettysburg room," he could look across the vacant lot on the east and get a glimpse of the yard between, two adjacent buildings which faced the canal and Carey Street, respectively, and he estimated the intervening space at about seventy feet. From the south windows, he looked out across a street upon the canal and James River, running parallel with each other, the two streams at this point being separated by a low and narrow strip of land. This strip periodically disappeared when protracted seasons of heavy rain came or when spring floods so rapidly swelled the river that the latter invaded the cellars of Libby. At such times it was common to see enormous swarms of rats come out from the lower doors and windows of the prison and make head for dry land in swimming platoons amid the cheers of the prisoners in the upper windows. On one or two occasions, Rose observed workmen descending from the middle of the south-side street into a sewer running through its center, and concluded that this sewer must have various openings to the canal both to the east and west of the prison.

The north portion of the cellar contained a large quantity of loose packing straw covering the floor to an average depth of two feet, and this straw afforded shelter, especially at night, for a large colony of rats, which gave the place the name of "Rat Hell."

In one afternoon's inspection of this dark end, Rose suddenly encountered a fellow prisoner, Major A. G. Hamilton of the 12th Kentucky Cavalry. A confiding friendship followed, and the two men entered at once upon the plan of gaining their liberty. They agreed that the most feasible scheme was a tunnel, to begin in the rear of the little kitchen-apartment at the southeast corner of Rat Hell. Without more ado they secured a broken shovel and two case knives and began operations.

Within a few days, the Confederates decided upon certain changes in the prison for the greater security of their captives. A week afterward the cook room was abandoned, the stairway nailed up, the prisoners sent to the upper floors, and all communication with the east cellar was cut off. This was a sore misfortune, for this apartment was the only possible base of successful tunnel operations. Colonel Rose now began to study other practicable means of escape and spent night after night examining the posts and watching the movements of the sentinels on the four sides of Libby. One very dark night, during a howling storm, Rose again unexpectedly met Hamilton in a place where no prisoner could reasonably be looked for at such an hour. For an instant the impenetrable darkness made it impossible for either to determine whether he had met a friend or foe: Neither had a weapon, yet each involuntarily felt for one, and each made ready to spring at the other's throat, when a flash of lightning revealed their identity. The two men had availed themselves of the darkness of the night and the roar of the storm to attempt an escape from a window of the upper west room to a platform that ran along the west outer wall of the prison, from which they hoped to reach the ground and elude the sentinels, whom they conjectured would be crouched in the shelter of some doorway or other partial refuge that might be available, but so vivid and frequent were the lightning flashes that the attempt was seen to be extremely hazardous.

Rose now spoke of the entrance from the south-side street to the middle cellar, having frequently noticed the entrance and exit of workmen at that point, and expressed his belief that, if an entrance could be effected to this cellar, it would afford them the only chance of slipping past the sentinels.

He hunted up a bit of pinewood, which he whittled into a sort of wedge, and the two men went down into the dark, vacant kitchen directly over this cellar. With the wedge Rose pried a floorboard out of its place and made an opening large enough to let himself through. He had never been in this middle cellar and was wholly ignorant of its contents or whether it was occupied by Confederates or workmen, but as he had made no noise and the place was in profound darkness, he decided to go down and reconnoiter.

He wrenched off one of the long boards that formed a table-seat in the kitchen and found that it was long enough to touch the cellar base and protrude a foot or so above the kitchen floor. By this means he easily descended, leaving Hamilton to keep watch above.

The storm still raged fiercely, and the faint beams of a streetlamp revealed the muffled form of the sentinel slowly pacing his beat and carrying his musket at "secure" arms. Creeping softly toward him along the cellar wall, he now saw that what he had supposed was a door was simply a naked opening to the street, and further inspection disclosed the fact that there was but one sentinel on the south side of the prison. Standing in the dark shadow, he could easily have touched this man with his hand as he repeatedly passed him. Groping about, he found various appurtenances indicating that the south end of this cellar was used for a carpenter's shop and that the north end was partitioned off into a series of small cells with padlocked doors and that through each door a square hole, a foot in diameter, was cut. Subsequently it was learned that these dismal cages were alternately used for the confinement of "troublesome prisoners"—i.e., those who had distinguished themselves by ingenious attempts to escape—and also for runaway slaves and Union spies under sentence of death.

At the date of Rose's first reconnaissance to this cellar, these cells were vacant and unguarded. The night was far spent, and Rose proceeded to return to the kitchen, where Hamilton was patiently waiting for him.

The very next day, a rare good fortune befell Rose. By an agreement between the commissioners of exchange, several bales of clothing and blankets had been sent by our government to the famishing Union prisoners on Belle Isle, a number of whom had already frozen to death. A committee of Union officers then confined in Libby consisting of General Neal Dow, Colonel Alexander von Shrader, Lieutenant Colonel Joseph F. Boyd, and Colonel Harry White, having been selected by the Confederates to supervise the distribution of the donation, Colonel White had, by a shrewd bit of finesse, "confiscated" a fine rope by which one of the bales was tied, and this he now presented to Colonel Rose. It was nearly a hundred feet long, an inch thick, and almost new.

It was hardly dark the following night before Rose and Hamilton were again in the kitchen, and as soon as all was quiet, Rose fastened his rope to one of the supporting posts, took up the floor plank as before, and both men descended to the middle cellar. They were not a little disappointed to discover that where there had been but one sentinel on the south side there were now two. On this and for several nights, they contented themselves with sly visits of observation to this cellar, during which Rose found and secreted various tools, among which were a broadax, a saw, two chisels, several files, and a carpenter's square. One dark night both men went down and determined to try their luck at passing the guards. Rose made the attempt and succeeded in passing the first man but unluckily was seen by the second. The latter called lustily for the corporal of the guard, and the first excitedly cocked his gun and peered into the dark door through which Rose swiftly retreated. The guard called, "Who goes there?" but did not enter the dark cellar. Rose and Hamilton mounted the rope and had just succeeded in replacing the plank when the corporal and a file of men entered the cellar with a lantern. They looked into every barrel and under every bench, but no sign of Yankees appeared, and as on this night it happened that several workmen were sleeping in an apartment at the north end, the corporal concluded that the man seen by the sentinel was one of these, notwithstanding their denial when awakened and questioned. After a long parley, the Confederates withdrew, and Hamilton and Rose, depressed in spirits, went to bed, Rose as usual concealing his rope.

Before the week was out, they were at it again. On one of these nights, Rose suddenly came upon one of the workmen and, swift as thought, seized the hidden broadax with the intention of braining him if he attempted an alarm, but the poor fellow was too much paralyzed to cry out, and when finally he did recover his voice and his wits, it was to beg Rose "for God's sake" not to come in there again at night. Evidently the man never mentioned the circumstance, for Rose's subsequent visits, which were soon resumed, disclosed no evidence of a discovery by the Confederates.

Hamilton agreed with Rose that there remained apparently but one means of escape, and that was by force. To overpower the two sentinels on the south side would have been an easy matter, but how to do it and not alarm the rest of the guard and, in consequence, the whole city was the problem. To secure these sentinels without alarming their comrades on the east, west, and north sides of the prison would require the swift action of several men of nerve acting in concert. Precious time was passing, and possibly further alterations might be decided upon that would shut them off from the middle cellar, as they had already been from their original base of operations. Moreover, a new cause of anxiety now appeared. It soon transpired that their nocturnal prowlings and close conferences together had already aroused the belief among many observant prisoners that a plan of escape was afoot, and both men were soon eagerly plied with guarded inquiries and besought by their questioners to admit them to their confidence.

Hamilton and Rose now decided to organize an escaping party. A number of men were then sworn to secrecy and obedience by Colonel Rose, who was the only recognized leader in all operations that followed. This party soon numbered seventy men. The band was then taken down by Rose in convenient details to the middle cellar or carpenter's shop on many nights to familiarize each man with the place and with his special part in the plot and also to take advantage of any favoring circumstances that might arise.

When all had by frequent visits become familiar with the rendezvous, Rose and the whole party descended one night with the determination to escape at whatever hazard. The men were assigned to their several stations as usual, and a selected few were placed by the leader close to the entrance, in front of which the sentinel was regularly passing. Rose commanded strict silence and placed himself near the exit preparatory to giving the signal. It was an exciting moment, and the bravest heart beat fast. A signal came but not the one they looked for. At the very moment of action, the man whom Rose had left at the floor opening in the kitchen gave the danger signal! The alert leader had, with consummate care, told every man beforehand that he must never be surprised by this signal—it was a thing to be counted upon— and that noise and panic were of all things to be avoided as fatal folly in their operations. As a consequence, when this signal came, Rose quietly directed the men to fall in line and reascend to the kitchen rapidly but without noise, which they did by the long rope which now formed the easy means of communication from the kitchen to the cellar.

Rose remained below to cover the retreat, and when the last man got up, he followed him, replaced the board in the floor, and concealed the rope. He had barely done so when a detail of Confederate guards entered the kitchen from the Carey Street door and, headed by an officer, marched straight in his direction. Meantime the party had disappeared up the stairway and swiftly made their way over their prostrate comrades' forms to their proper sleeping places. Rose, being the last up and having the floor to fix, had now no time to disappear like his companions, at least without suspicious haste. He accordingly took a seat at one of the tables and, putting an old pipe in his mouth, coolly awaited the approach of the Confederates. The officer of the guard came along, swinging his lantern almost in his face, stared at him for a second, and without a remark or a halt marched past him and ascended with his escort to the Chickamauga room. The entrance of a guard and their march around the prison, although afterward common enough after taps, was then an unusual thing, causing much talk among the prisoners, and to the mind of Rose and his fellow plotters was indicative of aroused suspicion on the part of the Confederates.

The whispering groups of men next day and the number of his eager questioners gave the leader considerable concern, and Hamilton suggested, as a measure of safety rather than choice, that some of the mischievous talk of escape would be suppressed by increasing the party. This was acted upon; the men, like the rest, were put under oath by Rose, and the party was thus increased to 420. This force would have been enough to overpower the prison guard in a few minutes, but the swift alarm certain to ensue in the streets and spread like wildfire over Richmond, the meager information possessed by the prisoners as to the strength and position of the nearest Federal troops, the strongly guarded labyrinth of breastworks that encircled the city, and the easy facilities for instant pursuit at the command of the Confederates put the success of such an undertaking clearly out of the range of probability, unless, indeed, some unusual favoring contingency should arise, such as the near approach of a cooperating column of Federal cavalry.

Nor was this an idle dream, as the country now knows, for even at this period General Kilpatrick was maturing his plans for that bold expedition for the rescue of the prisoners at Richmond and Belle Isle in which the lamented and heroic young cripple, Colonel Ulric Dahlgren, lost his life. Rose saw that a breakout of Libby without such outside assistance promised nothing but a fruitless sacrifice of life and the savage punishment of the survivors. Hence the project, although eagerly and exhaustively discussed, was prudently abandoned.

All talk of escape by the general crowd now wholly ceased, and the captives resigned themselves to their fate and waited with depressed spirits for the remote contingency of an exchange. The quiet thus gained was Rose's opportunity. He sought Hamilton and told him that they must by some stratagem regain access to Rat Hell and that the tunnel project must be at once revived. The latter assented to the proposition, and the two began earnestly to study the means of gaining an entrance without discovery into this coveted base of operations.

They could not even get into the room above the cellar they wanted to reach, for that was the hospital, and the kitchen's heavy wall shut them off therefrom. Neither could they break the heavy wall that divided this cellar from the carpenter's shop, which had been the nightly rendezvous of the party while the breakout was under consideration, for the breach certainly would be discovered by the workmen or Confederates, some of whom were in there constantly during daylight.

There was, in fact, but one plan by which Rat Hell could be reached without detection, and the conception of this device and its successful execution were due to the stout-hearted Hamilton. This was to cut a hole in the back of the kitchen fireplace; the incision must be just far enough to preserve the opposite or hospital side intact. It must then be cut downward to a point below the level of the hospital floor, then eastward into Rat Hell, the completed opening thus to describe the letter S. It must be wide enough to let a man through, yet the wall must not be broken on the hospital side above the floor nor marred on the carpenter's shop side below it. Such a break would be fatal, for both of these points were conspicuously exposed to the view of the Confederates every hour in the day. Moreover, it was imperatively necessary that all trace of the beginning of the opening should be concealed, not only from the Confederate officials and guards, who were constantly passing the spot every day, but from the hundreds of uninitiated prisoners who crowded around the stove just in front of it from dawn till dark.

Work could be possible only between the hours of ten at night, when the room was generally abandoned by the prisoners because of its inundated condition, and four o'clock in the morning, when the earliest risers were again astir. It was necessary to do the work with an old jackknife and one of the chisels previously secured by Rose. It must be done in darkness and without noise, for a vigilant sentinel paced on the Carey Street sidewalk just outside the door and within ten feet of the fireplace. A rubber blanket was procured, and the soot from the chimney carefully swept into it. Hamilton, with his old knife, cut the mortar between the bricks and pried a dozen of them out, being careful to preserve them whole.

The rest of the incision was made in accordance with the design described, but no conception could have been formed beforehand of the sickening tediousness of cutting an S-shaped hole through a heavy wall with a feeble old jackknife in stolen hours of darkness. Rose guarded his comrade against the constant danger of interruption by alert enemies on one side and by blundering friends on the other, and as frequently happens in human affairs, their friends gave them more trouble than their foes. Night after night passed, and still the two men got up after taps from their hard beds and descended to the dismal and reeking kitchen to bore for liberty. When the sentinel's call at Castle Thunder and at Libby announced four o'clock, the dislodged bricks were carefully replaced, and the soot previously gathered in the gum blanket was flung in handfuls against the restored wall, filling the seams between the bricks so thoroughly as to defy detection. At last, after many weary nights, Hamilton's heroic patience and skill were rewarded, and the way was open to the coveted base of operations, Rat Hell.

Now occurred a circumstance that almost revealed the plot and nearly ended in a tragedy. When the opening was finished, the long rope was made fast to one of the kitchen supporting posts, and Rose proceeded to descend and reconnoiter. He got partly through with ease but lost his hold in such a manner that his body slipped through so as to pinion his arms and leave him wholly powerless either to drop lower or return—the bend of the hole being such as to cramp his back and neck terribly and prevent him from breathing. He strove desperately, but each effort only wedged him more firmly in the awful vise. Hamilton sprang to his aid and did his utmost to effect his release, but powerful as he was, he could not budge him. Rose was gasping for breath and rapidly getting fainter, but even in this fearful strait, he refrained from an outcry that would certainly alarm the guards just outside the door. Hamilton saw that without speedy relief his comrade must soon smother. He dashed through the long, dark room up the stairway, over the forms of several hundred men, and disregarding consequences and savage curses in the dark and crowded room, he trampled upon arms, legs, faces, and stomachs, leaving riot and blasphemy in his track among the rudely awakened and now furious lodgers of the Chickamauga room. He sought the sleeping place of Major George H. Fitzsimmons, but he was missing. He, however, found Lieutenant F. F. Bennett of the 18th Regulars (since a major in the 9th United States Cavalry), to whom he told the trouble in a few hasty words. Both men fairly flew across the room, dashed down the stairs, and by their united efforts Rose, half-dead and quite speechless, was drawn up from the fearful trap.

Hamilton managed slightly to increase the size of the hole and provide against a repetition of the accident just narrated, and all being now ready, the two men entered eagerly upon the work before them. They appropriated one of the wooden spittoons of the prison and to each side attached a piece of clothesline, which they had been permitted to have to dry clothes on. Several bits of candle and the larger of the two chisels were also taken to the operating cellar. They kept this secret well and worked alone for many nights. In fact, they would have so continued, but they found that, after digging about four feet, their candle would go out in the vitiated air. Rose did the digging, and Hamilton fanned air into him with his hat; even then he had to emerge into the cellar every few minutes to breathe. Rose could dig but needed the light and air, and Hamilton could not fan and drag out and deposit the excavated earth and meantime keep a lookout. In fact, it was demonstrated that there was slim chance of succeeding without more assistance, and it was decided to organize a party large enough for effective work by reliefs. As a preliminary step and to afford the means of more rapid communication with the cellar from the fireplace opening, the long rope obtained from Colonel White was formed by Hamilton into a rope ladder with convenient wooden rungs. This alteration considerably increased its bulk and added to Rose's difficulty in concealing it from curious eyes.

He now made a careful selection of thirteen men besides himself and Hamilton and bound them by a solemn oath to secrecy and strict obedience. To form this party as he wanted it required some diplomacy, as it was known that the Confederates had on more than one occasion sent cunning spies into Libby disguised as Union prisoners for the detection of any contemplated plan of escape. Unfortunately, the complete list of the names of the party now formed has not been preserved, but among the party, besides Rose and Hamilton, were Captain John Sterling, 30th Indiana; Captain John Lucas, 5th Kentucky Cavalry; Captain Isaac N. Johnson, 6th Kentucky Cavalry; and Lieutenant F. F. Bennett, 18th Regulars.

The party being now formed were taken to Rat Hell and their several duties explained to them by Rose, who was invested with full authority over the work in hand. Work was begun in rear of the little kitchen room previously abandoned at the southeast corner of the cellar. To systematize the labor, the party was divided into squads of five each, which gave the men one night on duty and two off, Rose assigning each man to the branch of work in which experiments proved him the most proficient. He was himself, by long odds, the best digger of the party, while Hamilton had no equal for ingenious mechanical skill in contriving helpful, little devices to overcome or lessen the difficulties that beset almost every step of the party's progress.

The first plan was to dig down alongside the east wall and under it until it was passed, then turn southward and make for the large street sewer next the canal and into which Rose had before noticed workmen descending. This sewer was a large one, believed to be fully six feet high, and if it could be gained, there could be little doubt that an adjacent opening to the canal would be found to the eastward. It was very soon revealed, however, that the lower side of Libby was built upon ponderous timbers, below which they could not hope to penetrate with their meager stock of tools—such, at least, was the opinion of nearly all the party. Rose nevertheless determined that the effort should be made, and they were soon at work with old penknives and case knives hacked into saws. After infinite labor they at length cut through the great logs, only to be met by an unforeseen and still more formidable barrier. Their tunnel, in fact, had penetrated below the level of the canal. Water began to filter in—feebly at first, but at last it broke in with a rush that came near drowning Rose, who barely had time to make his escape. This opening was therefore plugged up, and to do this rapidly and leave no dangerous traces put the party to their wit's end.

An attempt was next made to dig into a small sewer that ran from the southeast corner of the prison into the main sewer. After a number of nights of hard labor, this opening was extended to a point below a brick furnace in which were incased several caldrons. The weight of this furnace caused a cave-in near the sentinel's path outside the prison wall. Next day, a group of officers were seen eying the break curiously. Rose, listening at a window above, heard the words *rats* repeated by them several times and took comfort. The next day he entered the cellar alone, feeling that, if the suspicions of the Confederates were really awakened, a trap would be set for him in Rat Hell and determined, if such were really the case, that he would be the only victim caught. He therefore entered the little partitioned corner room with some anxiety, but there was no visible evidence of a visit by the guards, and his spirits again rose.

The party now reassembled, and an effort was made to get into the small sewer that ran from the cook room to the big sewer which Rose was so eager to reach, but soon it was discovered, to the utter dismay of the weary party, that this wood-lined sewer was too small to let a man through it. Still it was hoped by Rose that by removing the plank with which it was lined the passage could be made. The spirits of the party were by this time considerably dashed by their repeated failures and sickening work, but the undaunted Rose, aided by Hamilton, persuaded the men to another effort, and soon the knives and toy saws were at work again with vigor. The work went on so swimmingly that it was confidently believed that an entrance to the main sewer would be gained on the night of January 26, 1864.

On the night of the 25th, two men had been left down in Rat Hell to cover any remaining traces of a tunnel, and when night came again, it was expected that all would be ready for the escape between eight and nine o'clock. In the meantime, the two men were to enter and make careful examination of the main sewer and its adjacent outlets. The party, which was now in readiness for its march to the Federal camps, waited tidings from these two men all next day in tormenting anxiety, and the weary hours went by on leaden wings. At last the sickening word came that the planks yet to be removed before they could enter the main sewer were of seasoned oak—hard as bone and three inches thick. Their feeble tools were now worn out or broken; they could no longer get air to work or keep a light in the horrible pit, which was reeking with cold mud; in short, any attempt at further progress with the utensils at hand was foolish.

Most of the party were now really ill from the foul stench in which they had lived so long. The visions of liberty that had first lured them to desperate efforts under the inspiration of Rose and Hamilton had at last faded, and one by one they lost heart and hope and frankly told Colonel Rose that they could do no more. The party was therefore disbanded, and the yet sanguine leader, with Hamilton for his sole helper, continued the work alone. Up to this time, thirty-nine nights had been spent in the work of excavation. The two men now made a careful examination of the northeast corner of the cellar, at which point the earth's surface outside the prison wall, being eight or nine feet higher than at the canal or south side, afforded a better place to dig than the latter, being free from water and with clay top enough to support itself. The unfavorable feature of this point was that the only possible terminus of a tunnel was a yard between the buildings beyond the vacant lot on the east of Libby. Another objection was that, even when the tunnel should be made to that point, the exit of any escaping party must be made through an arched wagonway under the building that faced the street on the canal side, and every man must emerge on the sidewalk in sight of the sentinel on the south side of the prison, the intervening space being in the full glare of the gas lamp. It was carefully noted, however, by Rose long before this that the west end of the beat of the nearest sentinel was between fifty and sixty feet from the point of egress, and it was concluded that by walking away at the moment the sentinel commenced his pace westward, one would be far enough into the shadow to make it improbable that the color of his clothing could be made out by the sentinel when he faced about to return toward the eastern end of his beat, which terminated ten to fifteen feet east of the prison wall. It was further considered that, as these sentinels had for their special duty the guarding of the prison, they would not be eager to burden themselves with the duty of molesting persons seen in the vicinity outside of their jurisdiction, provided, of course, that the retreating forms—many of which they must certainly see—were not recognized as Yankees. All others they might properly leave for the challenge and usual examination of the provost guard, who patrolled the streets of Richmond.

The wall of that east cellar had to be broken in three places before a place was found where the earth was firm enough to support a tunnel.

The two men worked on with stubborn patience, but their progress was painfully slow. Rose dug assiduously, and Hamilton alternately fanned air to his comrade and dragged out and hid the excavated dirt, but the old difficulty confronted him. The candle would not burn, the air could not be fanned fast enough with a hat, and the dirt hidden without better contrivances or additional help.

Rose now reassembled the party and selected from them a number who were willing to renew the attempt. Against the east wall stood a series of stone fenders abutting inward, and these, being at uniform intervals of about twenty feet, cast deep shadows that fell toward the prison front. In one of these dark recesses, the wall was pierced, well up toward the Carey Street end. The earth here has very densely compressed sand that offered a strong resistance to the broad-bladed chisel, which was their only effective implement, and it was clear that a long turn of hard work must be done to penetrate under the fifty-foot lot to the objective point. The lower part of the tunnel was about six inches above the level of the cellar floor, and its top, about two and a half feet. Absolute accuracy was, of course, impossible, either in giving the hole a perfectly horizontal direction or in preserving uniform dimensions, but a fair level was preserved, and the average diameter of the tunnel was a little over two feet. Usually one man would dig and fill the spittoon with earth; upon the signal of a gentle pull, an assistant would drag the load into the cellar by the clotheslines fastened to each side of this box and then hide it under the straw; a third constantly fanned air into the tunnel with a rubber blanket stretched across a frame, the invention of the ingenious Hamilton; a fourth would give occasional relief to the last two, while a fifth would keep a lookout.

The party now consisted of Colonel Thomas E. Rose, 77th Pennsylvania; Major A. G. Hamilton, 12th Kentucky; Captain Terrance

Clark, 79th Illinois; Major George H. Fitzsimmons, 30th Indiana; Captain John F. Gallagher, 2d Ohio: Captain W. S. B. Randall, 2d Ohio; Captain John Lucas, 5th Kentucky; Captain I. N. Johnson, 6th Kentucky; Major B. B. McDonald, 101st Ohio; Lieutenant N. S. McKean, 21st Illinois; Lieutenant David Garbett, 77th Pennsylvania; Lieutenant J. C. Fislar, 7th Indiana Artillery; Lieutenant John D. Simpson, 10th Indiana; Lieutenant John Mitchell, 79th Illinois; and Lieutenant Eli Foster, 30th Indiana. This party was divided into three reliefs as before, and the work of breaking the cellar wall was successfully done the first night by McDonald and Clark.

The danger of discovery was continual, for the guards were under instructions from the prison commandant to make occasional visits to every accessible part of the building, so that it was not unusual for a sergeant and several men to enter the south door of Rat Hell in the daytime, while the diggers were at labor in the dark north end. During these visits the digger would watch the intruders with his head sticking out of the tunnel, while the others would crouch behind the low stone fenders or crawl quickly under the straw. This was, however, so uninviting a place that the Confederates made this visit as brief as a nominal compliance with their orders permitted, and they did not often venture into the dark north end. The work was fearfully monotonous and the more so because absolute silence was commanded, the men moving about mutely in the dark. The darkness caused them frequently to become bewildered and lost, and as Rose could not call out for them, he had often to hunt all over the big dungeon to gather them up and pilot them to their places.

The difficulty of forcing air to the digger, whose body nearly filled the tunnel, increased as the hole was extended and compelled the operator to back often into the cellar for air, and for air that was itself foul enough to sicken a strong man.

But they were no longer harassed with the water and timbers that had impeded their progress at the south end. Moreover, experience was daily making each man more proficient in the work. Rose urged them on with cheery enthusiasm, and their hopes rose high, for already they had penetrated beyond the sentinel's beat and were nearing the goal.

The party off duty kept a cautious lookout from the upper east windows for any indications of suspicion on the part of the Confederates. In this extreme caution was necessary, both to avert the curiosity of prisoners in those east rooms and to keep out of the range of bullets from the guards, who were under a standing order to fire at a head if seen at a window or at a hand if placed on the bars that secured them. A sentinel's bullet one day cut a hole in the ear of Lieutenant Hammond; another officer was wounded in the face by a bullet, which fortunately first splintered against one of the window bars, and a captain of an Ohio regiment was shot through the head and instantly killed while reading a newspaper. He was violating no rule whatever and when shot was from eight to ten feet inside the window through which the bullet came. This was a wholly unprovoked and wanton murder; the cowardly miscreant had fired the shot while he was off duty and from the north sidewalk of Carey Street. The guards (home guards they were) used, in fact, to gun for prisoners' heads from their posts below, pretty much after the fashion of boys after squirrels; and the whizz of a bullet through the windows became too common an occurrence to occasion remark unless someone was shot.

Under a standing rule, the twelve hundred prisoners were counted twice each day, the first count being made about nine in the morning, and the last, about four in the afternoon. This duty was habitually done by the clerk of the prison, E. W. Ross, a civilian employed by the commandant. He was christened "Little Ross" by the prisoners because of his diminutive size. Ross was generally attended by either "Dick"

Turner, Adjutant Latouche, or Sergeant George Stansil of the 18th Georgia, with a small guard to keep the prisoners in four closed ranks during the count. The commandant of the prison, Major Thomas P. Turner (no relative of Dick's), seldom came upstairs.

To conceal the absence of the five men who were daily at work at the tunnel, their comrades of the party off digging duty resorted, under Rose's supervision, to a device of "repeating." This scheme, which was of vital importance to hoodwink the Confederates and avert mischievous curiosity among the uninformed prisoners, was a hazardous business that severely taxed the ingenuity and strained the nerve of the leader and his coadjutors. The manner of the fraud varied with circumstances, but in general it was worked by five of Rose's men, after being counted at or near the head of the line, stooping down and running toward the foot of the ranks, where a few moments later they were counted a second time, thus making Ross's book balance. The whole five, however, could not always do this undiscovered, and perhaps but three of the number could repeat. These occasional mishaps threatened to dethrone the reason of the puzzled clerk, but in the next count the "repeaters" would succeed in their game, and for the time all went well, until one day some of the prisoners took it into their heads, "just for the fun of the thing," to imitate the repeaters. Unconscious of the curses that the party were mentally hurling at them, the meddlers' sole purpose was to make "Little Ross" mad. In this they certainly met with signal success, for the reason of the mystified clerk seemed to totter as he repeated the count over and over in the hope of finding out how one careful count would show that three prisoners were missing and the next an excess of fifteen. Finally Ross, lashed into uncontrollable fury by the sarcastic remarks of his employers and the heartless merriment of the grinning Yanks before him, poured forth his goaded soul as follows: "Now, gentlemen, look yere. I can count a hundred as good as any blank man in this yere town, but I'll be blank blanked if I can count a hundred of you blanked Yankees. Now, gentlemen, there's one thing sho: There's eight or ten of you-uns yere that ain't yere!"

This extraordinary accusation "brought down the house," and the Confederate officers and guards and finally Ross himself were caught by the resistless contagion of laughter that shook the rafters of Libby.

The officials somehow found a balance that day on the books, and the danger was for this once over, to the infinite relief of Rose and his anxious comrades. But the Confederates appeared dissatisfied with something and came upstairs next morning with more officers and with double the usual number of guards, and some of these were now stationed about the room so as to make it next to impossible to work the repeating device successfully. On this day, for some reason, there were but two men in the cellar, and these were Major B. B. McDonald and Captain I. N. Johnson.

The count began as usual, and despite the guard in rear, two of the party attempted the repeating device by forcing their way through the center of the ranks toward the left, but the "fun of the thing" had now worn out with the unsuspecting meddlers, who resisted the passage of the two men. This drew the attention of the Confederate officers, and the repeaters were threatened with punishment. The result was inevitable: The count showed two missing. It was carefully repeated, with the same result. To the dismay of Rose and his little band, the prison register was now brought upstairs, and a long, tedious roll call by name was endured, each man passing through a narrow door as his name was called and between a line of guards.

No stratagem that Rose could now invent could avert the discovery by the Confederates that McDonald and Johnson had disappeared, and the mystery of their departure would be almost certain to cause an inquiry and investigation that would put their plot in peril and probably reveal it.

At last the Js were reached, and the name of I. N. Johnson was lustily shouted and repeated, with no response. The roll call proceeded until the name of B. B. McDonald was reached. To the increasing amazement of everybody but the conspirators, he also had vanished. A careful note was taken of these two names by the Confederates, and a thousand tongues were now busy with the names of the missing men and their singular disappearance.

The conspirators were in a tight place and must choose between two things. One was for the men in the cellar to return that night and face the Confederates with the most plausible explanation of their absence that they could invent, and the other alternative was the revolting one of remaining in their horrible abode until the completion of the tunnel.

When night came the fireplace was opened, and the unlucky pair were informed of the situation of affairs and asked to choose between the alternatives presented. McDonald decided to return and face the music, but Johnson, doubtful if the Confederates would be hoodwinked by any explanation, voted to remain where he was and wait for the finish of the tunnel.

As was anticipated, McDonald's return awakened almost as much curiosity among the inhabitants of Libby as his disappearance, and he was soon called to account by the Confederates. He told them he had fallen asleep in an out-of-the-way place in the upper west room, where the guards must have overlooked him during the roll call of the day before. McDonald was not further molested. The garrulous busybodies, who were Rose's chief dread, told the Confederate officials that they had certainly slept near Johnson the night before the day he was missed. Lieutenant J. C. Fislar (of the working party), who also slept next to Johnson, boldly declared this a case of mistaken identity and confidently expressed his belief to both Confederates and Federals who gathered around him that Johnson had escaped and was by this time, no doubt, safe in the Union lines. To this he added the positive statement that Johnson had not been in his accustomed sleeping place for a good many nights. The busybodies, who had indeed told the truth, looked at the speaker in speechless amazement but reiterated their statements. Others of the conspirators, however, took Fislar's bold cue and stoutly corroborated him.

Johnson, was, of course, nightly fed by his companions and gave them such assistance as he could at the work, but it soon became apparent that a man could not long exist in such a pestilential atmosphere. No tongue can tell how long were the days and nights the poor fellow passed among the squealing rats—enduring the sickening air; the deathly chill; the horrible, interminable darkness. One day out of three was an ordeal for the workers, who at least had a rest of two days afterward. As a desperate measure of relief, it was arranged, with the utmost caution, that late each night Johnson should come upstairs, when all was dark and the prison in slumber, and sleep among the prisoners until just before the time for closing the fireplace opening, about four o'clock each morning. As he spoke to no one and the room was dark, his presence was never known, even to those who lay next to him, and indeed he listened to many earnest conversations between his neighbors regarding his wonderful disappearance.

As a matter of course, the incidents above narrated made day work on the tunnel too hazardous to be indulged in on account of the increased difficulty of accounting for absentees, but the party continued the night work with unabated industry.

When the opening had been extended nearly across the lot, some of the party believed they had entered under the yard which was the intended terminus, and one night, when McDonald was the digger, so confident was he that the desired distance had been made that he turned his direction upward and soon broke through to the surface. A glance showed him his nearly fatal blunder, against which, indeed, he had been earnestly warned by Rose, who from the first had carefully estimated the intervening distance between the east wall of Libby and the terminus. In fact, McDonald saw that he had broken through in the open lot which was all in full view of a sentinel who was dangerously close. Appalled by what he had done, he retreated to the cellar and reported the disaster to his companions. Believing that discovery was now certain, the party sent one of their number up the rope to report to Rose, who was asleep. The hour was about midnight when the leader learned of the mischief. He quickly got up, went down to the cellar, entered the tunnel, and examined the break. It was not so near the sentinel's path as McDonald's excited report indicated, and fortunately the breach was at a point whence the surface sloped downward toward the east. He took off his blouse and stuffed it into the opening, pulling the dirt over it noiselessly, and in a few minutes, there was little surface evidence of the hole. He then backed into the cellar in the usual crab fashion and gave directions for the required depression of the tunnel and vigorous resumption of the work. The hole made in the roof of the tunnel was not much larger than a rat-hole and could not be seen from the prison. But the next night, Rose shoved an old shoe out of the hole, and the day afterward he looked down through the prison bars and saw the shoe lying where he had placed it and judged from its position that he had better incline the direction of the tunnel slightly to the left.

Meantime Captain Johnson was dragging out a wretched existence in Rat Hell and for safety was obliged to confine himself by day to the dark north end, for the Confederates often came into the place very suddenly through the south entrance. When they ventured too close, Johnson would get into a pit that he had dug under the straw as a hiding hole both for himself and the tunnelers' tools and quickly cover himself with a huge heap of short packing straw. A score of times he came near being stepped upon by the Confederates, and more than once the dust of the straw compelled him to sneeze in their very presence.

On Saturday, February 6, a larger party than usual of the Confederates came into the cellar, walked by the very mouth of the tunnel, and seemed to be making a critical survey of the entire place. They remained an unusually long time and conversed in low tones; several of them even kicked the loose straw about, and in fact everything seemed to indicate to Johnson—who was the only one of the working party now in the cellar—that the long-averted discovery had been made. That night he reported matters fully to Rose at the fireplace opening.

The tunnel was now nearly completed, and when Rose conveyed Johnson's message to the party, it caused dismay. Even the stouthearted Hamilton was for once excited, and the leader whose unflinching fortitude had thus far inspired his little band had his brave spirits dashed. But his buoyant courage rose quickly to its high and natural level. He could no longer doubt that the suspicions of the Confederates were aroused, but he felt convinced that these suspicions had not as yet assumed such a definite shape as most of his companions thought; still, he had abundant reason to believe that the success of the tunnel absolutely demanded its speedy completion, and he now firmly resolved that a desperate effort should be made to that end.

Remembering that the next day was Sunday and that it was not customary for the Confederates to visit the operating cellar on that day, he determined to make the most in his power of the now-precious time. He therefore caused all the party to remain upstairs, directing them to keep a close watch upon the Confederates from all available points of observation to avoid being seen in whispering groups—in short, to avoid all things calculated to excite the curiosity of friends or the suspicion of enemies—and to await his return.

Taking McDonald with him, he went down through the fireplace before daylight on Sunday morning, and bidding Johnson to keep a vigilant watch for intruders and McDonald to fan air into him, he entered the tunnel and began the forlorn hope. From this time forward, he never once turned over the chisel to a relief.

All day long he worked with the tireless patience of a beaver. When night came, even his single helper, who performed the double duty of fanning air and hiding the excavated earth, was ill from his hard, long task and the deadly air of the cellar. Yet this was as nothing compared with the fatigue of the duty that Rose had performed, and when at last, far into the night, he backed into the cellar, he had scarcely strength enough to stagger across to the rope ladder.

He had made more than double the distance that had been accomplished under the system of reliefs on any previous day, and the non-appearance of the Confederates encouraged the hope that another day without interruption would see the work completed. He therefore determined to refresh himself by a night's sleep for the finish. The drooping spirits of his party were revived by the report of his progress and his unalterable confidence.

Monday morning dawned, and the great prison with its twelve hundred captives was again astir. The general crowd did not suspect the suppressed excitement and anxiety of the little party that waited through that interminable day, which they felt must determine the fate of their project.

Rose had repeated the instructions of the day before and again descended to Rat Hell with McDonald for his only helper. Johnson reported all quiet, and McDonald taking up his former duties at the tunnel's mouth, Rose once more entered with his chisel. It was now the seventeenth day since the present tunnel was begun, and he resolved it should be the last. Hour after hour passed, and still the busy chisel was plied, and still the little wooden box with its freight of earth made its monotonous trips from the digger to his comrade and back again.

From the early morning of Monday, February 8, 1864, until an hour after midnight the next morning, his work went on. As midnight approached, Rose was nearly a physical wreck: The perspiration dripped from every pore of his exhausted body; food he could not have eaten if he had had it. His labors thus far had given him a somewhat exaggerated estimate of his physical powers. The sensation of fainting was strange to him, but his staggering senses warned him that to faint where he was meant at once his death and burial. He could scarcely inflate his lungs with the poisonous air of the pit; his muscles quivered with increasing weakness and the warning spasmodic tremor which their unnatural strain induced; his head swam like that of a drowning person.

By midnight he had struck and passed beyond a post which he felt must be in the yard. During the last few minutes, he had directed his course upward, and to relieve his cramped limbs, he turned upon his back. His strength was nearly gone; the feeble stream of air which his comrade was trying, with all his might, to send to him from a distance of fifty-three feet could no longer reach him through the deadly stench. His senses reeled; he had not breath or strength enough to move backward through his narrow grave. In the agony of suffocation, he dropped the dull chisel and beat his two fists against the roof of his grave with the might of despair—when, blessed boon! The crust gave way, and the loosened earth showered upon his dripping face, purple with agony; his famished eye caught sight of a radiant star in the blue vault above him; a flood of light and a volume of cool, delicious air poured over him. At that very instant, the sentinel's cry rang out like a prophecy—"Half past one, and all's well!"

Recovering quickly under the inspiring air, he dragged his body out of the hole and made a careful survey of the yard in which he found himself. He was under a shed, with a board fence between him and the east-side sentinels, and the gable end of Libby loomed grimly against the blue sky. He found the wagonway under the south-side building closed from the street by a gate fastened by a swinging bar, which, after a good many efforts, he succeeded in opening. This was the only exit to the street. As soon as the nearest sentinel's back was turned, he stepped out and walked quickly to the east. At the first corner, he turned north, carefully avoiding the sentinels in front of the "Pemberton Buildings" (another military prison northeast of Libby), and at the corner above this, he went westward, then south to the edge of the canal, and thus, by cautious moving, made a minute examination of Libby from all sides.

Having satisfied his desires, he retraced his steps to the yard. He hunted up an old bit of heavy plank, crept back into the tunnel feet first, drew the plank over the opening to conceal it from the notice of any possible visitors to the place, and crawled back to Rat Hell. McDonald was overjoyed, and poor Johnson almost wept with delight, as Rose handed one of them his victorious old chisel and gave the other some trifle he had picked up in the outer world as a token that the underground railroad to God's country was open.

Rose now climbed the rope ladder, drew it up, rebuilt the fireplace wall as usual, and, finding Hamilton, took him over near one of the windows and broke the news to him. The brave fellow was almost speechless with delight and, quickly hunting up the rest of the party, told them that Colonel Rose wanted to see them down in the dining room.

As they had been waiting news from their absent leader with feverish anxiety for what had seemed to them all the longest day in their lives, they instantly responded to the call and flocked around Rose a few minutes later in the dark kitchen, where he waited them. As yet, they did not know what news he brought, and they could scarcely wait for him to speak out, and when he announced, "Boys, the tunnel is finished," they could hardly repress a cheer. They wrung his hand again and again and danced about with childish joy.

It was now nearly three o'clock in the morning. Rose and Hamilton were ready to go out at once and indeed were anxious to do so, since every day of late had brought some new peril to their plans. None of the rest, however, were ready, and all urged the advantage of having a whole night in which to escape through and beyond the Richmond fortifications instead of the few hours of darkness which now preceded the day. To this proposition Rose and Hamilton somewhat reluctantly assented. It was agreed that each man of the party should have the privilege of taking one friend into his confidence and that the second party of fifteen thus formed should be obligated not to follow the working party out of the tunnel until an hour had elapsed. Colonel H. C. Hobart of the 21st Wisconsin was deputed to see that the program was observed. He was to draw up the rope ladder, hide it, and rebuild the wall and the next night was himself to lead out the second party, deputing some trustworthy leader to follow with still another party on the third night, and thus it was to continue until as many as possible should escape.

On Tuesday evening, February 9, at seven o'clock, Colonel Rose assembled his party in the kitchen and, posting himself at the fireplace, which he opened, waited until the last man went down. He bade Colonel Hobart goodbye, went down the hole, and waited until he had heard his comrade pull up the ladder and finally heard him replace the bricks in the fireplace and depart. He now crossed Rat Hell to the entrance into the tunnel and placed the party in the order in which they were to go out. He gave each a parting caution, thanked his brave comrades for their faithful labors, and, feelingly shaking their hands, bade them Godspeed and farewell.

He entered the tunnel first, with Hamilton next, and was promptly followed by the whole party through the tunnel and into the yard. He opened the gate leading toward the canal and signaled the party that all was clear. Stepping out on the sidewalk as soon as the nearest sentinel's back was turned, he walked briskly down the street to the east and a square below was joined by Hamilton. The others followed at intervals of a few minutes and disappeared in various directions in groups usually of three.

The plan agreed upon between Colonels Rose and Hobart was frustrated by information of the party's departure leaking out, and before nine o'clock, the knowledge of the existence of the tunnel and of the departure of the first party was flashed over the crowded prison, which was soon a convention of excited and whispering men. Colonel Hobart made a brave effort to restore order, but the frenzied crowd that now fiercely struggled for precedence at the fireplace was beyond human control.

Some of them had opened the fireplace and were jumping down like sheep into the cellar, one after another. The colonel implored the maddened men at least to be quiet and put the rope ladder in position and escaped himself.

My companion, Sprague, was already asleep when I lay down that night, but my other companion, Duenkel, who had been hunting for me, was very much awake, and seizing me by the collar, he whispered excitedly the fact that Colonel Rose had gone out at the head of a party through a tunnel. For a brief moment, the appalling suspicion that my friend's reason had been dethroned by illness and captivity swept over my mind, but a glance toward the window at the east end showed a quiet but apparently excited group of men from other rooms, and I now observed that several of them were bundled up for a march. The hope of regaining liberty thrilled me like a current of electricity. Looking through the window, I could see the escaping men appear one by one on the sidewalk below, opposite the exit yard, and silently disappear, without hindrance or challenge by the prison sentinels. While I was eagerly surveying this scene, I lost track of Duenkel, who had gone in search of further information, but ran against Lieutenant Harry Wilcox of the 1st New York, whom I knew and who appeared to have the "tip" regarding the tunnel. Wilcox and I agreed to unite our fortunes in the escape. My shoes were nearly worn out, and my clothes were thin and ragged. I was ill-prepared for a journey in midwinter through the enemy's country; happily I had my old overcoat, and this I put on. I had not a crumb of food saved up, as did those who were posted, but as I was ill at the time, my appetite was feeble.

Wilcox and I hurried to the kitchen, where we found several hundred men struggling to be first at the opening in the fireplace. We took our places behind them, and soon two hundred more closed us tightly in the mass. The room was pitch-dark, and the sentinel could be seen through the door cracks within a dozen feet of us. The fight for precedence was savage, though no one spoke, but now and then fainting men begged to be released. They begged in vain; certainly some of them must have been permanently injured. For my own part, when

I neared the stove, I was nearly suffocated, but I took heart when I saw but three more men between me and the hole. At this moment a sound as of tramping feet was heard, and some idiot on the outer edge of the mob startled us with the cry, "The guards, the guards!" A fearful panic ensued, and the entire crowd bounded toward the stairway leading up to their sleeping quarters. The stairway was unbanistered, and some of the men were forced off the edge and fell on those beneath. I was among the lightest in that crowd, and when it broke and expanded, I was taken off my feet, dashed to the floor senseless, my head and one of my hands bruised and cut and my shoulder painfully injured by the boots of the men who rushed over me. When I gathered my swimming wits, I was lying in a pool of water. The room seemed darker than before, and to my grateful surprise, I was alone. I was now convinced that it was a false alarm and quickly resolved to avail myself of the advantage of having the whole place to myself. I entered the cavity feet first but found it necessary to remove my overcoat and push it through the opening, and it fell in the darkness below.

I had now no comrade, having lost Wilcox in the stampede. Rose and his party, being the first out, were several hours on their journey, and I burned to be away, knowing well that my salvation depended on my passage beyond the city defenses before the pursuing guards were on our trail, when the inevitable discovery should come at roll call. The fact that I was alone I regretted, but I had served with McClellan in the Peninsula Campaign of 1862; I knew the country well from my frequent inspection of war maps, and the friendly north star gave me my bearings. The rope ladder had either become broken or disarranged, but it afforded me a short hold at the top, so I balanced myself, trusted to fortune, and fell into Rat Hell, which was a rayless pit of darkness, swarming with squealing rats, several of which I must have killed in my fall. I felt a troop of them run over my face and hands before I could regain my feet. Several times I put my hand on them, and once I flung one from my shoulder. Groping around, I found a stout stick or stave, put my back to the wall, and beat about me blindly but with vigor.

In spite of the hurried instructions given me by Wilcox, I had a long and horrible hunt over the cold surface of the cellar walls in my efforts to find the entrance to the tunnel, and in two minutes after I began feeling my way with my hands, I had no idea in what part of the place was the point where I had fallen; my bearings were completely lost, and I must have made the circuit of Rat Hell several times. At my entrance the rats seemed to receive me with cheers sufficiently hearty, I thought, but my vain efforts to find egress seemed to kindle anew their enthusiasm. They had received large reinforcements, and my march around was now received with deafening squeaks. Finally, my exploring hands fell upon a pair of heels which vanished at my touch. Here at last was the narrow road to freedom! The heels proved to be the property of Lieutenant Charles H. Morgan, 21st Wisconsin, a Chickamauga prisoner. Just ahead of him in the tunnel was Lieutenant William L. Watson of the same company and regiment. With my cut hand and bruised shoulder, the passage through the cold, narrow grave was indescribably horrible, and when I reached the terminus in the yard, I was sick and faint. The passage seemed to me to be a mile long, but the crisp, pure air and the first glimpse of freedom, the sweet sense of being out of doors, and the realization that I had taken the first step toward liberty and home had a magical effect in my restoration.

I have related before, in a published reminiscence, my experience and that of my two companions above named in the journey toward the Union lines and our recapture, but the more important matter relating to the plot itself has never been published. This is the leading motive of this article, and therefore I will not intrude the details of my personal experience into the narrative. It is enough to say that it was a chapter of hairbreadth escapes, hunger, cold, suffering, and—alas!—failure. We were run down and captured in a swamp several miles north of Charlottesville, and when we were taken, our captors pointed out to us the smoke over a Federal outpost. We were brought back to Libby and put in one of the dark, narrow dungeons. I was afterward confined in Macon, Georgia; Charleston and Columbia, South Carolina; and in Charlotte, North Carolina. After a captivity of just a year and eight months, during which I had made five escapes and was each time retaken, I was at last released on March 1, 1865, at Wilmington, North Carolina.

Great was the panic in Libby when the next morning's roll revealed to the astounded Confederates that 109 of their captives were missing, and as the fireplace had been rebuilt by someone and the opening of the hole in the yard had been covered by the last man who went out, no human trace guided the keepers toward a solution of the mystery. The Richmond papers having announced the "miraculous" escape of 109 Yankee officers from Libby, curious crowds flocked thither for several days, until someone, happening to remove the plank in the yard, revealed the tunnel.

Several circumstances at this time combined to make this escape peculiarly exasperating to the Confederates. In obedience to repeated appeals from the Richmond newspapers, iron bars had but recently been fixed in all the prison windows for better security, and the guard had been considerably reinforced. The columns of these same journals had just been aglow with accounts of the daring and successful escape of the Confederate general John Morgan and his companions from the Columbus (Ohio) jail. Morgan had arrived in Richmond on the 8th of January, exactly a month prior to the completion of the tunnel, and was still the lion of the Confederate capital.

At daylight a plank was seen suspended on the outside of the east wall; this was fastened by a blanket rope to one of the window bars and was, of course, a trick to mislead the Confederates. General John H. Winder, then in charge of all the prisoners in the Confederacy, with his headquarters in Richmond, was furious when the news reached him. After a careful external examination of the building and a talk, not of the politest kind, with Major Turner, he reached the conclusion that such an escape had but one explanation—the guards had been bribed. Accordingly the sentinels on duty were marched off under arrest to Castle Thunder, where they were locked up and searched for "greenbacks." The thousand and more prisoners still in Libby were compensated in a measure for their failure to escape by the panic they saw among the "Rebs." Messengers and dispatches were soon flying in all directions, and all the horse, foot, and dragoons of Richmond were in pursuit of the fugitives before noon. Only one man of the whole escaping party was retaken inside of the city limits. Of the 109 who got out that night, 59 reached the Union lines, 48 were recaptured, and 2 were drowned.

Colonel Streight and several other officers who had been chosen by the diggers of the tunnel to follow them out, in accordance with the agreement already referred to, lay concealed for a week in a vacant house, where they were fed by loyal friends, and escaped to the Federal lines when the first excitement had abated.

After leaving Libby, Rose and Hamilton turned northward and cautiously walked on a few squares, when suddenly they encountered some Confederates who were guarding a military hospital. Hamilton retreated quickly and ran off to the east, but Rose, who was a little in advance, walked boldly by on the opposite walk and was not challenged, and thus the two friends separated.

Hamilton, after several days of wandering and fearful exposure, came joyfully upon a Union picket squad, received the care he painfully needed, and was soon on his happy journey home.

Rose passed out of the city of Richmond to the York River Railroad and followed its track to the Chickahominy Bridge. Finding this guarded, he turned to the right, and as the day was breaking, he came upon a camp of Confederate cavalry. His blue uniform made it exceedingly dangerous to travel in daylight in this region, and seeing a large sycamore log that was hollow, he crawled into it. The February air was keen and biting, but he kept his cramped position until late in the afternoon, and all day he could hear the loud talk in the camp and the neighing of the horses. Toward night he came cautiously forth, and finding the Chickahominy fordable within a few hundred yards, he succeeded in wading across. The uneven bed of the river, however, led him into several deep holes, and before he reached the shore, his scanty raiment was thoroughly soaked. He trudged on through the woods as fast as his stiffened limbs would bear him, borne up by the hope of early deliverance, and made a brave effort to shake off the horrible ague. He had not gone far, however, when he found himself again close to some Confederate cavalry and was compelled once more to seek a hiding place. The day seemed of interminable length, and he tried vainly in sleep to escape from hunger and cold. His teeth chattered in his head, and when he rose at dark to continue his journey, his tattered clothes were frozen stiff. In this plight he pushed on resolutely and was obliged to wade to his waist for hundreds of yards through one of those deep and treacherous morasses that proved such deadly fever pools for McClellan's army in the campaign of 1862. Finally he reached the high ground, and as the severe exertion had set his blood again in motion and loosened his limbs, he was making better progress, when suddenly he found himself near a Confederate picket. This picket he easily avoided, and keeping well in the shadow of the forest and shunning the roads, he pressed forward with increasing hopes of success. He had secured a box of matches before leaving Libby, and as the cold night came on and he felt that he was really in danger of freezing to death, he penetrated into the center of the cedar grove and built a fire in a small and secluded hollow. He felt that this was hazardous, but the necessity was desperate, since with his stiffened limbs he could no longer move along fast enough to keep the warmth of life in his body. To add to his trouble, his foot, which had been broken in Tennessee previous to his capture, was now giving him great pain and threatened to cripple him wholly; indeed, it would stiffen and disable the best of limbs to compass the journey he had made in darkness over strange, uneven, and hard-frozen ground, and through rivers, creeks, and bogs, and this without food or warmth.

The fire was so welcome that he slept soundly—so soundly that, waking in the early morning, he found his bootlegs and half his uniform burned up, the ice on the rest of it probably having prevented its total destruction.

Resuming his journey much refreshed, he reached Crump's Crossroads, where he successfully avoided another picket. He traveled all day, taking occasional short rests, and before dark had reached New Kent Courthouse. Here again he saw some pickets but by cautious flanking managed to pass them, but in crossing an open space a little farther on, he was seen by a cavalryman, who at once put spurs to his horse and rode up to Rose and, saluting him, inquired if he belonged to the New Kent Cavalry. Rose had on a gray cap and, seeing that he had a stupid sort of fellow to deal with, instantly answered, "Yes," whereupon the trooper turned his horse and rode back. A very few moments were enough to show Rose that the cavalryman's report had failed to satisfy his comrades, whom he could see making movements for his capture. He plunged through a laurel thicket and had no sooner emerged than he saw the Confederates deploying around it in confidence that their game was bagged. He dashed on as fast as his injured foot would let him and entered a tract of heavily timbered land that rose to the east of this thicket. At the border of the grove, he found another picket post and barely escaped the notice of several of the men. The only chance of escape lay through a wide, clear field before him, and even this was in full view from the grove that bordered it, and this he knew would soon swarm with his pursuers.

Across the center of this open field, which was fully half a mile wide, a ditch ran, which, although but a shallow gully, afforded a partial concealment. Rose, who could now hear the voices of the Confederates nearer and nearer, dove into the ditch as the only chance and, dropping on his hands and knees, crept swiftly forward to the eastward. In this cramped position, his progress was extremely painful, and his hands were torn by the briers and stones, but forward he dashed, fully expecting a shower of bullets every minute. At last he reached the other end of the half-mile ditch, breathless and half-dead but without having once raised his head above the gully.

Emerging from this field, he found himself in the Williamsburg Road, and bordering the opposite side was an extensive tract thickly covered with pines. As he crossed and entered this tract, he looked back and could see his enemies, whose movements showed that they were greatly puzzled and off the scent. When at a safe distance, he sought a hiding place and took a needed rest of several hours.

He then resumed his journey and followed the direction of the Williamsburg Road, which he found picketed at various points, so that it was necessary to avoid open spaces. Several times during the day, he saw squads of Confederate cavalry passing along the road so near that he could hear their talk. Near nightfall he reached Diasen Bridge, where he successfully passed another picket. He kept on until nearly midnight, when he lay down by a great tree and, cold as he was, slept soundly until daylight. He now made a careful reconnaissance and found near the road the ruins of an old building, which, he afterward learned, was called "Burnt Ordinary."

He now found himself almost unable to walk with his injured foot, but nerved by the yet bright hope of liberty, he once more went his weary way in the direction of Williamsburg. Finally he came to a place where there were some smoking fagots and a number of tracks, indicating it to have been a picket post of the previous night. He was now nearing Williamsburg, which, he was inclined to believe from such meager information as had reached Libby before his departure, was in possession of the Union forces. Still, he knew that this was territory that was frequently changing hands and was therefore likely to be under a close watch. From this on, he avoided the roads wholly and kept under cover as much as it was possible, and if compelled to cross an open field at all, he did so in a stooping position. He was now moving in a southeasterly direction, and coming again to the margin of a wide opening, he saw, to his unutterable joy, a body of Union troops advancing along the road toward him.

Thoroughly worn out, Rose, believing that his deliverers were at hand, sat down to await their approach. His pleasant reverie was disturbed by a sound behind and near him, and turning quickly he was startled to see three soldiers in the road along which the troops first seen were advancing. The fact that these men had not been noticed before gave Rose some uneasiness for a moment, but as they wore blue uniforms and moreover seemed to take no note of the approaching Federal troops, all things seemed to indicate that they were simply an advanced detail of the same body. This seemed to be further confirmed by the fact that the trio were now moving down the road, apparently with the intent of joining the larger body, and as the ground to the east rose to a crest, both of the bodies were a minute later shut off from Rose's view.

In the full confidence that all was right, he rose to his feet and walked toward the crest to get a better view of everything and greet his comrades of the loyal blue. A walk of a hundred yards brought him again in sight of the three men, who now noticed and challenged him.

In spite of appearances, a vague suspicion forced itself upon Rose, who, however, obeyed the summons and continued to approach the party, who now watched him with fixed attention. As he came closer to the group, the brave but unfortunate soldier saw that he was lost.

For the first time, the three seemed to be made aware of the approach of the Federals and to show consequent alarm and haste. The unhappy Rose saw before the men spoke that their blue uniform was a disguise, and the discovery brought a savage expression to his lips. He hoped and tried to convince his captors that he was a Confederate but all in vain; they retained him as their prisoner and now told him that they were Confederates. Rose, in the first bitter moment of his misfortune, thought seriously of breaking away to his friends so temptingly near, but his poor broken foot and the slender chance of escaping three bullets at a few yards made this suicide, and he decided to wait for a better chance, and this came sooner than he expected.

One of the men appeared to be an officer, who detailed one of his companions to conduct Rose to the rear in the direction of Richmond. The prisoner went quietly with his guard; the other two men tarried a little to watch the advancing Federals, and now Rose began to limp like a man who was unable to go farther. Presently the ridge shut them off from the view of the others. Rose, who had slyly been staggering closer and closer to the guard, suddenly sprang upon the man and, before he had time to wink, had twisted his gun from his grasp, discharged it into the air, flung it down, and ran off as fast as his poor foot would let him toward the east and so as to avoid the rest of the Confederates. The disarmed Confederate made no attempt at pursuit, nor indeed did the other two, who were now seen retreating at a run across the adjacent fields.

Rose's heart bounded with new hope, for he felt that he would be with his advancing comrades in a few minutes at most. All at once a squad of Confederates, hitherto unseen, rose up in his very path and beat him down with the butts of their muskets. All hands now rushed around and secured him, and one of the men called out excitedly, "Hurry up, boys; the Yankees are right here!" They rushed their prisoner into the wooded ravine, and here they were joined by the man whom Rose had just disarmed. He was in a savage mood and declared it to be his particular desire to fill Rose full of Confederate lead. The officer in charge rebuked the man, however, and compelled him to cool down, and he went along with an injured air that excited the merriment of his comrades.

The party continued its retreat to Barhamsville, thence to the White House on the Pamunkey River, and finally to Richmond, where Rose was again restored to Libby and, like the writer, was confined for a number of days in a narrow and loathsome cell. On the 30th of April, his exchange was effected for a Confederate colonel, and on the 6th of July, 1864, he rejoined his regiment, in which he served with conspicuous gallantry to the close of the war.

As already stated, Hamilton reached the Union lines safely after many vicissitudes and did brave service in the closing scenes of the rebellion. He is now a resident of Reedyville, Kentucky. Johnson, whose enforced confinement in Rat Hell gave him a unique fame in Libby, also made good his escape and now lives at North Pleasantville, Kentucky.

Of the fifteen men who dug the successful tunnel, four are dead; viz., Fitzsimmons, Gallagher, Garbett, and McDonald. Captain W. S. B. Randall lives at Hillsboro, Highland County, Ohio; Colonel Terrance Clark at Paris, Edgar County, Illinois; Captain Eli Foster at Chicago; Colonel N. S. McKean at Collinsville, Madison County, Illinois; and Captain J. C. Fislar at Lewiston, I. T. The addresses of Captains Lucas, Simpson, and Mitchell are unknown at this writing.

Colonel Rose has served faithfully almost since the end of the war with the 16th United States Infantry, in which he holds a captain's commission. No one meeting him now would hear from his reticent lips or read in his placid face the thrilling story that links his name in so remarkable a manner with the history of the famous Bastille of the Confederacy.

2

THE LAST PIRATE

BY ARTHUR HUNT CHUTE

Mogul Mackenzie loved the frigid waters off the coast of Maine. There were plenty of wealthy and unsuspecting targets—coastal traders and clippers and whalers and packet ships—headed to Boston and beyond. For a pirate, it was easy pickings. Or so he thought.

In the farther end of the Bay of Fundy, about a mile off from the Nova Scotian coast, is the Isle of Haut. It is a strange, rocky island that rises several hundred feet sheer out of the sea, without any bay or inlets. A landing can only be effected there in the calmest weather, and on account of the tremendous ebb of the Fundy tides, which rise and fall sixty feet every twelve hours, the venturesome explorer cannot long keep his boat moored against the precipitous cliffs.

Because of this inaccessibility, little is known of the solitary island. Within its rampart walls of rock, they say there is a green valley, and in its center is a fathomless lake, where the Micmac Indians used to bury their dead, and hence its dread appellation of the "Island of the Dead." Beyond these bare facts, nothing more is certain about the secret valley and the haunted lake. Many wild and fabulous descriptions are current, but they are merely the weavings of fancy.

Sometimes on a stormy night, the unhappy navigators of the North Channel miss the coast lights in the fog, and out from the Isle of Haut a gentle undertow flirts with their bewildered craft. Then little by little, they are gathered into a mighty current, against which all striving is in vain, and in the white foam among the iron cliffs, their ship is pounded into splinters. The quarry which she gathers in so softly at first and so fiercely at last, however, is soon snatched away from the siren shore. The ebb tide bears every sign of wreckage far out into the deeps of the Atlantic, and not a trace remains of the ill-starred vessel or her crew. But one of the boats in the fishing fleet never comes home, and from lonely huts on the coast, reproachful eyes are cast upon the "Island of the Dead."

On the long winter nights, when the "boys" gather about the fire in Old Steele's General Stores at Hall's Harbor, their hard, gray life becomes bright for a spell. When a keg of hard cider is flowing freely, the grim fishermen forget their taciturnity, the ice is melted from their speech, and the floodgates of their souls pour forth. But ever in the background of their talk, unforgotten, like a haunting shadow, is the "Island of the Dead." Of their weirdest and most blood-curdling yarns, it is always the center, and when at last, with uncertain steps, they leave the empty keg and the dying fire to turn homeward through the drifting snow, fearful and furtive glances are cast to where the island looms up like a ghostly sentinel from the sea. Across its high promontory, the northern lights scintillate and blaze, and out of its moving brightness, the terrified fishermen behold the war canoes of dead Indians freighted with their redskin braves; the forms of *cœur de bois* and desperate

Frenchmen swinging down the skyline in a ghastly snake dance; the shapes and spars of ships long since forgotten from the "Missing List"; and always, most dread-inspiring of them all, the distress signals from the sinking ship of Mogul Mackenzie and his pirate crew.

Captain Mogul Mackenzie was the last of the pirates to scourge the North Atlantic seaboard. He came from that school of freebooters that was let loose by the American Civil War. With a letter of marque from the Confederate States, he sailed the seas to prey on Yankee shipping. He and his fellow privateers were so thorough in their work of destruction that the Mercantile Marine of the United States was ruined for a generation to come. When the war was over, the defeated South called off her few remaining bloodhounds on the sea. But Mackenzie, who was still at large, had drunk too deeply of the wine of a wild, free life. He did not return to lay down his arms but began on a course of shameless piracy. He lived only a few months under the black flag, until he went down on the Isle of Haut. The events of that brief and thrilling period are unfortunately obscure, with only a ray of light here and there. But the story of his passing is the most weird of all the strange yarns that are spun about the "Island of the Dead."

In May 1865, a gruesome discovery was made off the coast of Maine, which sent a chill of fear through all the seaport towns of New England. A whaler bound for New Bedford was coming up Cape Cod one night long after dark. There was no fog, and the lights of approaching vessels could easily be discerned. The man on the lookout felt no uneasiness at his post, when, without any warning of bells or lights, the sharp bow of a brigantine suddenly loomed up, hardly a ship's length in front.

"What the blazes are you trying to do?" roared the mate from the bridge, enraged at this unheard-of violation of the right of way. But no voice answered his challenge, and the brigantine went swinging by, with all her sails set to a spanking breeze. She bore directly across the bow of the whaler, which just grazed her stern in passing.

"There's something rotten onboard there," said the mate.

"Ay," said the captain, who had come on the bridge. "There's something rotten there right enough. Swing your helm to port, and get after the devils," he ordered.

"Ay, ay, sir!" came the ready response, and the helmsman changed his course to follow the eccentric craft. She was evidently bound on some secret mission, for not otherwise would she thus tear through the darkness before the wind without the flicker of a light.

The whaler was the swifter of the two ships, and she could soon have overhauled the other, but fearing some treachery, the captain refrained from running her down until daylight. All night long she seemed to be veering her course, attempting to escape from her pursuer. In the morning, off the coast of Maine, she turned her nose directly out to sea. Then a boat was lowered from the whaler and rowed out to intercept the oncoming vessel. When they were directly in her course, they lay on their oars and waited. The brigantine did not veer again but came steadily on, and soon the whalemen were alongside and made themselves fast to a dinghy, which she had in tow. A few minutes of apprehensive waiting followed, and as nothing happened, one of the boldest swung himself up over the tow rope onto the deck. He was followed by the others, and they advanced cautiously with drawn knives and pistols.

Not a soul was to be seen, and the men, who were brave enough before a charging whale, trembled with fear. The wheel and the lookout were alike deserted, and no sign of life could be discovered anywhere below. In the galley were the embers of a dead fire, and the table in the captain's cabin was spread out ready for a meal which had never been eaten. On deck everything was spick and span, and not the slightest evidence of a storm or any other disturbance could be found. The theory of a derelict was impossible. Apparently all had been well onboard, and they had been sailing with good weather, when, without any warning, her crew had been suddenly snatched away by some dread power.

The sailors with one accord agreed that it was the work of a sea serpent. But the mate had no place for the ordinary superstitions of the sea, and he still scoured the hold, expecting at any minute to encounter a dead body or some other evil evidence of foul play. Nothing more, however, was found, and the mate at length had to end his search with the unsatisfactory conclusion that the *St. Clare*, a brigantine registered from Hartpool with cargo of lime, had been abandoned on the high seas for no apparent reason. Her skipper had taken with him the ship's papers and had not left a single clue behind.

A crew was told off to stand by the *St. Clare* to bring her into port, and the others climbed into the longboat to row back to the whaler.

"Just see if there is a name on that there dinghy, before we go," said the mate.

An exclamation of horror broke from one of the men as he read on the bow of the dinghy the name: *Kanawha*.

The faces of all went white with a dire alarm as the facts of the mystery suddenly flashed before them. The *Kanawha* was the ship in which Captain Mogul Mackenzie had made himself notorious as a privateersman. Everyone had heard her awe-inspiring name, and every Yankee seafaring man prayed that he might never meet her on the seas. After the *Alabama* was sunk and the *Tallahassee* was withdrawn, the *Kanawha* still remained to threaten the shipping of the North. For a long time, her whereabouts had been unknown, and then she was discovered by a Federal gunboat, which gave chase and fired upon her. Without returning fire, she raced in for shelter among the dangerous islands off Cape Sable and was lost in the fog. Rumor had it that she ran on the rocks off that perilous coast and sank with all onboard. As time went by and there was no more sign of the corsair, the rumor was accepted as proven. Men began to spin yarns in the forecastle about Mogul Mackenzie, with an interest that was tinged with its former fear. Skippers were beginning to feel at ease again on the grim waters, when suddenly, like a bolt from the blue, came the awful news of the discovery of the *St. Clare.*

Gunboats put off to scour the coastline, and again with fear and trembling, the lookout began to eye suspiciously every new sail coming up on the horizon.

One afternoon, toward the end of May, a schooner came tearing into Portland harbor, with all her canvas, crowded on, and flying distress signals. Her skipper said that off the island of Campobello he had seen a long, gray sailing ship with auxiliary power sweeping down upon him. As the wind was blowing strong inshore, he had taken to his heels and made for Portland. He was chased all the way, and his pursuer did not drop him until he was just off the harbor bar.

Many doubted his story, however, saying that no one would dare to chase a peaceful craft so near to a great port in broad daylight. And, again, it was urged that an auxiliary vessel could easily have overhauled the schooner between Campobello and Portland. The fact that the captain of the schooner was as often drunk as sober and that, when he was under the influence of drink, he was given to seeing visions was pointed to as conclusive proof that his yarn was a lie. After the New Bedford whaler came into port with the abandoned *St. Clare*, it was known beyond doubt that the *Kanawha* was still a real menace. But nobody cared to admit that Mogul Mackenzie was as bold as the schooner's report would imply, and hence countless arguments were put forward to allay such fears.

But a few days later, the fact that the pirates were still haunting their coast was absolutely corroborated. A coastal packet from Boston arrived at Yarmouth with the news that she had not only sighted *Kanawha* in the distance but they had crossed each other's paths so near that the name could be discerned beyond question with a spyglass. She was heading up the Bay of Fundy and did not pause or pay any heed to the other ship.

This news brought with it consternation, and every town and village along the Fundy was ahum with stories and theories about the pirate ship. The interest, instead of being abated, was augmented as the days went by with no further report. In the public houses and along the quays, it was almost the only topic of conversation. The excitement became almost feverish when it was known that several captains, outward bound, had taken with them a supply of rifles and ammunition. The prospect of a fight seemed imminent.

About a week after the adventure of the Boston packet, Her Majesty's ship *Buzzard* appeared off Yarmouth Harbor. The news of the *Kanawha* had come to the admiral at Halifax, and he had dispatched the warship to cruise about the troubled coast.

"That'll be the end of old Mogul Mackenzie, now that he's got an English ship on his trail," averred a Canadian as he sat drinking in the "Yarmouth Light" with a group of seafaring men of various nationalities. "It takes the British jack-tar to put the kibosh on this pirate game. One of them is worth a shipload of Yankees at the business."

"Well, don't you crow too loud now," replied a Boston skipper. "I reckon that that Nova Scotian booze artist, who ran into Portland the other day scared of his shadow, would not do you fellows much credit."

"Yes, but what about your gunboats that have had the job of fixing the *Kanawha* for the last three years and haven't done it yet?" The feelings between Canada and the United States were none too good just after the Civil War, and the Canadian was bound not to lose this opportunity for horseplay. "You're a fine crowd of seadogs, you are, you fellows from the Boston Tea Party. Three years after one little half-drowned rat, and haven't got him yet. Wouldn't Sir Francis Drake or Lord Nelson be proud of the record that you long-legged, slab-sided Yankees have made on the sea!"

"Shut your mouth, you blue-nosed, down-East herring choker!" roared the Yankee skipper. "I reckon we've given you traitors that tried to stab us in the back a good enough licking, and if any more of your dirty dogs ever come nosing about down south of Mason and Dixon's Line, I bet they'll soon find out what our record is."

"Well, you fools can waste your tongue and wind," said a third man, raising his glass, "but for me here's good luck to the *Buzzard*."

"So say we all of us," chimed in the others, and the Yankee and the Canadian drank together to the success of the British ship, forgetting their petty jealousies before a common foe.

Everywhere the news of the arrival of the British warship was hailed with delight. All seemed to agree that her presence assured the speedy extermination of the pirate crew. But after several days of futile cruising about the coast, her commander, to escape from a coming storm, had to put into St. Mary's Bay, with the object of his search still eluding his vigilance. He only arrived in time to hear the last chapter of the *Kanawha*'s tale of horrors.

The night before, Dominic Lefountain, a farmer living alone at Meteighan, a little village on the French shore, had been awakened from his sleep by the moaning and wailing of a human voice. For days the imminent peril of an assault from the pirates had filled the people of the French coast with forebodings. And now, awakened thus in the dead of night, the lonely Frenchman was well-nigh paralyzed with terror. With his flesh creeping and his eyes wide, he groped for his rifle and waited in the darkness, while ever and anon came those unearthly cries from the beach. Nearly an hour passed before he could gather himself together sufficiently to investigate the cause of the alarm. At last, when the piteous wailing had grown weak and intermittent, the instinct of humanity mastered his fears, and he went forth to give a possible succor to the one in need.

On the beach, lying prostrate, with the water lapping about his feet, he found a man in the last stage of exhaustion. The blood was flowing from his mouth, and as Dominic turned him over to stanch its flow, he found that his tongue had been cut out and hence the unearthly wailing which had roused him from his sleep. The beach was deserted by this time, and it was too dark to see far out into the bay.

Dominic carried the unfortunate man to his house and nursed him there for many weeks. He survived his frightful experiences and lived on for twenty years, a pathetic and helpless figure supported by the big-hearted farmers and fishermen of the French shore. Evidently he had known too much for his enemies, and they had sealed his mouth forever. He became known as the "Mysterious Man of Meteighan," and his deplorable condition was always pointed to as a mute witness of the last villainy of Mogul Mackenzie.

On the night following the episode of the "Mysterious Man of Meteighan," a wild and untoward storm swept down the North Atlantic and over the seaboard far and near. In the Bay of Fundy that night, the elements met in their grandest extremes. Tide rips and mountain waves opposed each other with titanic force. All along the bleak and rock-ribbed coast, the boiling waters lay churned into foam. Over the breakwaters the giant combers crashed and soared far up into the troubled sky, while out under the black clouds of the night, the whirlpools and the tempests met. Was ever a night like this before? Those onshore thanked God, and those with fathers on the sea gazed out upon a darkness where no star of hope could shine.

Now and again through the Stygian gloom, a torrent of sheet lightning rolled down across the heavens, bringing in its wake a moment of terrible light. It was in one of these brief moments of illumination that the wan watchers at Hall's Harbor discerned a long, gray ship being swept like a specter before the winds toward the Isle of Haut. Until the flash of lightning, the doomed seamen appeared to have been unconscious of their fast-approaching fate, and then, as if suddenly awakened, they sent a long, thin trail of light to wind itself far up into the darkness. Again and again the rockets shot upward from her bow, while above the noises of the tempest came the roar of a gun.

The people on the shore looked at each other with blanched faces, speechless, helpless. A lifetime by that shore had taught them the utter puniness of the sons of men. Others would have tried to do something with what they thought was their strong arm. But the fishermen knew too well that the Fundy's arm was stronger. In silence they waited with bated breath while the awful moments passed. Imperturbable they stood there, with their feet in the white foam and their faces in the salt spray, and gazed at the curtain of the night, behind which a tragedy was passing, as dark and dire as any in the annals of the sea.

Another flash of lightning, and there, dashing upon the iron rocks, was a great ship with all her sails set and a cloud of lurid smoke trailing from her funnel. She was gray-colored, with auxiliary power, and as her lines dawned upon those who saw her in the moment of light, they burst out with one accord, "It's the *Kanawha*! It's the *Kanawha*!" As if an answer to their sudden cry, another gun roared, and another shower of rockets shot up into the sky, and then all was lost again in the darkness and the voices of the tempest.

Next morning the winds had gone out with the tide, and when in the afternoon the calm waters had risen, a boat put off from Hall's Harbor and rowed to the Isle of Haut. For several hours the rocky shores were searched for some traces of the wreck, but not a spar or splinter could be found. All about, the bright waters laughed, with naught but the sunbeams on their bosom, and not a shadow remained from last night's sorrow on the sea.

So Mogul Mackenzie, who had lived a life of stress, passed out on the wings of storm. In his end, as always, he baffled pursuit and was sought but could not be found. His sailings on the sea were in secret, and his last port in death was a mystery. But, as has been already related, when the northern lights come down across the haunted island, the distress signals of his pirate crew are still seen shooting up into the night.

3

A LYNCHING IN GOLDEN

BY D. J. COOK

The two men who murdered a beloved Colorado rancher thought they had pulled off the perfect crime. It had been months since they'd escaped, and no one seemed to be on the trail. The Rocky Mountain Detective Agency and the angry citizens of Golden were persistent. They had their own ideas about justice.

In all the criminal history of Colorado—in all the register of the achievements of the Rocky Mountain Detective Association—the ensanguined pages show no more causeless, unprovoked murder than that of R. B. Hayward in September 1879. The difficulties met and overcome by the detectives and the prompt and tragic end of the criminals lend an additional interest to the case and make it one of the most famous in the far West, as it is most assuredly one of the most noted in Colorado in some of its features. The absence of any material temptation; the temporary escape of the murderers; the accidental finding of the body of the victim; the patient search of the officers; the final arrest of the men hundreds of miles away; the identification and confession; and then the lynching, so rich in dramatic detail, form a narrative reading more like a sensational romance than the cold facts of an actual reality.

On the 10th of August, 1879, Gen. D. J. Cook, superintendent of the Rocky Mountain Detective Association, received a dispatch from Sheriff Besey, of Grand County, Colorado, telling him to keep a sharp lookout for a man looking very much like an Asian who was wanted for the robbery of the house of Mr. Frank Byers in Middle Park. The robber had secured a watch and a few trinkets of more or less value and then, helping himself to a mule, had departed for other fields. This robbery had occurred on the 8th, and the intricate machinery of the detectives was put in motion as soon as notified, for Mr. Byers was a well-known citizen, and presently information began to take shape and flow through the properly appointed channels to headquarters.

It was found that on the 12th, four days after the Byers robbery and two after the detectives had been notified, the robber had appeared in Georgetown and called upon Dr. William A. Burr, giving his name as Joseph F. Seminole and stating that he came from Emerson Kinney of Hot Sulphur Springs, who desired the medical gentleman's immediate presence, as Mrs. Kinney was dangerously ill.

"When you get about six miles out of town on the road to Empire," said the cool and crafty scoundrel, "stop at the ranch of Mr. Lindstrom and get my mule, which I left there. It will be much better for you to use my animal than to ride your own on such a long and hard trip. When you reach the Summit house in Berthoud pass, just present this order, and the proprietor will furnish you with a horse and buggy."

The order that was given read as follows:

Please give to Dr. W. A. Burr horse and buggy, and charge same
to Emerson Kinney of Hot Sulphur Springs on same order as
before.

> J. F. SEMINOLE.

When the doctor reached Lindstrom's place, he exchanged his horse
for the mule left by Seminole and continued on his way. At the Summit
house, the foregoing order was presented, but the proprietor declined
to furnish a conveyance on the strength of it, saying that he did not
know Seminole at all but offering a horse and buggy if the doctor
would be personally responsible for it, a proposition which the latter accepted. At last Mr. Kinney's ranch was reached, and to his utter
stupefaction, the doctor found that his expected patient was not only
never in better health but had not the slightest idea of being sick.
Breathing vengeance deep and dire, the good-hearted but exasperated
doctor started on his return, and when Lindstrom's was again reached,
he was greeted with the intelligence that Seminole had been there and
secured his horse, and to this day that animal has never been seen or
even heard of.

Thus far the detectives got and then were balked. To them it was
but a case of robbery—they never dreamed how soon it was to develop
into a ghastly murder. Somewhat piqued at their nonsuccess, although
the crime was comparatively but a paltry one, they continued their
efforts and after a while traced Seminole to Leadville, where, on the
7th of September, he, in company with a man known as Tom Johnson, whose correct name proved to be Samuel Woodruff, hired two
horses for the avowed purpose of merely taking a little ride. While

skirmishing around, they noticed a Mr. Aldrich draw two hundred dollars from a bank and learned that he was going immediately to Georgetown. They followed behind him and, when six miles from his destination, rode up to him, drew their pistols, and called upon him to halt and deliver. Aldrich, however, was not of that kind and jerked his own weapon and turned loose, though, unfortunately, not hitting either of the two scoundrels, who turned and fled precipitately. When he arrived in Georgetown, he promptly notified the sheriff of Clear Creek County, and that official immediately struck the trail and followed it up without the loss of a moment. So rapidly did he gain on the fleeing desperadoes that they dismounted from their horses, turned the animals loose, and made their escape in the brush. The animals were returned to their owners, and the sheriff abandoned the pursuit of the men.

The rascals continued on foot until September 10. They reached the place of Mr. Anderson and hired him to drive them to Denver. They stated that they had no money, but an uncle of theirs kept a livery stable in Denver, and he would pay for all the trouble. While on the trip, Anderson noticed that his passengers did have money and remarked that they had better pay the toll charges at least, as he was not willing to spend cash right out of his pocket and trust them besides. But they refused, and then Anderson said he would go no farther, but upon being confronted by two cocked pistols, he changed his mind and drove on. About a mile farther, two wagons were seen coming from the direction of Denver and going in that of Georgetown, and when almost within hailing distance, Messrs. Seminole and Johnson jumped out and took to the brush, evidently fearing that Anderson would call for assistance. Relieved of his undesirable passengers, Anderson joined the other wagons and in their company returned to Georgetown.

That same afternoon, about half past four, this pair of precious scoundrels came to the house of R. B. Hayward near Big Hill, Jefferson County, and engaged him to gear up and take them to a cattle camp they said they were hunting, supposed to be near A. Rooney's place near Green Mountain, just outside of Hogback. They passed the Mt. Vernon tollgate at about half past six that evening, and from here the fate of Mr. Hayward was an unfathomed mystery until his body was found.

Of course Mr. Hayward's people became uneasy on account of his failure to return the evening after he left, and when he did not come the next day, Mrs. Hayward took steps to inform the Jefferson County authorities of the circumstances under which her husband had gone away from home and of his prolonged absence. They made thorough search but failed to discover anything, either concerning Mr. Hayward's whereabouts as to what disposition had been made of his team or where the men were who had gone away with him.

On the 16th of September, C. P. Hoyt of the Rocky Mountain Detective Association reported the facts of the mysterious absence of Mr. Hayward to Superintendent Cook and gave the description of the two men last seen with the missing man.

In the meantime, on September 11, the same two men (though the fact of the murder was not then known) went to Brown & Marr of the bus barn on Arapahoe Street, Denver, and hired two bay mares and a top-rig buggy, paying four dollars in advance. This was about two o'clock in the afternoon, and they said they merely wanted to take a little spin around town and would return at a certain specified hour. As this time had long been passed, Brown & Marr placed the matter in the hands of the detective association late in the evening of the 11th, and they telegraphed all over a description of the missing rig. About eleven o'clock on the morning of the 12th, Superintendent Cook received a message from the town of Loveland in Larimer County, stating that two men had abandoned a buggy, answering the description of the missing one, and had mounted the mares and ridden off. An officer was immediately dispatched to the scene, and sure enough it was the identical vehicle taken from the Denver stable.

As it was now ascertained that the thieves had gone north, Superintendent Cook notified Assistant Superintendent Carr at Cheyenne to be on the lookout, and on the 14th of the month, Gen. Cook received information from him that two men, answering the description of the two who had hired the horses and buggy, had remained all night in the vicinity of a ranch near La Porte, Larimer County. The men represented to the owner of the ranch that they belonged to a cattle outfit and that the cattle were down in the bottoms near at hand, while the wagon containing the camping outfit was far to the rear. They were obliged to be with their cattle, they said, and would like to borrow a couple of buffalo robes until morning. The kind-hearted ranchman acceded to their request and never again beheld his robes, nor in the morning could he find any signs or traces of cattle.

On the 22d of the same month, a gentleman named Leech, while riding from Laramie City to Cheyenne on horseback, met two men mounted on bay mares, with folded buffalo robes as saddles, at the crossing of the Union Pacific Railroad, four miles east of Sherman Station. They stopped him, asked him what time it was and where he lived, and as they had a hard look about them, he assured them he lived about two hundred yards from there, on the other side of a little butte, though the truth of the matter was, there wasn't a house within four miles of the spot. When Mr. Leech reached Cheyenne, he met Detective Carr and mentioned this meeting near Sherman, and when the officer gave a description of the missing horses and thieves, Mr. Leech recognized it immediately.

Carr then went diligently to work and after a while ascertained that on the 23d two men riding bay mares with no saddles but buffalo robes in lieu thereof had come to the ranch of Nick Janise near Sidney Bridge on the North Platte. This information was forwarded to Gen. Cook, and Mr. Leech, having come down to Denver on business, was interviewed at his hotel by Detective Joe Arnold as a representative of Chief Cook, who had, as did also Gen. Cook, shrewd suspicions that the murderers of Hayward and the horse thieves were the same parties. He showed Mr. Leech a description of the men who had engaged Mr. Hayward to drive them to the cattle ranch, and that gentleman immediately recognized them, being especially sure because of the white bone-handled knife and the revolvers carried by the suspicious-looking strangers.

The result of this interview was that Detective W. W. Ayres of the Rocky Mountain Association was sent in pursuit of the men, starting from Denver on the 4th of October. By this time the Hayward murder had become state talk, as the mystery was still unsolved and as the cold-blooded nature of the affair had also become generally known. Currency was also given to the fact that he had left an intelligent wife and two bright daughters just budding into womanhood to watch and wait for the return of the husband and father who would never return.

There remained hardly any trace of doubt that Mr. Hayward had been murdered by the two men with whom he had started out. This suspicion was greatly strengthened by learning the late history of the two men who had gone with him, which history has been given in the beginning of this story.

Mrs. Hayward was for a while almost frantic with grief at the loss of her husband, but she soon rallied with the genuine pluck which is the characteristic of most western women and determined to do what she might to avenge his death. She offered a reward of $200 for the capture of the murderers. This offer was followed by one from Jefferson County, agreeing to pay $500 for their capture, and soon Gov. Pitkin proclaimed a reward on the part of the state of $1,000 for their apprehension, making $1,700 the aggregate sum offered for the fugitives.

As related above, Gen. Cook had already formed the theory, though he kept it to himself, that the two men who had stolen the horses were the Hayward murderers, and he decided to have them followed to "the jumping-off place" if necessary or get them. He had already formed a pretty definite theory as to the destination of the two men. He had learned, among numerous other facts which he had gathered together, that Seminole was a half-breed Sioux Indian and that he belonged at Pine Ridge Agency, Dakota, where he had a family, going there by the name of J. S. Leuischammesse. As has already been seen, the men who stole the horses had turned their attention in that direction, and thitherward Cook directed Mr. Ayres, never informing him, however, that he had any suspicion that they were guilty of any crime greater than that of horse stealing, wisely concluding that, if Seminole's fellow Indians knew that he was charged with murder and likely to be hanged, they would not permit the detective to bring him away and believing that the best way of keeping this fact from them was to impart it to no one. On the other hand, they would perhaps even assist the detective in getting him for horse stealing.

Mr. Ayres had a long and arduous journey before him, as he could look forward to at least a thousand miles of stagecoaching and horseback riding in the north, with winter coming on and with many hardships to endure in a land of savages. But he started out undaunted by the prospect, and the result shows how faithfully he worked and how successfully he wrought.

While he is making his way across the almost pathless plains of Wyoming and Dakota, it is necessary to stop for a moment to relate to the reader the fact of the discovery of the body of Mr. Hayward. It was found on the 7th of October, three days after Ayres had left the city and almost a month after Mr. Hayward had left home, in an old culvert on the Golden Road, five miles from Denver. The body bore no testimony as to the manner or cause of death. It was greatly decayed but still was not beyond identification, and the coroner's jury brought in the verdict that death was caused in all probability by dislocation of the neck at the hand of a party or parties unknown. No wound or mark of violence could be found anywhere on the body, and the theories were that either the murderers had broken his neck with some dull instrument or else had poisoned him.

In the meantime Detective Ayres had gone to Cheyenne, taken horse there, and ridden to Horse Creek; from there to Big Horse Creek, thence to Hawk Springs, and into old Red Cloud Agency on the Platte. Here he got information of the men he was after and without loss of time pushed on to Running Water; from there to Camp Robinson, thence to Camp Sheridan, and then into Pine Ridge Agency. The Indian agent, Mr. V. T. McGillycuddy, proffered all assistance, and Joseph Seminole was soon under arrest. Not without considerable trouble, however, as shall appear.

Mr. Ayres had taken letters to the agent and the military and had been assured that he should have every assistance, as the Rocky Mountain Detective Agency was well known and highly respected in that faraway section.

Not only the officers and the soldiers, but the Indian police as well, were anxious and willing to assist in running Seminole down. They recognized the description as soon as it was given them and told the officer from the faraway region that they would find him forthwith and volunteered to lead him to his place of abode. Ayres told them all he knew of the crimes charged against Seminole, the worst being that of horse thieving, and assured them that he was wanted on no more serious charge than that of showing his undue love for horseflesh. They professed great indignation that their nation should have been disgraced by the stealing of a single horse and avowed that he should be sent back forthwith to answer for the offense. They seemed to dislike the fellow anyway, possibly because he was a half-breed but most likely for the reason that he was better educated than the rest of them and held himself in a manner aloof from them. At any rate, they were quite willing to take the officer to him, saying that Seminole should not only be arrested but that they would see that the officer should get away with him in good shape.

This was as good a thing as Mr. Ayres wanted, and when he was well rested, the Indians, true to their promise, led him to the wigwam of the culprit.

It may not have been a picture of peace and plenty which Seminole presented, but he certainly seemed to be quite contented, surrounded as he was by his squaw and papooses, who prattled about in the dirt, while he sat enjoying the bliss of a long-stemmed pipe. The surroundings were rude and coarse, but the half Indian appeared to be perfectly at home and at ease.

But the officer of the law cannot stand back on account of any qualms of conscience or foolish sentiment when there are arrests to be made. His is not the part of preserving domestic felicity.

When broken in upon, the murderer did not show any signs of fear, and when introduced to Mr. Ayres as an officer from Colorado in search of him, he manifested no disposition to make resistance. It may be that he asked rather impetuously to know the charge against him, but Ayres's answer that it was that of horse stealing reassured him, and he submitted quietly and walked out of his wigwam stolidly, though with apparent willingness.

The officer was led to believe that he had accomplished a big job with but little effort and was mentally congratulating himself accordingly. But all was not accomplished. There was much yet to be done. He felt that he had a wide and wild stretch of country to cover in getting home, and the idea of going through an Indian region alone in charge of a half Indian was not a cheerful one. Not by any means.

When Seminole was once out of his house, the detective undertook to handcuff him. But the fellow had had time for a little self-introspection and meditation. The Hayward murder undoubtedly came into his mind, and he began to feel that, whatever the charge upon which he was to be brought back to Denver, he would be in danger of being discovered as the murderer, and he began to show fight at the sight of the handcuffs. He would not agree to have them put on and, when the officer attempted to force them on, struck at him. He was a strong man and able to get the best of the officer had he been unaided. But the Indian police came nobly to Ayres's rescue, and they laid Mr. Seminole low in very short order, and while he was prone upon the ground and kicking and scratching, the irons were adjusted. The scene was as wild a one in the interest of justice as ever fell to the lot of man to witness.

The capture was now completed, and one of the murderers of "old man" Hayward was in the hands of an officer of the law, though on a different charge and far away from the scene of the tragedy or the bounds of civilization.

The officer found that, on September 29, Seminole had sold his stolen bay mare to an Indian chief named Woman's Dress, giving a bill of sale and signing thereto the name of Joseph Leuischammesse, which, upon being compared upon arrival at Denver with the writing of the order to the proprietor of the Summit house, proved that it was written by the same hand, the letters being formed identically alike. The other man, Tom Johnson, as he is still called, was not there.

With an armed escort of Sioux Indians, Ayres started back with his prisoner. He parted with his escort at Camp Robinson and at Pine Bluffs boarded a freight train and took up quarters in the caboose.

About three o'clock of the next morning, after taking passage on the freight, Mr. Ayres found himself minus the prisoner to capture whom he had risked so much and undergone so many hardships. He had allowed the man to be out of his sight for a moment, and that moment had been embraced by the fellow to regain his liberty. The train was rattling along at more than ordinary freight train speed, so that Mr. Ayres did not dream of the handcuffed man's jumping from the train. But Seminole was a man who dared anything, and he boldly plunged out of the caboose into the darkness and was once more free. Mr. Ayres's efforts to refind his man proved utterly futile, and nothing was left to him but to notify his chief.

A great deal had been gained, but now everything seemed lost. By this time Cook had become entirely convinced that Seminole, or Leuis-chammesse, was one of the murderers of Hayward, and for that reason he determined to leave no stone unturned to recover his man. Consequently the matter was again placed in the hands of Assistant Superintendent Carr, and through the aid of the telegraph, but a very few hours had elapsed when there were no less than fifteen cowboys scouring the plains under the leadership of Cattle Detective Cowles in the neighborhood of the point at which the escape was made, and in nine hours from the time of the escape, the recapture had been effected.

What could better serve to show the complete system upon which the Rocky Mountain Detective Association is organized?

Without further incident of note, the wily rascal was brought to Denver and taken to the county jail. He had become moody and cross and was generally pronounced a rough customer by those with whom he came in contact. He would not talk at first at all. It was evident to Gen. Cook—who had kept his suspicion concerning the connection of Seminole with the Hayward murder to himself, even up to that time—that the fellow was living in dread of having his identity discovered. But Cook preserved a discreet silence. Mr. Ayres did not yet know the importance of the arrest which he had made.

As soon as the fellow was securely locked in, Gen. Cook sent for Mrs. Hayward, the widow of the murdered man, who was brought to Denver by Detective Hoyt of Golden. Taking her to the jail building, he had seven or eight prisoners, including Seminole, and all of them, corresponding in some respects in appearance with him, placed in a row in a room.

Into this room Mrs. Hayward was guided, having been told what was expected of her, namely, that she should have an opportunity to identify the probable murderer of her husband. She was told to walk along the line in which Seminole stood as stolid as a block of stone and find among the array, if she could, the guilty party. She passed rapidly down the line, looking at one man at a time, without stopping to hesitate, until she came to Seminole, when, getting a full view of him, she threw up her hands and exclaimed, "My God! That's the man. Take him away from me!"

The identification was positive and was a death blow to the half breed's hopes. Besides this, he was identified by Brown & Marr, by Dr. Burr, and others, so that no doubt as to his identity could by any possibility be entertained. Seeing that he was in for it, Seminole made a full confession.

While Seminole was in jail here, Detective Cook determined to obtain from him some information which would lead to the apprehension of Woodruff, of whom all trace had now been lost. He accordingly sent a detective to the jail in response to Seminole's request for a lawyer and who, while professing to be a legal adviser, obtained from Seminole all he knew of his companion in crime and the particulars of the murder. He stated that, while riding with Mr. Hayward, they rode behind, the old man in front, driving; that Johnson suddenly clutched Hayward about the throat and choked him to death, while he, Seminole, took the lines and handled the horses; that the breakage of the neck was occasioned when they heaved the body out of the wagon when about to shove him under the little bridge where it was found; that at half-past ten the same night, they drove the wagon and mules into Denver and put up at the Western barn; that in the morning they took the outfit around to Paul & Strickler's on Fifteenth Street and tried to have it sold at auction, but learning that the sale would not take place until afternoon, they went back to the barn and finally sold it to a Leadville teamster for $190, Woodruff giving the bill of sale and signing the name Thomas Logan to it; that they then went to Brown & Marr's and hired the buggy and mares and followed exactly the route as traced and that at Sidney Bridge they separated, Woodruff going to the right, in the direction of the Niobrara River, while he kept straight on to the Pine Ridge Agency, where he was captured.

As to his companion, Seminole said his right name was Woodruff, though he had been known only as Tom Johnson in Colorado. He knew that Woodruff was a stonecutter by trade and that he had been pardoned out of the Wyoming penitentiary after serving three years for killing a man named John Friehl, with whose wife Woodruff had been too intimate. The fellow gave a complete description of Woodruff and seemed decidedly reckless as to whether his companion in crime should be caught or not. He made his confession in a cold-blooded manner and gave no reason for the murder of Hayward, except that they wanted his team and thought it would be best to have the owner conveniently hidden away while they were carrying forward their operations in Denver and getting out of the country.

Gen. Cook concluded that the best place to look for Woodruff was the place at which he had last been seen by Seminole and consequently sent detectives to the Niobrara region. This time Mr. Ayres, who had captured Seminole, was sent out and was accompanied by Mr. C. A. Hawley, who, being one of the most courageous as well as one of the shrewdest members of the association, was selected for this task because it was believed that there would be some lively work in arresting Woodruff, who was known to be desperate as well as cunning.

"But you must get him, Hawley," said Cook to his deputy when he left. "I trust the work to you and expect you to do it up in good shape."

"If he is to be had, you can depend on me," said Hawley. "I am ready for him and go to find him."

The two detectives made the trip to Niobrara with all possible haste. When they arrived there, they began to look around for their man. One day when they came close upon an individual who answered the general description of Woodruff, that individual, finding that he was closely watched by the officers and suspecting them to be officers, jumped on his horse and rode off at a lively gait. Inquiry revealed the fact that this man was known as Tom Johnson. They felt convinced that he was the man that they wanted, and they went after him with all possible haste. A wild chase he led them, too, over the uninhabited country of western Nebraska. Knowing the lay of the land better than the officers did, he was able to evade them for a long time, and at the end of a week of as hard work as often falls to the lot of detectives, they overtook and captured him.

After taking the fellow, they had doubts as to whether he was the man they were seeking but concluded that a man who would act as suspiciously as he had been acting must be guilty of some crime, and whether it was that of the murder of the Colorado ranchman or some other mattered little to them. Hence they determined to bag him and to bring him to Denver, which determination they put into execution, landing here with him near the middle of November. The fellow proved not to be Woodruff, but it was soon ascertained that he was a fugitive from justice from Omaha, where he had been guilty of horse stealing, and it may be remarked in passing that he was sent to that city and tried and that he had to serve out a seven-years' sentence in the penitentiary of Nebraska. Thus the officers only brought down the wrong game when they fired, though they did not waste their ammunition. Shakespeare tells us that conscience makes cowards of us all. Johnson's conscience certainly put him behind the bars at Lincoln City.

This episode did not delay matters a great deal. Gen. Cook had been on the qui vive while his officers were out and had learned that Woodruff had relatives living either in Iowa or eastern Nebraska, and he had come to the conclusion that the fugitive murderer would most likely fly to them for protection and to escape detection. The sequel will prove that in this case, as in most others where he forms a theory as to the conduct of fugitive criminals, he was right. Hence he decided to send Hawley to look up Woodruff's relatives, with the hope of also finding Woodruff. He had heard that they resided in the country before Hawley started and suggested to him that it would be a good idea for him to play the role of a granger, in case it would serve his purpose. It was also decided to make the most of the capture of Johnson, the story of which was published in the newspapers in such a way as to lead to the inference that Johnson was the man wanted, the belief being that Woodruff would see the papers and, seeing this article, would conclude that the officers had been outwitted and taken the wrong man; he would become careless, and hence be all the more easily come up with.

While the people were reading the story of Johnson's capture, the next morning after his arrival from Niobrara, believing that the murderer had really been overtaken, Hawley was preparing to start upon a second excursion in search of that individual. He again started out to find his man. This time he did find him, "and no foolin'," either.

There was one important point to be gained in making the search. No one knew definitely where Woodruff's relatives lived, though they were known to be residents of the vicinity of Council Bluffs or Omaha.

Going first to Omaha and then crossing the Missouri to Council Bluffs, the detective took a train on the Chicago, Burlington, and Quincy Railroad and went down the road about fifty miles, keeping his eyes and ears widely open in the hope of getting the slightest trace of the party he was after and then, disgusted, returned to Council Bluffs and went to his hotel. From a man whom he met there, he learned that James W. Woodruff, known to a brother of Sam, lived at Big Grove, thirty miles distant.

Disguising himself as a granger, he got a pony and a letter from Mr. Phelps of the Ogden Hotel to his foreman, Walter Farwell, on his stock ranch near the house of the Woodruffs and started off. The stock ranch was about twenty-eight and a half miles from Council Bluffs, and here Hawley hired out as a corn-husker and went to work. James Woodruff's place was about a mile and a half farther on.

Hawley passed under the name of Charles Albert and, after working one day at corn-husking, prevailed upon the foreman to send him out the following morning, looking for lost stock. It must be mentioned that, while husking corn, the detective was incidentally told by Mr. Farwell of the late arrival of a brother of James Woodruff, said to be direct from the Black Hills and with a $9,000 bank account in Deadwood. He had been home but ten days, and Hawley shrewdly suspected that this brother was the Samuel he was after. So in the course of his rambles about after lost stock, he stopped at the Woodruff farm and learned that they had moved into the town of Big Grove. The officer thereupon circled and rode into the little village from the east and spotted the Woodruff house, returning immediately thereafter to Phelps's stock place.

After unsaddling his pony and getting something to eat, he started for Council Bluffs, leaving at about eleven in the morning and arriving at about four in the afternoon. Here, on the 25th of November, he swore out a warrant for the arrest of Samuel Woodruff before Justice Baird, and securing the services of Constable Theodore Guittar, they took a two-seated buggy and at ten that night started for the stock farm again, getting there about three o'clock in the morning and seeking the barn for rest. But two hours later, they were rudely awakened by an attendant, who didn't "sabe" the presence of two rough-looking tramps.

After feeding their horses and obtaining breakfast, they drove down to Big Grove and, leaving their team concealed in the bushes on the outskirts, walked into the town. They noticed their man at work near the Woodruff house, but as soon as he saw the two strangers, he stopped his labors and went within. The officers then walked on down to the store of a Mr. Freeman, and while Hawley talked about the chances of getting work on the railroad, his companion went out and borrowed a double-barreled shotgun.

The detective discharged both barrels out of the back door and then carefully loaded the weapon with a handful of buckshot in each barrel, stating to Guittar that it meant "death to either himself or Woodruff," in case of an escape or failure to capture. A little later James Woodruff, the brother, came driving down the street and hitched his team a short distance from Freeman's store and, coming up to the latter place, began a series of questioning and requestioning, evidently endeavoring to pump the disguised detective, however with little success.

Perhaps an hour was consumed in this manner, and then he left, and a few minutes later Hawley saw the two Woodruffs coming down the street together. James carried an axe, and Sam, a revolver.

The detective pulled back the hammers of his shotgun and watched the men through the window.

As they neared the store, Hawley stepped out, apparently closely examining something about the locks of his weapon, and when the brothers reached the store, the officer brought the gun to his shoulder and said, "Sam Woodruff, throw up your hands; I want you."

Quick as a flash, the desperado's fist sought his revolver. But the cool, quiet tones of the officer, "Pull that pistol one inch, and I'll blow daylight through you," caused him to let go his grip and throw up his hands above his head.

Constable Guittar then applied the handcuffs and shackles and disarmed the man, and he was immediately marched down the street a little way, while a boy was sent after the officers' team. The brother, James, attempted a few demonstrations, but Hawley's revolver, cocked and held in position, quieted his ardor.

Five minutes later, and the officers and their prisoner were driving toward Council Bluffs at full speed, and as soon as identified by Justice Baird and turned over to Hawley, he was taken to Omaha and there lodged in jail.

Hawley, being out of funds, now telegraphed Sheriff Cook for money, and though instantly forwarded, through some red-tapeism of the telegraph company, he was delayed until too late to catch the train of that day. On the next, however, the detective and his prisoner left, reaching Cheyenne on the 29th at one o'clock in the afternoon. Before starting, the officer telegraphed Sheriff Gregg at Fremont and Sheriff Con. Groner of North Platte to meet him for the purpose of identification of his prisoner. This these officers did and fully identified the man as Samuel Woodruff. At North Platte, in addition to the sheriff, Martin Oberst, night clerk of the Railroad Hotel, recognized him as having stopped at the house two or three weeks before, when he signed his correct name. At Cheyenne he was further identified by the sheriff and T. Jeff Carr of the detective association, and upon arrival in Denver the next day, Mr. Hunter, who was in the city on business, recognized him as having stopped at his ranch on the Niobrara River on or about the 18th of September.

When brought to the sheriff's office, Woodruff refused to say anything, though on the journey he had denied all knowledge of the murder. He was driven over to the jail and his copartner in crime, Joseph Seminole, brought into his presence.

"Hello, Clarke," was Woodruff's exclamation. "What are you doing here?"

To this Seminole merely shrugged his shoulders.

"I used to know that man as Clarke when we were together in the penitentiary at Laramie City," Woodruff added, explanatorily, to the officers.

And with this these two scoundrels were locked up in separate cells. One thing worthy of note was that Seminole's description of the revolver carried by Woodruff tallied exactly with the weapon which Woodruff wore when arrested.

Much of the above is taken from the *Denver Tribune*, as told its reporter by the detectives. At this stage of the proceedings, the *Tribune* was led to remark,

To the Rocky Mountain Detective Agency, a great deal of credit is deservedly due for the able and persistent manner in which this matter has been worked up, and this final capture had added increased lustre to the reputation already borne by this excellent organization. To D. J. Cook, C. A. Hawley, W. W. Ayres, Joe Arnold, T. J. Carr, and C. P. Hoyt, the officers who have worked up the affair, special honor is due. They have been untiring in their efforts and unsparing in their expenditures and now have the pleasure of seeing total success crown their labors. Officers Cook and Arnold have secured the wagon that belonged to the murdered man from a Mr. Todd in Douglas country and will soon have the mules.

On the 3d of December, three days after Woodruff's arrival in the city, Mrs. Hayward and her two daughters, Minnie and Cora, aged then thirteen and fifteen, respectively, arrived in the city accompanied by Detective Hoyt of Golden and proceeded to the jail to identify the prisoner. When all was ready, Woodruff was brought from his cell into the parlor of the jail. Mrs. Hayward sat upon the sofa facing the door, Cora on her left and Minnie on the right. Sheriff Cook stood at the head of the sofa, and the other officials, near the windows and the door. As Woodruff entered the room, he shot one glance out of his dark eyes at the visitor on the sofa and then dropped them, never again raising them during the remainder of the interview except once, and then to reply to a question. His nervousness was quite apparent, the trembling and twitching of his hands being very perceptible.

A moment's silence after he had taken his seat, and then Mrs. Hayward said, "Minnie, is that the man?"

"Yes," was the positive and quick reply of the little girl, never raising her eyes from the close scrutiny with which she had regarded the prisoner from his entrance.

"You are sure he is the man," continued Mrs. Hayward, and the answer was as quick and as positive as before.

The other daughter, Cora, now spoke. "I know that is the man," she said, and the mother, turning to Sheriff Cook, said slowly, "Yes, that is the man—there is no mistake."

At this moment Joseph Seminole was brought into the room. "And there is the other," said Mrs. Hayward—the two daughters agreeing in like words. Then Gen. Cook asked Woodruff if he desired to ask any questions to test the visitors' belief and received the reply, "My lawyer will do my talking."

There was no longer any room for doubt. The two scoundrels who had killed an innocent man and who had led the officers such a chase as few criminals before or since their time ever did had been overtaken by the Rocky Mountain Detective Association. It had been a long but a successful chase. They had been taken and securely locked in the Arapahoe County jail, where they had been fully identified and where they awaited orders from the Jefferson County authorities.

The last chapter of this somewhat remarkable story at last opens. It is, if anything, the most thrilling of the series, as it relates the tragic end of the two men who have figured in these pages to considerable length and with whom we began when we left Middle Park in August of 1879. It is now December 28 of the same year, and the story is drawing to its close. Over three months have elapsed since Mr. Hayward, the quiet citizen and loving father and husband, was killed by these villains, but his neighbors, who knew him and appreciated his worth, had not forgotten the horror of the crime nor allowed the passing days to carry with them their desire to avenge the great wrong that had been committed.

The scene is now laid at Golden. Gen. Cook, for the Rocky Mountain Detective Association, had taken the murderers to Golden, that being the county seat of Jefferson County, on the 9th of December, and, hearing that there was a likelihood of an effort being made to lynch the scamps, took precautions to prevent such a result. It had long been his boast that no prisoner had ever been taken from his hands and lynched, and he did not propose to have his creditable reputation blackened now. He was fully prepared to meet any attempt upon the lives of the men that might be made, and appreciating the sort of man they were dealing with, the Jefferson vigilantes wisely decided to await "a more convenient season" for the putting into execution of any designs they might have. The prisoners feared lynching and trembled when Cook and his party left them after they had been identified and placed in jail. Woodruff said, "I fear those old farmers who were Hayward's neighbors. They are a great deal more determined and bitter than miners."

His fears were well founded. The dreadful hour came shortly after midnight on the cool, crisp Sunday morning of Christmas week of '79.

A few minutes before twelve o'clock Saturday night, the late habitués of saloons and billiard halls, as well as others who happened to be awake at that hour, noticed the riding along the principal street of numerous horsemen, who came from apparently all directions and in little squads of two, three, half a dozen, or so. They noticed that these silent horsemen all rode toward the jail, and all seemed to be intent on some urgent business. Then, remembering the oft-repeated murmurs of lynching made against the imprisoned murderers of poor old Hayward, a number of citizens followed in the wake of the strangers, who made at the jail a cavalcade of at least a hundred men, armed to the teeth and grimly seated upon their horses, not even talking or whispering among themselves.

A consultation between the chief and his lieutenants took place upon the steps leading to the first floor above the basement of the courthouse, and a few minutes later, without noise or confusion, a large circle of guards was spread around the jail and some two or three hundred yards distant from it. These grim sentinels were but a few paces apart, and some were mounted and some on foot. Every member of this avenging band wore a mask or a handkerchief across the face or had his features blackened with burnt cork, so that recognition was absolutely impossible. No one was permitted to pass this cordon of guards, no matter what the excuse. One man climbed a telegraph pole, and the telephone wire from the jail was cut, and thus all communication to and from the building was ended. Then the horses were ridden to a vacant lot opposite and tied, while the riders dismounted and closed in upon the jail. There was no noise or confusion. Everything had been carefully planned, and every man had a certain position and a certain duty assigned, and he silently took the one and performed the other.

There were in the building, aside from the prisoners in the cells, Under-Sheriff Joseph Boyd, who was asleep with his family in a rear room, and an extra watchman, Edgar Cox, who was lying upon a bench in the sheriff's office. Hearing the sound of feet on the frozen earth outside, Cox rose to a sitting position and looked up at the windows, the curtains of which were raised. At each window he saw, to his stupefaction, two or three men, who had rifles in their hands. Their gleaming barrels pointed directly at him, and a stern voice simply said, "Don't move, or you'll get hurt."

Under the circumstances Cox did not move but sat gazing at the deadly weapons which so steadily and unrelentingly covered him, while he could hear the heavy tramp of men marching in at the front door and filing down the inside stairs to the basement.

This same *tramp, tramp* of many feet, foretelling something unusual, reached the ears of Under-Sheriff Boyd, who was in bed, and he suddenly awoke with the feeling that there was trouble ahead. Hastily pulling on his clothes, he rushed out of his room and saw the two rooms, from which the two doors open into the jail part, teeming with masked and armed men, who apparently paid no attention to him whatever. As he passed the "feeding" door—so termed because through this the prisoners' meals are taken in to them—he noticed that the outer wooden door was splintered and the lock broken off. Pushing his way through to the front room, he mounted to the third step of the stairs leading to the first floor and, raising his voice, said, "Gentlemen, listen to me one moment. You are, or I take you to be, law-abiding and law-loving citizens, and yet you are now engaged in unlawful proceedings. I beg of you to cease and not in your indignation or passionate feelings take the law into your own hands. Rest assured justice will be obtained, even though it take a little longer."

At this juncture three men at the foot of the stairs pulled their revolvers and covered the speaker, while one said, "Hands up, sir—we know our business."

To which Boyd replied, "I'll not hold up my hands. I know you have not come here to harm me," and recommenced his expostulation and entreaty to the men in front of him.

In the meantime, a number of the vigilantes had attacked the iron-grated door with sledge hammers and crowbars. Every blow told, and sinewy and muscular arms sent the heavy instruments to the points where they would do the most good.

The under-sheriff still continued his address to the men, and finally the leader, a tall, well-built man, ordered three of his fellows to take Boyd into custody and remove him. They instantly complied, and the officer was taken into the inner room, where he still continued his protestations. The blows fell thick and fast upon the great, strong lock, and at last with a crash, it gave way and the door swung open, and those terrible, determined men swarmed within.

Previous to all this, the prisoners were sound asleep in their cells, save one, Joseph Murphy, in for petty larceny and who was out of his cell, being on duty in keeping up the fire and such other little chores as might be necessary.

As the assault began upon the bolts of the iron door, Woodruff awoke with a start and sprang to the grating of his cell, where he glared in tremulous anxiety upon the bars that were trembling beneath the rain of blows. Seminole, too, awoke about the same time and began a low moaning in his terrible fear, though he did not arise from his bed, but as the door at last gave way and the crowd rushed in, he gave vent to a cry which is described as being more like the shriek of some wild animal than any other noise.

Without loss of time, the vigilantes attacked the padlocks on cells fourteen and twelve, the former being Woodruff's and the latter Seminole's. Noticing the liberty of Murphy and supposing that he might attempt to escape in the confusion, the leader of these midnight dispensers of justice went to Boyd, who was still under guard, and told him he had better lock up such prisoners as might be loose.

"Will you pledge your word of honor for yourself and men that you will not touch the keys if I get them?" asked the faithful official.

"Yes," was the brief but evidently earnest reply.

Calling the watchman, Cox, and accompanied still by his masked guard, Boyd went to the vault and began to work the combination that opened it. Before giving the last twist, however, he turned to his silent captors, and said, "You have heard the pledge given by your captain or chief or whatever you call him in relation to the keys; have I your words of honor also?"

They bowed a grim assent, and a moment later the bolt shot back and the iron door turned on its hinges. Taking the keys the official entered the jail and locked Murphy up. As he passed the cells containing two burglars, they begged to be released, fearing lest the vigilantes would also make an example of them. Boyd assured them that they would not be harmed, or at least he would do all in his power to protect them.

In the meantime cold chisels had cut into the cell padlocks, and sledge hammers completed the job. Woodruff was on his feet and showed fight, but his visitors were determined men, and the cold-blooded murderer was soon rendered docile, a few raps with the butt of a revolver being administered on the top of his head. He was carried out and laid upon his stomach on the floor, his face resting upon his left side, while skillful and willing hands bound his wrists together behind his back. As he was being taken from his cell, he made but one remark, "Gentlemen, you are mistaken. I am innocent of this crime."

When the tying was completed, he was lifted up to a sitting posture and asked for the captain, referring to Boyd, and that officer immediately came forward.

Laying hand upon the shoulder of the prisoner, Boyd said, "Well, Woodruff, what can I do for you?"

Woodruff raised his dark eyes to the kindly face above him and, with a low voice, inexpressibly sad and full of feeling, said, "Captain, write to my wife—and to my brother, and tell them all about this, will you? Don't forget it. Write to (and a name was given which the officer forgets) and tell him to avenge my death—he'll do it."

"Gentlemen," he said, turning to his captors, "this is not the last of this."

Then Boyd said, "Is that all I can do for you, Sam?"

"Yes," said the prisoner, "all—all."

During all this time, the men had been hammering away at Seminole's cell, and as Woodruff finished speaking, the door was opened and a number of men sprang within. Seminole was lying upon his face, moaning fearfully in his terror. He was quickly picked up and carried out and his hands bound behind him in like manner to Woodruff's.

Without further hesitation or delay and in perfect silence, the prisoners, the manacles on their ankles clanking a dismal dead march, were taken out through the front door of the basement and taken in the direction of the Golden and South Platte Railroad, three or four hundred yards distant. Woodruff refused to walk and was half carried and half pushed, but Seminole did what he could in the way of locomotion, and in a few minutes, the men were on the railroad bridge that crosses Kinney Creek.

The bridge is a timber one, having three spans, supported on spiles resting on wooden foundations. A rope three-eighths of an inch in diameter was produced, which was supposed to be long enough to hang both men, but being found too short, a delay occurred while a new one, an inch in diameter, was obtained. Woodruff was stationed on the end nearest Denver and Seminole just five sleepers farther away. With nooses about their necks, the other ends of the ropes being fastened to the projecting ends of the timbers (notches being cut to prevent any slipping), the men stood.

"Sam Woodruff, do you wish to say anything?" was the grim question of the masked leader.

The man addressed looked around upon the crowd in silence a few moments and then without further preface, said, "Gentleman, you are hanging an innocent man, but I trust God will forgive you, as I do. May I say my prayers?"

Assent being given, the doomed man knelt and silently prayed to the Almighty. When he had finished, he arose to his feet and, looking once more upon his captors, said, "I have one last request to make. Permit me to jump off the bridge; don't push me to my death."

But his request was not granted, and a few moments later a dozen hands pushed him off the edge—off the edge into eternity.

When Seminole was asked if he had anything to say, he choked a moment and then, in a clear, distinct voice, said,

Gentlemen, I have but little to say, and I address myself to those among you who may be erring ones. Beware of the first bad step. The after ones are not to be feared; it is the beginnings. But for my first evil break, I would not be standing here tonight with this rope about my neck and death staring me in the face. In relation to this murder, gentlemen, we two are the guilty ones. We committed the crime. I have no excuse to offer, nothing to say.

And then, raising his head toward heaven, his lips moving tremulously, he broke out with, "O, God Almighty, have mercy on my sinful soul; and as Thou hast shown Thy love and tenderness in times past to weak and guilty ones, show such to me now. Guard, oh, I pray Thee, my mother and brothers, and let not them follow in my footsteps or take my sinful path. Forgive me my transgressions, O God, and"—his voice broke slightly—"take me to Thee, sinful though I am." And then, in simple but beautiful and eloquent terms, he prayed for the well-being and salvation of his captors and executioners.

During this prayer the vigilantes stood around, with hats removed and heads bowed, in reverential listening. It was a somber, impressive picture. The moonlight shining cold and clear upon the scene; the fated man, with eyes turned toward the zenith, one foot upon the iron rail of the track, the other upon the tie to which was attached the rope that drooped from his neck; the swinging, twitching body of his companion in crime dangling in awful solitude below; the congregated men with uncovered and bent heads, and their faces hid beneath grim masks; the polished barrels of rifles and guns gleaming in the moonbeams, and the grave-like silence alone broken by the earnest, feeling words of the speaker—a picture never to be forgotten. And when at last the lips were closed and the fatal push was given, even the stern executioners of inexorable law felt a tremor run through their stalwart, muscular limbs.

Seminole died instantly, his neck being broken in the fall, but swinging past the spiles the skin on the knuckles of his right hand was rubbed off. Woodruff died hard, his struggles for breath being distinctly heard, and his limbs twitching convulsively.

The work was done, and the vigilantes slowly retraced their steps to their horses and without a word mounted to their saddles, while the two bodies hanging beneath the bridge twisted and twirled and finally rested motionless, stirred only now and then by a passing breeze that played fitfully with their fast-stiffening forms.

During the confusion in securing the prisoners in the jail, Mr. Boyd managed to get to the telephone and attempted to communicate with the town. But in vain. Then he sent Cox, the watchman, off to alarm Sheriff Belcher, but ere the messenger had proceeded a dozen yards, he was stopped and returned to the building. The sheriff was asleep at his home when, about one o'clock, he was awakened by his brother-in-law, Archer DeFrance, who told him that something was going on at the jail, and a few moments later, a black watchman named Baker, who had been especially instructed in view of such an emergency, came in with the alarm also. A few minutes later, and the sheriff was hastening at the top of his speed toward the jail on the hill. But he was too late. The murderers of R. B. Hayward had gone to their final account, and the vigilantes, with the exception of a guard on the ridge near the bodies, had disappeared as quietly and mysteriously as they had come. Then the sheriff went for the coroner, Dr. Joseph W. Anderson, and without loss of time, that officer arrived upon the ground. While he was examining the bodies, the coroner was hailed by the vigilantes with, "What are you doing?"

"Examining into your devilish work."

"Are they dead?"

"Yes; deader than hell."

"All right. Hayward is avenged. Good night." And the sentinel horsemen rode off with a parting wave of their hands.

As the main body of men left the scene of the lynching, they fired a farewell shot from their pistols, and as their number was variously estimated at from one hundred to a hundred and fifty, it made quite a volley.

After viewing the hanged men, the coroner ordered the sheriff to cut them down, which was done, and D. P. Maynard having been sent for and arriving with his express wagon, the corpses were taken up and conveyed to an unoccupied storeroom on Ford Street. Here they were placed under the care of two watchers and, about nine o'clock in the morning, were conveyed to the courthouse, where, an hour later, the jury impaneled by the coroner held the inquest and brought in a verdict to the effect that Seminole and Woodruff "came to their death upon the 28th day of December, 1879, being taken from the jail and custody of the said jailer of said county by force and violence, between the hours of twelve and one o'clock a.m. and hanged by the neck by parties unknown to this jury and with felonious intent."

After the tragedy the undertaker laid the bodies out in plain pine boxes, painted black on the outside, and, untying their hands, crossed them in front. Woodruff was dressed in a dark check shirt, duck overall, and cotton stockings, without shoes. His eyes were half-open, and his mouth, with its lips slightly apart, disclosed his regular teeth beneath. During his confinement in Golden, he had not shaved, and a rough growth of beard covered his cheeks and chin. His forehead was covered with blood that dripped from the wounds on the top of his head caused by the necessary rapping given with the pistol butt when taking him out of his cell.

Seminole wore a checkered vest and a dark sack coat over his undershirt. Dark pantaloons, brown mixed stockings, and Indian moccasins completed the balance of his attire. His mouth and eyes were firmly closed, and from either corner of the shut lips, a streak of blood ran down upon his neck, while watery matter oozed slightly from his left eye. His face was considerably swollen, and decomposition soon set in. The knots on both nooses had slipped around to the front, immediately beneath the chin, and had cut somewhat into the flesh of both men. The back of Woodruff's neck was badly cut and much swollen, and blood marked the courses on both necks followed by the rope. In order to accommodate Woodruff's body, a box six feet, seven inches, long was necessary, and six feet, one inch, for Seminole.

Monday afternoon, succeeding the day of the lynching, no answer having been received from relatives, both Seminole and Woodruff were buried in the Golden cemetery.

And thus Samuel Woodruff and Joseph Seminole pass out of the world's daily history, and another terrible example is recorded to give terror to all evildoers.

Recording the tragedy as above related, the *Tribune* of December 30 said,

In wandering through the town of Golden yesterday and conversing with business men of all grades of social and intellectual standing, the reporter failed to find one solitary person who condemned this recent lynching. On every side the popular verdict seemed to be that the hanging was not only well merited but a positive gain to the county, saving it at least five or six thousand dollars. In plumply asking the question from thirteen representative men, the *Tribune* commissioner met with the unvarying response, "It was the best thing possible, and we are all glad of it."

4

A TRAGEDY OF THE SIERRAS

BY C. F. MCGLASHAN

The promise of a new and fruitful life drew thousands to California. And why not? There was a welcoming climate and more land than they could imagine. All they needed to do was make the journey across the Sierras, and it was theirs. What could be the problem?

On the evening of the second day after leaving Donner Lake, Reed's party and the little band of famished emigrants found themselves in a cold, bleak, uncomfortable hollow, somewhere near the lower end of Summit Valley. Here the storm broke in all its fury upon the doomed company. In addition to the cold, sleet-like snow, a fierce, penetrating wind seemed to freeze the very marrow in their bones. The relief party had urged the tired, hungry, enfeebled emigrants forward at the greatest possible speed all day in order to get as near the settlements as they could before the storm should burst upon them. Besides, their provisions were exhausted, and they were anxious to reach certain caches of supplies which they had made while going to the cabins. Fearing that the storm would prevent the party from reaching these caches, Mr. Reed sent Joseph Jondro, Matthew Dofar, and Hiram Turner forward to the first cache, with instructions to get the provisions and return to the suffering emigrants. That very night the storm came, and the three men had not been heard from.

The camp was in a most inhospitable spot. Exposed to the fury of the wind and storm, shelterless, supperless, overwhelmed with discouragements, the entire party sank down exhausted upon the snow. The entire party? No! There was one man who never ceased to work. When a fire had been kindled and nearly everyone had given up, this one man, unaided, continued to strive to erect some sort of shelter to protect the defenseless women and children. Planting large pine boughs in the snow, he banked up the snow on either side of them so as to form a wall. Hour after hour, in the darkness and raging storm, he toiled on alone, building the sheltering breastwork which was to ward off death from the party who by this time had crept shiveringly under its protection. But for this shelter, all would have perished before morning. At midnight the man was still at work. The darting snow particles seemed to cut his eyeballs, and the glare of the fire and the great physical exhaustion under which he was laboring gradually rendered him blind. Like his companions, he had borne a child in his arms all day over the soft, yielding snow. Like them, he was drenched to the skin, and his clothing was frozen stiff and hard with ice. Yet he kept up the fire, built a great sheltering wall about the sufferers, and went here and there among the wailing and dying. With unabated violence the storm continued its relentless fury. The survivors say it was the coldest night they ever experienced. There is a limit to human endurance. The man was getting stone-blind. Had he attempted to speak, his tongue would have cloven to the roof of his mouth. His senses were chilled, blunted, dead. Sleep had stilled the plaintive cries of those about him. All was silent, save the storm. Without knowing it, this heroic man was yielding to a sleep more powerful than that which had overcome his companions. While trying to save those who were weaker than himself, he had been literally freezing. Sightless, benumbed, moving half-unconsciously about his work, he staggered, staggered, staggered, and finally sank in the snow. All slept! As he put no more fuel upon the fire, the flames died down. The logs upon which the fire had rested gave way, and most of the coals fell upon the snow. They were in almost total darkness.

Presently someone awoke. It was Mrs. Breen, whose motherly watchfulness prevented more than a few consecutive moments' sleep. The camp was quickly aroused. All were nearly frozen. Hiram Miller's hands were so cold and frosted that the skin on the fingers cracked open when he tried to split some kindlings. At last the fire was some-how renewed. Meantime they had discovered their leader—he who had been working throughout the night—lying cold, speechless, and apparently dead upon the snow. Hiram Miller and William McCutchen carried the man to the fire, chafed his hands and limbs, rubbed his body vigorously, and worked with him as hard as they could for two hours before he showed signs of returning consciousness. Redoubling their exertions, they kept at work until the cold, gray morning dawned, ere the man was fully restored. Would you know the name of this man, this hero? It was James Frazier Reed.

From this time forward, all the toil, all the responsibility, devolved upon William McCutchen and Hiram Miller. Jondro, Dofar, and Turner were caught in the drifts ahead. The fishers or other wild animals had almost completely devoured the first cache of provisions, and while these men were trying to reach the second cache, the storm imprisoned them. They could neither go forward nor return. Cady and Stone were between Donner Lake and Starved Camp and were in a like helpless condition. McCutchen and Miller were the only ones able to do anything toward saving the poor creatures who were huddled together at the miserable camp. All the other men were completely disheartened by the fearful calamity which had overtaken them. But for the untiring exertions of these two men, death to all would have been certain. McCutchen had on four shirts, and yet he became so chilled while trying to kindle the fire that in getting warm he burned the back out of his shirts. He only discovered the mishap by the scorching and burning of his flesh.

What a picture of desolation was presented to the inmates of Starved Camp during the next three days! It stormed incessantly. One who has not witnessed a storm on the Sierra cannot imagine the situation. A quotation from Bret Harte's *Gabriel Conroy* will afford the best idea of the situation:

Snow. Everywhere. As far as the eye could reach fifty miles, looking southward from the highest white peak. Filling ravines and gulches and dropping from the walls of canyons in white shroud-like drifts, fashioning the dividing ridge into the likeness of a monstrous grave, hiding the bases of giant pines, and completely covering young trees and larches, rimming with porcelain the bowl-like edges of still, cold lakes, and undulating in motionless white billows to the edge of the distant horizon. Snow lying everywhere on the California Sierra and still falling. It had been snowing in finely granulated powder; in damp, spongy flakes; in thin, feathery plumes; snowing from a leaden sky steadily, snowing fiercely, shaken out of purple-black clouds in white flocculent masses, or dropping in long level lines like white lances from the tumbled and broken heavens. But always silently! The woods were so choked with it, it had so cushioned and muffled the ringing rocks and echoing hills, that all sound was deadened. The strongest gust, the fiercest blast, awoke no sigh or complaint from the snow-packed, rigid files of forest. There was no cracking of bough nor crackle of underbrush; the overladen branches of pine and fir yielded and gave away without a sound. The silence was vast, measureless, complete!

In alluding to these terrible days in his diary, Mr. Reed says, under date of March 6,

With the snow there is a perfect hurricane. In the night there is a great crying among the children, and even with the parents there is praying, crying, and lamentation on account of the cold and the dread of death from hunger and the howling storm. The men up nearly all night making fires. Some of the men began praying. Several of them became blind. I could not see the light of the fire blazing before me nor tell when it was burning. The light of heaven is, as it were, shut out from us. The snow blows so thick and fast that we cannot see twenty feet looking against the wind. I dread the coming night. Three of my men only able to get wood. The rest have given out for the present. It is still snowing and very cold. So cold that the few men employed in cutting the dry trees down have to come and warm about every ten minutes. "Hungry! Hungry!" is the cry with the children, and nothing to give them. "Freezing!" is the cry of the mothers, who have nothing for their little, starving, freezing children. Night closing fast, and with it the hurricane increases.

March 7. Thank God day has once more appeared, although darkened by the storm. Snowing as fast as ever, and the hurricane has never ceased for ten minutes at a time during one of the most dismal nights I have ever witnessed. I hope I shall never witness another such in a similar situation. Of all the praying and crying I ever heard, nothing ever equaled it. Several times I expected to see the people perish of the extreme cold. At one time our fire was nearly gone, and had it not been for McCutchen's exertions, it would have entirely disappeared. If the fire had been lost, two-thirds of the camp would have been out of their misery before morning; but, as God would have it, we soon had it blazing comfortably, and the sufferings of the people became less for a time. Hope began to animate the bosoms of many, young and old, when the cheering blaze rose through the dry pine logs we had piled together. One would say, "Thank God for the fire!" Another, "How good it is!" The poor, little, half-starved, half-frozen children would say, "I'm glad, I'm glad we have got some fire! Oh, how good it feels! It is good our fire didn't go out!" At times the storm would burst forth with such fury that I felt alarmed for the safety of the people on account of the tall timber that surrounded us.

Death entered the camp on the first night. He came to claim one who was a true, faithful mother. One who merits greater praise than language can convey. Though comparatively little has been told concerning her life by the survivors, doubt not that Mrs. Elizabeth Graves was one of the noblest of the mothers of the Donner Party. Her charity is kindly remembered by all who have spoken her name. To her companions in misfortune, she always gave such food as she possessed; for her children she now gave her life. The last morsels of food, the last grain of flour, she had placed in the mouths of her babes, though she was dying of starvation.

Mrs. Farnham, who talked personally with Mrs. Breen, gives the following description of that terrible night:

Mrs. Breen told me that she had her husband and five children together, lying with their feet to the fire and their heads under shelter of the snow breast-work. She sat by them, with only moccasins on her feet and a blanket drawn over her shoulders and head, within which and a shawl she constantly wore, she nursed her poor baby on her knees. Her milk had been gone several days, and the child was so emaciated and lifeless that she scarcely expected at any time on opening the covering to find it alive. Mrs. Graves lay with her babe and three or four older children at the other side of the fire. The storm was very violent all night, and she watched through it, dozing occasionally for a few minutes and then rousing herself to brush the snow and fly-ing sparks from the covering of the sleepers. Toward morning she heard one of the young girls opposite call to her mother to cover her. The call was repeated several times impatiently, when she spoke to the child, reminding her of the exhaustion and fatigue her mother suffered in nursing and carrying the baby and bidding her cover herself, and let her mother rest. Presently she heard the mother speak, in a quiet, unnatural tone, and she called to one of the men near her to go and speak to her. He arose after a few minutes and found the poor sufferer almost past speaking. He took her infant and, after shaking the snow from her blanket, covered her as well as might be. Shortly after, Mrs. Breen observed her to turn herself slightly and throw one arm feebly up, as if to go to sleep. She waited a little while, and seeing her remain quite still, she walked around to her. She was already cold in death. Her poor starving child wailed and moaned piteously in the arms of its young sister, but the mother's heart could no more warm or nourish it.

The members of the second relief party realized that they were themselves in imminent danger of death. They were powerless to carry the starving children over the deep, soft, treacherous snow, and it was doubtful if they would be able to reach the settlements unencumbered. Isaac Donner, one of the sons of Jacob and Elizabeth Donner, perished during one of the stormy nights. He was lying on the bed of pine boughs between his sister Mary and Patty Reed and died so quietly that neither of the sleeping girls awoke.

The relief party determined to set out over the snow, hasten to the settlements, and send back relief. Solomon Hook, Jacob Donner's oldest boy, insisted that he was able to walk and therefore joined the party. Hiram Miller, an old friend of the Reed family, took little Thomas Reed in his arms and set out with the others. Patty Reed, full of hope and courage, refused to be carried by her father and started on foot.

With what emotions did the poor sufferers in Starved Camp watch the party as it disappeared among the pines! There was no food in camp, and death had already selected two of their number. What a pitiable group it was! Could a situation more desolate or deplorable be imagined? Mr. Breen, as has been heretofore mentioned, was feeble, sickly, and almost as helpless as the children. Upon Mrs. Breen devolved the care, not only of her husband, but of all who remained in the fatal camp, for all others were children. John Breen, their eldest son, was the strongest and most vigorous in the family, yet the following incident shows how near he was to death's door. It must have occurred the morning the relief party left. The heat of the fire had melted a deep, round hole in the snow. At the bottom of the pit was the fire. The men were able to descend the sides of this cavity and frequently did so to attend to the fire. At one time, while William McCutchen was down by the fire, John Breen was sitting on the end of one of the logs on which the fire had originally been kindled. Several logs had been laid side by side, and the fire had been built in the middle of the floor thus constructed. While the central logs had burned out and let the fire descend, the outer logs remained with their ends on the firm snow. On one of these logs John Breen was sitting. Suddenly overcome by fatigue and hunger, he fainted and dropped headlong into the fire pit. Fortunately, Mr. McCutchen caught the falling boy and thus saved him from a horrible death. It was some time before the boy was fully restored to consciousness. Mrs. Breen had a small quantity of sugar, and a little was placed between his clenched teeth. This seemed to revive him, and he not only survived but is living today, the head of a large family in San Benito County.

Mrs. Breen's younger children, Patrick, James, Peter, and the nursing babe, Isabella, were completely helpless and dependent. Not less helpless were the orphan children of Mr. and Mrs. Graves. Nancy was only about nine years old, and upon her devolved the task of caring for the babe, Elizabeth. Nancy Graves is now the wife of the earnest and eloquent divine Rev. R. W. Williamson of Los Gatos, Santa Clara County. To her lasting honor be it said, that although she was dying of hunger in Starved Camp, yet she faithfully tended, cared for, and saved her baby sister. Aside from occasional bits of sugar, this baby and Mrs. Breen's had nothing for an entire week, save snow water. Besides Nancy and Elizabeth, there were of the Graves children Jonathan, aged seven, and Franklin, aged five years. Franklin soon perished. Starvation and exposure had so reduced his tiny frame that he could not endure these days of continual fasting.

Mary M. Donner, whom all mention as one of the most lovely girls in the Donner Party, met with a cruel accident the night before the relief party left Starved Camp. Her feet had become frozen and insensible to pain. Happening to lie too near the fire, one of her feet became dreadfully burned. She suffered excruciating agony yet evinced remarkable fortitude. She ultimately lost four toes from her left foot on account of this sad occurrence.

Seven of the Breens, Mary Donner, and the three children of Mr. and Mrs. Graves, made the eleven now waiting for relief at Starved Camp. Mrs. Graves, her child Franklin, and the boy, Isaac Donner, who lay stark in death upon the snow, completed the fourteen who were left by the relief party.

Meantime, how fared it with those who were pressing forward toward the settlements? At each step they sank two or three feet into the snow. Of course those who were ahead broke the path, and the others, as far as possible, stepped in their tracks. This, Patty Reed could not do because she was too small. So determined was she, however, that, despite the extra exertion she was compelled to undergo, she would not admit being either cold or fatigued. Patty Reed has been mentioned as only eight years old. Many of the survivors speak of her, however, in much the same terms as John Breen, who says, "I was under the impression that she was older. She had a wonderful mind for one of her age. She had, I have often thought, as much sense as a grown person." Over Patty's large, dark eyes on this morning gradually crept a film. Previous starvation had greatly attenuated her system, and she was far too weak to endure the hardship she had undertaken. Gradually the snow-mantled forests, the forbidding mountains, the deep, dark canyon of Bear River, and even the forms of her companions faded from view. In their stead came a picture of such glory and brightness as seldom comes to human eyes. It was a vision of angels and of brilliant stars. She commenced calling her father and those with him and began talking about the radiant forms that hovered over her. Her wan, pale face was illumined with smiles, and with an ecstasy of joy, she talked of the angels and stars and of the happiness she experienced. "Why, Reed," exclaimed McCutchen, "Patty is dying!" And it was too true.

For a few moments, the party forgot their own sufferings and trials and ministered to the wants of the spiritual child, whose entrance into the dark valley had been heralded by troops of white-winged angels. At Starved Camp, Reed had taken the hard, frozen sacks in which the provisions had been carried and, by holding them to the fire, had thawed out the seams and scraped therefrom about a teaspoonful of crumbs. These he had placed in the thumb of his woolen mitten to be used in case of emergency. Little did he suppose that the emergency would come so soon. Warming and moistening these crumbs between his own lips, the father placed them in his child's mouth. Meantime they had wrapped a blanket around her chilled form and were busily chafing her hands and feet. Her first return to consciousness was signaled by the regrets she expressed at having been awakened from her beautiful dream. To this day she cherishes the memory of that vision as the dearest, most enchanting of all her life. After this, some of the kindhearted Frenchmen in the party took turns with Reed in carrying Patty upon their backs.

Past-midshipman S. E. Woodworth is a name that in most published accounts figures conspicuously among the relief parties organized to rescue the Donner Party. At the time Reed and his companions were suffering untold horrors on the mountains and those left at Starved Camp were perishing of starvation, Woodworth, with an abundance of supplies, was lying idle in camp at Bear Valley. This was the part that Selim E. Woodworth took in the relief of the sufferers.

The three men who had been sent forward to the caches left the remnant of the provisions which had not been destroyed where it could easily be seen by Reed and his companions. Hurrying forward, they reached Woodworth's camp, and two men, John Stark and Howard Oakley, returned and met Reed's party. It was quite time. With frozen feet and exhausted bodies, the members of the second relief were in a sad plight. They left the settlements strong, hearty men. They returned in a half-dead condition. Several lost some of their toes on account of having them frozen, and one or two were crippled for life. They had been three days on the way from Starved Camp to Woodworth's. Cady and Stone overtook Reed and his companions on the second day after leaving Starved Camp. On the night of the third day, they arrived at Woodworth's.

When Patty Reed reached Woodworth's and had been provided with suitable food, an incident occurred which fully illustrates the tenderness and womanliness of her nature. Knowing that her mother and dear ones were safe, knowing that relief would speedily return to those on the mountains, realizing that for her there was to be no more hunger or snow and that she would no longer be separated from her father, her feelings may well be imagined. In her quiet joy, she was not wholly alone. Hidden away in her bosom, during all the suffering and agony of the journey over the mountains, were a number of childish treasures. First, there was a lock of silvery gray hair which her own hand had cut from the head of her Grandmother Keyes way back on the Big Blue River. Patty had always been a favorite with her grandma, and when the latter died, Patty secured this lock of hair. She tied it up in a little piece of old-fashioned lawn, dotted with wee blue flowers, and always carried it in her bosom. But this was not all. She had a dainty little glass saltcellar, scarcely larger than the inside of a hummingbird's nest, and, what was more precious than this, a tiny, wooden doll. This doll had been her constant companion. It had black eyes and hair and was indeed very pretty. At Woodworth's camp, Patty told "Dolly" all her joy and gladness, and who cannot pardon the little girl for thinking her dolly looked happy as she listened?

Patty Reed is now Mrs. Frank Lewis of San Jose, California. She has a pleasant home and a beautiful family of children. Yet oftentimes the mother, the grown-up daughters, and the younger members of the family gather with tear-dimmed eyes about a little sacred box. In this box is the lock of hair in the piece of lawn, the tiny saltcellar, the much loved "Dolly," and an old woolen mitten, in the thumb of which are yet the traces of fine crumbs.

Very noble was the part which Mrs. Margaret Breen performed in this Donner tragedy, and very beautifully has that part been recorded by a woman's hand. It is written so tenderly, so delicately, and with so much reverence for the maternal love which alone sustained Mrs. Breen that it can hardly be improved. This account was published by its author, Mrs. Farnham, in 1849 and is made the basis of the following sketch. With alterations here and there made for the sake of brevity, the article is as it was written:

> There was no food in Starved Camp. There was nothing to eat, save a few seeds tied in bits of cloth that had been brought along by someone and the precious lump of sugar. There were also a few teaspoonfuls of tea. They sat and lay by the fire most of the day, with what heavy hearts, who shall know! They were upon about thirty feet of snow. The dead lay before them, a ghastlier sight in the sunshine that succeeded the storm than when the dark clouds overhung them. They had no words of

cheer to speak to each other, no courage or hope to share, but those which pointed to a life where hunger and cold could never come, and their benumbed faculties were scarcely able to seize upon a consolation so remote from the thoughts and wants that absorbed their whole being.

A situation like this will not awaken in common natures religious trust. Under such protracted suffering, the animal outgrows the spiritual in frightful disproportion. Yet the mother's sublime faith, which had brought her thus far through her agonies with a heart still warm toward those who shared them, did not fail her now. She spoke gently to one and another, asked her husband to repeat the litany and the children to join her in the responses, and endeavored to fix their minds upon the time when the relief would probably come. Nature, as unerringly as philosophy could have done, taught her that the only hope of sustaining those about her was to set before them a termination to their sufferings.

What days and nights were those that went by while they waited! Life waning visibly in those about her; not a morsel of food to offer them; her own infant—and the little one that had been cherished and saved through all by the mother now dead—wasting hourly into the more perfect image of death; her husband worn to a skeleton; it needed the fullest measure of exalted faith, of womanly tenderness and self-sacrifice, to sustain her through such a season. She watched by night as well as by day. She gathered wood to keep them warm. She boiled the handful of tea and dispensed it to them, and when she found one sunken and speechless, she broke with her teeth a morsel of the precious sugar and put it in his lips. She fed her babe freely on snow water, and scanty as was the wardrobe she had, she managed to get fresh clothing next to its skin two or three times a week. Where, one asks in wonder and reverence, did she get the strength and courage for all this? She sat all night by her family, her elbows on her knees, brooding over the meek little victim that lay there, watching those who slept, and occasionally dozing with a fearful consciousness of their terrible condition always upon her. The sense of peril never slumbered. Many times during the night, she went to the sleepers to ascertain if they all still breathed. She put her hand under their blankets and held it before the mouth. In this way she assured herself that they were yet alive. But once her blood curdled to find, on approaching her hand to the lips of one of her own children, there was no warm breath upon it. She tried to open his mouth and found the jaws set. She roused her husband, "Oh! Patrick, man! Arise and help me! James is dying!" "Let him die!" said the miserable father. "He will be better off than any of us." She was terribly shocked by this reply. In her own expressive language, her heart stood still when she heard it. She was bewildered and knew not where to set her weary hands to work, but she recovered in a few moments and began to chafe the breast and hands of the perishing boy. She broke a bit of sugar and with considerable effort forced it between his teeth with a few drops of snow water. She saw him swallow, then a slight convulsive motion stirred his features, he stretched his limbs feebly, and in a moment more opened his eyes and looked upon her. How fervent were her thanks to the Great Father, whom she forgot not day or night.

Thus she went on. The tea leaves were eaten, the seeds chewed, the sugar all dispensed. The days were bright and, compared with the nights, comfortable. Occasionally, when the sun shone, their voices were heard, though generally they sat or lay in a kind of stupor from which she often found it alarmingly difficult to arouse them. When the gray evening twilight drew its deepening curtain over the cold glittering heavens and the icy waste, and when the famishing bodies had been covered from the frost that pinched them with but little less keenness than the unrelenting hunger, the solitude seemed to rend her very brain. Her own powers faltered. But she said her prayers over many times in the darkness as well as the light and always with renewed trust in Him who had not yet forsaken her, and thus she sat out her weary watch. After the turning of the night, she always sat watching for the morning star, which seemed, every time she saw it rise clear in the cold eastern sky, to renew the promise, "As thy day is, so shall thy strength be."

Their fire had melted the snow to a considerable depth, and they were lying on the bank above. Thus they had less of its heat than they needed and found some difficulty in getting the fuel she gathered placed so it would burn. One morning after she had hailed her messenger of promise and the light had increased so as to render objects visible in the distance, she looked as usual over the white expanse that lay to the southwest to see if any dark, moving specks were visible upon its surface. Only the treetops, which she had scanned so often as to be quite familiar with their appearance, were to be seen. With a heavy heart, she brought herself back from that distant hope to consider what was immediately about her. The fire had sunk so far away that they had felt but little of its warmth the last two nights, and casting her eyes down into the snow pit, whence it sent forth only a dull glow, she thought she saw the welcome face of beloved mother Earth. It was such a renewing sight after their long, freezing separation from it. She immediately aroused her eldest son, John, and, with a great deal of difficulty and repeating words of cheer and encouragement, brought him to understand that she wished him to descend by one of the treetops which had fallen in so as to make a sort of ladder and see if they could reach the naked earth and if it were possible for them all to go down. She trembled with fear at the vacant silence in which he at first gazed at her, but at length, after she had told him a great many times, he said "Yes, Mother," and went.

He reached the bottom safely and presently spoke to her. There was naked, dry earth under his feet; it was warm, and he wished her to come down. She laid her baby beside some of the sleepers and descended. Immediately she determined upon taking them all down. How good, she thought, as she descended the boughs, was the God whom she trusted. By perseverance, by entreaty, by encouragement, and with her own aid, she got them into this snug shelter.

Relief came not, and as starvation crept closer and closer to himself and those about him, Patrick Breen determined that it was his duty to employ the means of sustaining life which God seemed to have placed before them. The lives of all might be saved by resorting to such food as others, in like circumstances, had subsisted upon. Mrs. Breen, however, declared that she would die and see her children die before her life or theirs should be preserved by such means. If ever the father gave to the dying children, it was without her consent or knowledge. She never tasted nor knew of her children partaking. Mrs. Farnham says that, when Patrick Breen ascended to obtain the dreadful repast, his wife, frozen with horror, hid her face in her hands and could not look up. She was conscious of his return and of something going on about the fire, but she could not bring herself to uncover her eyes till all had subsided again into silence. Her husband remarked that perhaps they were wrong in rejecting a means of sustaining life of which others had availed themselves, but she put away the suggestion so fearfully that it was never renewed nor acted upon by any of her family. She and her children were now, indeed, reaching the utmost verge of life. A little more battle with the grim enemies that had pursued them so relentlessly, twenty-four or at most forty-eight hours of such warfare, and all would be ended. The infants still breathed but were so wasted they could only be moved by raising them bodily with the hands. It seemed as if even their light weight would have dragged the limbs from their bodies. Occasionally through the day, she ascended the tree to look out. It was an incident now and seemed to kindle more life than when it only required a turn of the head or a glance of the eye to tell that there was no living thing near them. She could no longer walk on the snow, but she had still strength enough to crawl from tree to tree to gather a few boughs, which she threw along before her to the pit and piled them in to renew the fire. The eighth day was passed. On the ninth morning, she ascended to watch for her star of mercy. Clear and bright it stood over against her beseeching gaze, set in the light liquid blue that overflows the pathway of the opening day. She prayed earnestly as she gazed, for she knew that there were but few hours of life in those dearest to her. If human aid came not that day, some eyes that would soon look imploringly into hers would be closed in death before that star would rise again. Would she herself, with all her endurance and resisting love, live to see it? Were they at length to perish? Great God! Should it be permitted that they, who had been preserved through so much, should die at last so miserably?

Her eyes were dim and her sight wavering. She could not distinguish trees from men on the snow, but had they been near, she could have heard them, for her ear had grown so sensitive that the slightest unaccustomed noise arrested her attention. She went below with a heavier heart than ever before. She had not a word of hope to answer the languid, inquiring countenances that were turned to her face, and she was conscious that it told the story of her despair. Yet she strove with some half-insane words to suggest that somebody would surely come to them that day. Another would be too late, and the pity of men's hearts and the mercy of God would surely bring them. The pallor of death seemed already to be stealing over the sunken countenances that surrounded her, and weak as she was, she could remain below but a few minutes together. She felt she could have died had she let go her resolution at any time within the last forty-eight hours. They repeated the litany. The responses came so feebly that they were scarcely audible, and the protracted utterances seemed wearisome. At last it was over, and they rested in silence.

The sun mounted high and higher in the heavens, and when the day was three or four hours old, she placed her trembling feet again upon the ladder to look out once more. The corpses of the dead lay always before her as she reached the top—the mother and her son and the little boy, whose remains she could not even glance at since they had been mutilated. The blanket that covered them could not shut out the horror of the sight.

The rays of the sun fell on her with a friendly warmth, but she could not look into the light that flooded the white expanse. Her eyes lacked strength and steadiness, and she rested herself against a tree and endeavored to gather her wandering faculties in vain. The enfeebled will could no longer hold rule over them.

She had broken perceptions, fragments of visions, contradictory and mixed—former mingled with latter times. Recollections of plenty and rural peace came up from her clear, tranquil childhood, which seemed to have been another state of existence; flashes of her latter life—its comfort and abundance—gleams of maternal pride in her children who had been growing up about her to ease and independence.

She lived through all the phases which her simple life had ever worn in the few moments of repose after the dizzy effort of ascending; as the thin blood left her whirling brain and returned to its shrunken channels, she grew more clearly conscious of the terrible present and remembered the weary quest upon which she came. It was not the memory of thought; it was that of love, the old tugging at the heart that had never relaxed long enough to say, "Now I am done; I can bear no more!" The miserable ones down there—for them her wavering life came back; at thought of them, she turned her face listlessly the way it had so often gazed. But this time something caused it to flush as if the blood, thin and cold as it was, would burst its vessels! What was it? Nothing that she saw, for her eyes were quite dimmed by the sudden access of excitement! It was the sound of voices! By a superhuman effort, she kept herself from falling! Was it reality or delusion? She must at least live to know the truth. It came again and again. She grew calmer as she became more assured, and the first distinct words she heard uttered were, "There is Mrs. Breen alive yet, anyhow!" Three men were advancing toward her. She knew that now there would be no more starving. Death was repelled for this time from the precious little flock he had so long threatened, and she might offer up thanksgiving unchecked by the dreads and fears that had so long frozen her.

5

EYEWITNESS
The Raid at Harpers Ferry

BY REVEREND SAMUEL VANDERLIP LEECH

The story of John Brown's attack on Harpers Ferry has been recounted for years in history books but never as it was by a man who watched it unfold and knew its importance. Was it heroic or ill-fated folly? A firsthand view from the front lines.

The town of Harpers Ferry is located in Jefferson County, West Virginia. Lucerne, in Switzerland, does not excel it in romantic grandeur of situation. On its northern front, the Potomac sweeps along to pass the national capital and the tomb of Washington in its silent flow toward the sea. On its eastern side, the Shenandoah hurries to empty its waters into the Potomac, that in perpetual wedlock they may greet the stormy Atlantic. Across the Potomac the Maryland Heights stand out as the tall sentinels of nature. Beyond the Shenandoah are the Blue Ridge Mountains, fringing the westward boundary of Loudon County, Virginia. Between these rivers and nestling inside of their very confluence reposes Harpers Ferry. Back of its hills lies the famous Shenandoah Valley, celebrated for its natural scenery, its historic battles, and "Sheridan's ride." At Harpers Ferry the United States authorities early located an arsenal and an armory.

Before the Civil War, the Baltimore Conference of the Methodist Episcopal Church was constituted of five extensive districts in Virginia, stretching from Alexandria to Lewisburg, and two great districts north of the Potomac, including the cities of Washington and Baltimore. The first three years of my ministerial life, I spent on Shepherdstown, West Loudon, and Hillsboro Circuits, being then all in Virginia. The state of West Virginia, now embracing Harpers Ferry, had not been organized by Congress as a war measure out of the territory of the mother state. Our Methodist Episcopal Church was theoretically an antislavery organization, but our Virginia and Maryland members held thousands of inherited and many purchased slaves. These were generally well-cared-for and contented. Being close to the free soil of Pennsylvania, they could have gotten there in a night had they wished to escape bondage, and then they could have easily reached Canada by that Northern aid called the "Underground Railroad."

On the Sunday night when John Brown and his men invaded Virginia, I slept within a half mile of Harpers Ferry. That day I inaugurated revival services at my westward appointment called "Ebenezer" in Loudon County, two miles from Harpers Ferry. I was twenty-two years of age.

Three months before this raid, Captain John Brown with two of his sons, Owen and Oliver, and Jeremiah G. Anderson, calling themselves "Isaac Smith and Sons," rented a small farm on the Maryland side of the Potomac, four miles from Harpers Ferry. It was known as the "Booth-Kennedy Place." They also carried on across the mountains at Chambersburg, Pennsylvania, a small hardware store managed by John H. Kagi. It was a depot for the munitions of war to be hauled to their Maryland farm. Another of Brown's men, John E. Cook, sold maps in the vicinity. He was a relative of Governor Willard of Indiana, who secured the services of Hon. Daniel W. Voorhees, attorney general of Indiana, to defend Cook at his after-trial in Virginia. It was a time of profound national peace. Brown and his men represented themselves as geologists, miners, and speculators. They had a mule and wagon with which to haul their boxes from Chambersburg. A wealthy merchant of Boston, Mr. George Luther Stearns, chairman of the Massachusetts Aid Society, had financed Brown's Kansas border warfare work, as well as his approaching Harpers Ferry raid. Other Northern friends assisted. Brown had completed his preparations and collected his twenty-one helpers early in October 1859. He had hidden in an old log cabin on the place 200 Sharpe's rifles; 13,000 rifle cartridges; 950 long iron pikes; 200 revolving pistols; 100,000 pistol caps; 40,000 percussion caps; 250 pounds of powder; 12 reams of cartridge paper; and other warlike materials. He organized his twenty-two men, himself included, into a "military provisional government" to superintend the possible uprising of the slaves of Virginia. Thirteen of these men had engaged in border warfare in Kansas in a successful effort to prevent Kansas from becoming a slave state. He, sixteen other white men, and five negroes constituted his entire Virginia army. The white men were Captain John Brown; Adjutant General John H. Kagi; and Captains Owen Brown, Oliver Brown, Watson Brown, Aaron D. Stephens, John E. Cook, Dauphin Adolphus Thompson, George P. Tidd, William Thompson, and Edwin Coppoc. The lieutenants were Jeremiah G. Anderson, Albert Hazlitt, and William Henry Leeman. The privates numbered eight. Three of them were white men and five were negroes. The whites were Francis J. Merriam, Barclay Coppoc, and Steward Taylor. The negroes were Dangerfield Newby, Osborne P. Anderson, John A. Copeland, Sherrard Lewis Leary, and Shields Green.

On Sunday morning, October 16th, 1859, Brown assembled his men and informed them that on that night their invasion into Virginia would take place. They took the oath of allegiance to the "provisional government." Adjutant General Kagi presented to each officer his commission.

The contents of the armory, arsenal, and Hall's Rifle Works were daily open to public inspection. Captain John Brown well knew that Daniel Whelan was the only watchman during the nighttime at the armory grounds. He believed that if he could secure the arms and ammunition in these buildings, carry them into the fastnesses of the adjacent mountains, and then unfurl the flag of freedom for all slaves who would flock to his standard, the result would be a general uprising of the negro population throughout the border states. A more idiotic and senseless theory never entered an American mind. In the superlative degree, it was unreasonable and ridiculous. I personally know of the general loyalty of the slaves to their masters in that locality at that period in our national history. Federal generals were astonished at the devotion of the negroes to their masters everywhere in the South after the war had begun. This was especially true along the border states. But John Brown—honest, enthusiastic, and intensely fanatical on the slavery question—issued his commands. On this Sunday he assigned to each his earliest work. Captain Owen Brown, Barclay Coppoc, and Francis J. Merriam were to remain at the farm to guard the arms and ammunition. Hence only nineteen left the Kennedy farm. They were to walk down the river road on the Maryland side to the Maryland end of the Baltimore and Ohio Railroad bridge. The Virginia end was close to the depot, hotel, armory, and the arsenal. Captain John Brown was to ride in the wagon with the necessary guns, pistols, and tools. Captains Cook and Tidd were to go in advance and cut the telegraph wires on the Maryland side. Captain Stephens and Adjutant General Kagi were to capture Mr. Williams, the guard of the bridge. Captain Watson Brown and Taylor were to hold up the passenger train due from the west at 1:40 a.m. It would be bound for Washington and Baltimore. Captain Oliver Brown and Thompson were to hold the bridges spanning the two rivers. Captain Dauphin Adolphus Thompson and Lieutenant Anderson were to hold the first building in the armory grounds, popularly known afterward as "John Brown's Fort." It was the engine house where Brown held his most distinguished prisoners. From the portholes of it that they made after his entrance, his men did their final fighting. Captain Coppoc and Lieutenant Hazlitt were to hold the arsenal outside and opposite the armory gates. Adjutant General Kagi and Copeland were to seize and retain Hall's Rifle Works. They were half of a mile up the western shore of the Shenandoah. Captain Stephens and such men as he might select were to go out to the home of Colonel Lewis W. Washington, the grandnephew of General George Washington, and bring him and some of his adult male slaves to the engine house. They were also to secure the swords presented to General George Washington by Frederick the Great and by General Lafayette. For this object Stephens selected as his helpers Captains Tidd and Cook and Privates Leary, Green, and Anderson. Brown made the raid at 11:30 that night. Mr. Williams, the bridge guard, was captured by Stephens and Kagi. The watchman at the armory, Daniel Whelan, refused Brown and his men admission to the grounds. They broke the locks with tools, captured Whelan, and took possession of the armory and also of the arsenal outside. The following prisoners were brought in early on Monday and placed in the engine house: Jesse W. Graham, who was master workman; Colonel Lewis W. Washington; Terence Byrne; John M. Allstadt; John Donohue, who was clerk of the railroad company; Benjamin F. Mills, the master armorer; Armstead M. Ball, the master machinist; Archibald M. Kitzmiller, assistant superintendent; Isaac Russell, a justice of the peace; George D. Shope of Frederick; and J. Bird, arsenal armorer. The white prisoners were to be held as hostages, and the blacks were to be armed and placed in Brown's army. Cook and Tidd evidently mistrusted their surroundings. During the night they made their way back to the farm and hastily escaped into Pennsylvania. Captain Watson Brown and Taylor held up the train bound for Baltimore, detaining it for three hours. The colored porter of the depot, Shepherd Hayward, went out on the bridge to hunt for Williams. He was brutally shot by one of Brown's bridge guards. Hayward managed to crawl to the baggage room, where he died at noon on Monday. Dr. John Starry dressed his wounds and ministered to his every want. The physician was under the impression that a band of train robbers had captured the depot. He told this to Mr. Kitzmiller before Kitzmiller's imprisonment. Captain E. P. Dangerfield, clerk to the paymaster, entered the grounds and was hustled into the engine house quite early in the morning. Numerous arriving workmen were imprisoned in an adjoining building. Colonel Washington said that fully sixty men were imprisoned by eight o'clock on Monday morning. The citizens were hearing of the situation. Newby and Green, negroes, were stationed at the junction of High and Shenandoah Streets. Newby shot at and killed Captain George W. Turner, a graduate of West Point. Green shot and killed Mr. Thomas Boerley, a grocer. Dr. Claggett attended Boerley, who also soon died. After the mulatto had shot Turner, a man named Bogert entered the residence of Mrs. Stephenson by a rear door. Having no bullet he put a large nail into his gun, went upstairs, and shot Newby, the nail cutting his throat from ear to ear. He was also shot in the stomach by someone else. I saw him die in great agony, with an infuriated crowd around him. About ten o'clock in the morning, armed citizens crossed the Potomac and Shenandoah Rivers to prevent the escape by the bridges or by water of any of the raiders. Some walked down the Maryland river road and wounded Captain Oliver Brown on the bridge. He reached the engine house but soon died beside his father. Citizens seized the uninjured prisoner, Captain Thompson, and put him under guard at the Galt Hotel. Captain Stephens tried to reach the hotel to propose, as he stated, terms of surrender. George Chambers wounded him and then assisted him into the Galt Hotel, where his wounds were dressed. About eleven o'clock in the morning, the Jefferson Guards from Charlestown commanded by Captain J. W. Rowen arrived. A half hour passed, and the Hamtramck Guards under Captain V. M. Butler came to the Ferry. They were followed by the Shepherdstown Mounted Troop commanded by Captain Jacob Reinhart. Then a military company from Martinsburg, twenty miles distant, reached the place, under the command of Captain Alburtis. Colonels W. R. Baylor and John T. Gibson took the general direction of the military affairs. Some soldiers crossed the Shenandoah along with armed citizens to intercept the four raiders Kagi, Leary, Leeman, and Copeland, when they should be driven out of Hall's Rifle Works. These raiders also had in these works one of Colonel Washington's slaves pressed into their service. All of them ran out into the river to swim across to the Loudon County shore. All were shot to death in the river with the exception of Copeland. He threw up his hands and surrendered. During the excitement Hazlitt and the negro Anderson left the arsenal and, undetected, escaped into Pennsylvania. Early in the morning, Captain Owen Brown, Barclay Coppoc, and Merriam had deserted the Kennedy farm and gone north. Thus seven of the twenty-two men fled to the North. Cook and Hazlitt were captured. They were returned to Virginia, tried, and executed.

By two o'clock p.m., the town and hills swarmed with militia and citizens. Brown had barricaded the engine house doors with the engine and reel. Inside were Captains John Brown and his son Watson; also Captain Oliver Brown, who was soon dead; Shields Green, Captain Edwin Coppoc, Lieutenant Jeremiah G. Anderson, Captain Dauphin Adolphus Thompson, and ten white prisoners. The numerous prisoners, mostly workmen, in the adjoining structure had all escaped from the grounds, Brown having no portholes on that side of his fort. The militia were afraid to fire into the portholes for fear of killing some of the prominent prisoners. About four o'clock the mayor, Mr. Fontaine Beckham, aged sixty years, who was also station agent of the railroad company, went out on the platform unarmed. He was shot dead by the negro Shields Green. Captain Watson Brown in the engine house received his death wound soon afterward. Mayor Beckham was very much beloved by the people. A number of citizens hurried into the hotel and brutally seized Captain Thompson, threw him over the wall into the Potomac, and riddled him with bullets. Mrs. Foulke of the hotel and her colored porter went to the platform and brought in the dead body of the mayor.

As night was settling on the excited city, a military company from Winchester, Virginia, commanded by Captain B. B. Washington arrived by a Shenandoah Valley train. Shortly thereafter a Baltimore and Ohio Railroad train brought several companies of soldiers from Frederick, Maryland. They were commanded by Colonel Shriver. Soon several independent companies from Baltimore, accompanied by the Second Light Brigade, arrived under the general command of General Charles C. Edgerton. Colonel Robert E. Lee of the United States Army overtook these troops at Sandy Hook, a mile and a half below the Ferry on the Maryland side. He had come from Washington with several companies of marines. He was accompanied by Lieutenant J. E. B. Stuart, afterward a famous Confederate cavalry general, also by Major Russell and by Lieutenant Israel Green, who died several months ago in the West. All were regular army officers. Colonel Lee regarded it as unwise to attack the engine house that night, fearing that Colonel Lewis W. Washington or other prisoners might be killed. Early in the morning, he sent Lieutenant J. E. B. Stuart, who had once held Brown as a prisoner in Kansas, to demand an immediate and unconditional surrender. Brown refused to trust himself and men to the United States officers. About this time Colonel Robert E. Lee got within range of Captain Coppoc's rifle. Prisoners said that Mr. Graham knocked the muzzle aside. Lee's life was saved. Had he been then killed, who knows that the battles of Antietam, Gettysburg, and the final conflicts north of the Appomattox would have ever been fought? On the Confederate side, no abler general or more magnificent man ever sat on a saddle than Robert E. Lee. He was the son of "Light Horse Harry Lee," a brave major general of the Revolutionary War. He was the father of William Henry Fitzhugh Lee, who became a major general of the Confederate forces of Virginia at a later date. General Robert E. Lee made a brilliant record in the Mexican War as chief engineer of the United States Army. After surrendering his decimated army to General Ulysses S. Grant at Appomattox, he accepted the political situation with dignity. He became president of the Washington University at Lexington, Virginia. The South lavished on him every possible honor. During the late summer, the Virginia legislature placed in the National Hall of Fame at the United States Capitol two fine statues of two representative men of their state. One was the statue of General George Washington, the other that of General Robert E. Lee.

By the advice of Colonel Lewis W. Washington, all of Brown's prisoners mounted the fire engine and the reel carriage and lifted up their hands when the attack began. Three marines undertook to batter down the doors with heavy sledgehammers. They were not successful. Then twelve marines struck the doors with the end of a strong ladder. They opened. Lieutenant Green entered first of all amid a shower of bullets. Discovering Brown reloading his rifle, he sprang on him with his sword and cut his head and stomach. The raider Captain Anderson rose to shoot Green. A marine named Luke Quinn ran his bayonet through him. Another raider shot Luke Quinn, who soon died. Two other marines were wounded. I saw Captains Anderson and Watson Brown as they lay dying on the grass after their capture. The dead body of Captain Oliver Brown lay beside them. Captain Watson Brown had been dying for sixteen hours. Captain John Brown, bleeding profusely, and Captain Stephens from the hotel were carried into the paymaster's office. Brown's long gray beard was stained with wet blood. He was bare-headed. His shirt and trousers were gray in color. His trousers were tucked into the top of his boots. Captain Coppoc and the negro Green were also taken prisoners. They were not wounded.

As Brown lay on the floor of the paymaster's office, he was very cool and courageous. Governor Henry A. Wise, United States Senator J. M. Mason of Virginia, and Honorable Clement L. Vallandingham of Ohio plied him with many questions. To all he gave intelligent and fearless replies. He refused to involve his Northern financiers and advisers. He took the entire responsibility on himself. He told Governor Wise that he, Brown, was simply "an instrument in the hands of Providence." He said to some newspaper correspondents and others: "I wish to say that you had better—all you people of the South—prepare for a settlement of this question. You may dispose of me very easily. I am nearly disposed of now. But this question is yet to be settled—this negro question I mean. The end is not yet." Before thirteen months had passed, one of the greatest Americans of any century, Abraham Lincoln, had been elected president of the United States; the Republican Party was for the first time dominating national affairs, and soon thereafter, the Civil War was begun, which culminated in the physical freedom of every slave in this republic.

On Wednesday Captains John Brown, Stephens, and Coppoc, along with Copeland and Green, were removed to the county jail at Charlestown, ten miles south of Harpers Ferry. Being acquainted with the jailor, Captain John Avis, I was permitted to visit Brown on one occasion. Captain Aaron D. Stephens was lying on a cot in the same room. I was told that Brown had ordered out of his room a Presbyterian minister named Lowrey when he had proposed to offer prayer. He had also said to my first colleague, Rev. James H. March, "You do not know the meaning of the word *Christianity*. Of course I regard you as a gentleman but only as a heathen gentleman." I was advised to say nothing to him about prayer. He had told other visitors that he wanted no minister to pray with him who would not be willing to die to free a slave. I was not conscious that I was ready for martyrdom from Brown's standpoint. I have never been anxious to die to save the life of anybody. My life is as valuable to me and my family as any other man's is to him and his family. But young as I was, I hated American slavery. I was a "boy minister" of a great antislavery denomination of Christians. For more than a century, the Methodist Episcopal Church has carried in its disciplines its printed testimony against slavery. It is today the largest fully organized antislavery society on earth. I would have gladly offered prayer in Brown's room at Charlestown if an honorable opportunity had been afforded.

At his preliminary examination before five justices, Colonel Davenport presiding, Brown said,

Virginians! I did not ask for quarter at the time I was taken. I did not ask to have my life spared. Your governor assured me of a fair trial. If you seek my blood, you can have it at any time without this mockery of a trial. I have no counsel. I have not been able to advise with anyone. I know nothing of the feelings of my fellow prisoners and am utterly unable to attend to my own defense. If a fair trial is to be allowed, there are mitigating circumstances to be urged. But, if we are forced with a mere form, a trial for execution, you might spare yourselves that trouble. I am ready for my fate.

Two very able Virginia attorneys were assigned as a matter of state form as counsel for Brown. They were Honorable Charles J. Faulkner of Martinsburg, afterward United States envoy extraordinary to France, and Judge Green, ex-mayor of Charlestown. The county grand jury indicted Brown on three separate charges: first, conspiracy with slaves for purposes of insurrection; second, treason against the commonwealth of Virginia; third, murder in the first degree. Mr. Faulkner withdrew from the case, and Mr. Lawson Botts took his place. Mr. Samuel Chilton, a learned lawyer of Washington, DC, and Judge Henry Griswold of Ohio, another distinguished attorney, volunteered their services as counsel for John Brown and were accepted. Some of Brown's friends sent an excellent young lawyer named George H. Hoyt from Boston as additional counsel. These attorneys made an able defense, whatever may have been their private opinion as to Brown's guilt or innocence. The prosecuting attorney for the state of Virginia was Andrew Hunter, an exceptionally brilliant orator and able lawyer. He was a courtly and commanding speaker. He was gifted with a rich and powerful voice. After the indictment of Brown by the court of justices, the prosecuting attorney of Jefferson County,

Mr. Charles B. Harding, left the prosecution almost exclusively to Mr. Andrew Hunter, who represented the state. So, too, after the arrival of Brown's chosen outside counsel, Judge Green and Mr. Lawson Botts withdrew in good taste from his defense.

At the regular trial, Brown's counsel requested a postponement on account of the prisoner's health. But Dr. Mason, his physician, attested the physical ability of his patient to undergo the strain. The state was spending almost a thousand dollars a day for military guards and other items. When Brown's counsel presented telegrams from his relatives asking for delay until they could forward proofs of his insanity, Brown said, "I will say, if the court will allow me, that I look on this as a miserable artifice and trick of those who ought to take a different course in regard to me, if they take any at all. I view it with contempt more than otherwise. I am perfectly unconscious of insanity, and I reject, so far as I am capable, any attempts to interfere in my behalf on that score."

On the last day of the trial, October 31st, after six hours of argument by Hunter, Chilton, and Griswold, the jury delivered the following verdict: "Guilty of treason and of conspiring and advising with slaves and others to rebel and of murder in the first degree." On Wednesday, November the 2nd, he was brought into court to receive his sentence. The county clerk, Robert H. Brown, asked, "Have you anything to say why sentence should not be passed on you?" Brown, leaning on a cane, slowly arose from his chair and with plaintive emphasis addressed Judge Parker as follows:

I have, may it please the court, a few words to say. In the first place, I deny everything but what I have all along admitted, the design on my part to free the slaves. I certainly intended to have made a clean thing of that matter as I did last winter when I went into Missouri and took slaves without the snapping of a gun on either side, moved them through the country, and finally left them in Canada. I designed to have done the same thing again on a larger scale. That was all I intended. I never did intend murder or treason or the destruction of property or to excite or incite slaves to rebellion or to make insurrection. I have another objection, and that is that it is unjust that I should suffer such a penalty. Had I interfered in the manner which I admit and which I admit has been fairly proved, for I admire the truthfulness and candor of the greater portion of the witnesses who have testified in this case—had I so interfered in behalf of the rich, the powerful, the intelligent, the so-called great or in behalf of any of their friends, either father, mother, sister, brother, wife, or children, or any of that class and suffered and sacrificed what I have in this interference, it would have been all right, and every man in this court would have deemed it an act worthy of reward rather than punishment. This court acknowledges, as I suppose, the validity of the law of God. I see a book kissed here, which I suppose is the Bible or at least the New Testament. That teaches me that all things, whatsoever I would that men should do to me, I should do even unto them. It teaches me further to "Remember them that are in bonds as bound with them." I endeavored to act up to that instruction. I say that I am yet too young to understand that God is any respecter of persons. I believe that to have interfered as I have done, as I have always admitted freely I have done, in behalf of His despised poor was not wrong but right. Now if it is deemed necessary that I should forfeit my life for the furtherance of the ends of justice and mingle my blood further with the blood of my children and with the blood of millions in this slave country, whose rights are disregarded by wicked, cruel, and unjust enactments, I submit. So let it be done.

Let me say one word further. I feel entirely satisfied with the treatment I have received on my trial. Considering all the circumstances, it has been more generous than I expected. But I feel no consciousness of guilt. I never had any design against the life of any person nor any disposition to commit treason or excite slaves to rebellion or make any general insurrection. I never encouraged any man to do so but always discouraged any idea of the kind.

Let me say a word in regard to the statements made by some of those connected with me. I hear it has been stated by some of them that I induced them to join me. But the contrary is true. I do not say this to injure them but as regards their weakness. There is not one of them but joined me of his own accord and the greater part of them at their own expense. A number of them I never saw and never had a word of conversation with till the day they came to me, and that was for the purpose I have stated. Now I am done.

Brown's statement was not exactly sustained by the facts. Why had he collected the Sharpe's rifles, the pikes, the kegs of powder, many thousands of caps, and much warlike material at the Kennedy farm? Why did he and other armed men break into the United States armory and arsenal, make portholes in the engine house, shoot and kill citizens, and surround their own imprisoned persons with prominent men as hostages? But everybody in the courthouse believed the old man when he said that he did everything with a solitary motive, the liberation of the slaves.

Judge Parker could, under his oath, do nothing else than to sentence him to be hung. He fixed the date for Friday, the 2nd of December. Brown's counsel appealed to the Supreme Court of Virginia. Its five judges unanimously sustained the action of the Jefferson County court.

Brown was hung on the bright and beautiful morning of December 2nd at 11:15 o'clock. At his request Andrew Hunter wrote his will. He then visited his fellow prisoners, who were all executed at a later date. He rode to his death between Sheriff Campbell and Captain Avis in a furniture wagon drawn by two white horses. He did not ride seated on his coffin as some of his chief eulogists have affirmed. The wagon was escorted to the scaffold by state military companies. No citizens were allowed near to the jail. Hence he did not kiss any negro baby as he emerged from his prison, as Mr. Whittier has described in a poem on the event and as artists have memorialized in paintings. The utter absurdity of such an incident occurring under such surroundings any Virginian will see. Avis, Campbell, and Hunter publicly denied it. But the story will doubtless have immortality. In one of the companies of soldiers walked the actor John Wilkes Booth, the infamous assassin of Abraham Lincoln. At the head of the Lexington cadets walked Professor Thomas Jefferson Jackson, who became an able Confederate general and is best known to the world as "Stonewall Jackson." As the party neared the gallows, Brown gazed on the glorious panorama of mountain and landscape scenery. Then he said, "This is a beautiful country." He wore a black slouch hat with the front tipped up. Reaching the scaffold the numerous state troops formed into a hollow square. Brown mounted the platform without trepidation. Standing on the drop, he said to the sheriff and his assistants, "Gentlemen! I thank you for your kindness to me. I am ready at any time. Do not keep me waiting." The drop fell, and in ten minutes Dr. Mason pronounced him dead. That evening Mrs. Brown and her friends received the casket at Harpers Ferry and accompanied it to the old home at North Elba, New York. His funeral, as reported by the metropolitan papers, took place there six days after his execution. An immense concourse was in attendance. The conspicuous and brilliant orator Wendell Phillips delivered the address. He closed it with these words: "In this cottage he girded himself and went forth to battle. Fuller success than his heart ever dreamed of God had granted him. He sleeps in the blessings of the crushed and the poor. Men believe more firmly in virtue now that such a man has lived." Personally I remained in Virginia.

On the day that Brown was hung, martyr services, as they were called, were held in many Northern localities. At Concord, Dr. Edmund Sears read a poem in which are these stanzas:

> Not any spot, six feet by two
> Will hold a man like thee
> John Brown will tramp the shaking earth
> From Blue Ridge to the sea
> Till the strong angel comes at length
> And opes each dungeon door:
> And God's Great Charter holds and waves
> O'er all the humble poor.
> And then the humble poor may come
> In that far distant day,
> And from the felon's nameless grave
> Will brush the leaves away:
> And gray old men will point the spot
> Beneath the pine tree's shade,
> As children ask with streaming eyes
> Where old John Brown was laid.

6

DELUGE

Heroics in the Johnstown Flood

FROM REPORTS BY
THE *POLICE GAZETTE*

The gentle Conemaugh River flowed unnoticed for the most part through the rolling hills around Johnstown, Pennsylvania. A poorly maintained dam and a powerful storm changed all that in a few moments of horror for thousands of unsuspecting residents.

There is not one chance in a million that the Conemaugh River would ever have been heard of in history had it not been for its action on Friday evening, May 31.

The Conemaugh River is, or rather was, a simple little stream that meandered through northwestern Pennsylvania and made glad by its peaceful murmurings those who dwelt by its bankside or bore tokens of affection in the way of pleasure-seeking picnickers, moonlight parties, or across-stream excursionists upon its placid bosom. It was one of those inoffensive creeks, termed by courtesy a river, that the Hudson River of the East, the Mississippi of the Middle, or the Red River of the West might call a stripling.

There are times when even the still, small voice arises in its might and asserts its supremacy, and the wee small river of Conemaugh did that self-same thing on Friday evening, May 31. All along the banks of the listless yet ever flowing, little alleged river, the farmers were preparing for their anticipated harvests; the fishermen of the section—amateur fishermen indeed, for they were only equal to the fish—small and incomplete as was the Conemaugh, such as you and I, reader, who took pleasure in flinging their worm-crowded hooks into the stomach of a log and then going home for more bait; bonny fairies; brisk young tillers of the soil; toilers; and seeming-tired miners; these and all other human concomitants that go to make up such a quiet, thriving bailiwick dwelt in the locality.

And so went on the listless life of the denizens of the Conemaugh Valley, nestling at the foot of the Allegheny range. Snuggling in the coziest nook, right where no prying reporter or trout-fishing president ever bent his way, was Johnstown. The word *was* is used advisedly; Johnstown is no more. At four o'clock on the fateful day, all was serene. At six o'clock, all was desolation and destruction.

The "big dam" had broken, and the little brooklet had burst its sides for very glee at being dubbed a creek and was making itself known in history. The Brooklyn Theatre holocaust, with its dead three hundred, paled into insignificance. The Mud Run and Reading disasters had to take a backseat.

"Let me alone for horror," murmured the Conemaugh, "and I'll get there!"

It did get there.

Right above Johnstown on the self-same Conemaugh, or rather where the North Fork glides into that erstwhile inoffensive stream, was a reservoir. The reservoir is on the site of the old lake, which was one of the feeders of the Pennsylvania Canal. It is the property of a number of wealthy gentlemen in Pittsburgh, who formed themselves into the corporation, the title of which is the South Fork Fishing and Hunting Club. This sheet of water was formerly known as Conemaugh Lake. It is from two hundred to three hundred feet above the level of Johnstown, being in the mountains. It is about three and one-half miles long and from a mile to one and one-fourth miles in width, and in some places it is one hundred feet in depth. It holds more water than any other reservoir, natural or artificial, in the United States. The lake has been quadrupled in size by artificial means and was held in check by a dam from seven hundred to one thousand feet wide. It was 90 feet in thickness at the base, and the height was 110 feet. The top has a breadth of over twenty feet.

From what could be ascertained by the writer, the reservoir banks had not been considered absolutely safe by the people of the big and growing town. The reservoir was an artificial rather than a natural lake. The art came in when the South Fork Club, a corporation of gentlemen, took charge of the reservoir and dammed it. The South Fork Club had the dam inspected once a month by the Pennsylvania Railroad engineers, and their investigation showed that nothing less than some convulsion of nature would tear the barrier away and loosen the weapon of death. The steady rains of the past forty-eight hours had increased the volume of water in all the small mountain streams, which had already been swelled by the lesser rains earlier in the week. At this time it was evident that something in the nature of a cloudburst must have occurred just before the waters broke through the embankment.

Then the water came. It came with a rush that astonished the natives. There was a low murmuring at first and then a rushing, hissing noise; then crevices appeared in the dam side. Then the embankment gave away, and onward rushed the torrent. It meant death and destruction to the fairest country on God's footstool. Johnstown became a City of the Dead, and the once-pleasant valley was the Valley of Death.

Only those who were on the spot at the time can or could tell of the terrible scenes that ensued, and even they could not depict them in their real colors. It would take the pen of a mightier than human hand to write the story and a brush of a heaven-inspired artist to delineate the action. All was desolation, death, and destruction. Men, women, and children, animals, houses, furniture were swept on the hell-bent waters!

All through Cambria came the flood. Then on to Cooperdale. Frantic mothers with children born and unborn were compelled to flee and then had to succumb to the deluge. The cruel, onrushing tide had nothing in its instincts humanitarian. The death-tide rolled onward, and suckling babes were swept from their mother's breasts, even as if the King of Old had proclaimed.

So on to St. Florence in Fairfield—well-named. The people at Ninevah and the quiet, easygoing folk of the cruel-river towns counted their losses by hundreds.

"Ten thousand dead," was the announcement that came over the wires.

The effect can never be told. Centuries may come and go, but no century can make its mark in the history of time like that of the nineteenth, with its aide, the Conemaugh. Hundreds upon hundreds of lives were lost. The number cannot even be approximated, for in such regions there are always innumerable people—what the careless world calls its floating population—who would not be missed or accounted for until the Judgment roll is called.

Even on Monday, three days after the horror, mothers meandered about frantically, begging that their children might be returned to them, and men with hearts brushed tears from their eyes and endeavored to make them believe that their dear ones had been rescued. Children pleadingly prayed that they might be saved, but the cruel, ever-onward-rushing flood gathered them in and swept them onward.

To add to the horror, the Johnstown Bridge, as if to add terror to terror and to make confusion worse confounded, swept from its approaches and precipitated the horror-stricken multitude into the torrent. An overturned stove in a dwelling inaugurated a conflagration. Nearly a hundred people were literally burned to death, thus adding holocaust to the far more preferable death by drowning.

Scarcely had the news of the terrible disaster been sent abroad than the alert newspapers had their commissioners speedily on their way to the scene. Only the most meager accounts had been given to the public for the reason that every mode of communication via telegraph or train had been cut off. When the newspaper representatives reached Johnstown, the scene was a pitiable one. The former town was a swamp. Debris was piled here, there, and everywhere, and the pestilential stench from the dead bodies was next to unbearable.

The scene beggars description. Even the trained newspaper men turned their eyes aside and held their nostrils. Corpses everywhere. Dank corpses at that, with glazed, fishy eyes and sloppy, wet hair that made the onlooker feel aweary and not overanxious to handle.

In a single hole, after the waters had passed by, 150 bodies were found. Just imagine it! Two hours before, these 150 souls were alive, but there they were, huddled together as if they had been congregated for the purpose which had asserted itself.

East Conemaugh was almost depopulated, and Franklinborough, on the north of Johnstown, was entirely swept away. Mineral Point, between Johnstown and the viaduct, was blotted out of existence. If any of the six hundred souls that formerly resided there are alive, the reporters could not find them. Ninevah, just below the Conemaugh furnace, is a city of corpses. Indeed, from South Fork to Bolivar and for a distance of a dozen miles or so, the banks of the old-time river are literally strewn with corpses. After the death-dealing current had gone on, the work of tallying began. It will never be ended.

Then the fiends in human shape began their ghoulish work of robbing the dead. Summary punishment was dealt out to some of them. A vigilance committee, hastily organized, ran a score of them into the river, and that was the end of them.

At five o'clock on Monday evening, hundreds upon hundreds of citizens are arriving upon the scene. Coffins are coming in by the carload, and the result of philanthropic and necessary aid began to pour in. More relief is needed.

The best story of the horror can be gathered from the tale of an eyewitness, C. W. Linthicum. Said he,

My train left Pittsburgh Friday morning for Johnstown. The train was due at Sang Hollow at 4:02 but was five minutes late.

At Sang Hollow, just as we were about to pull out, we heard that the flood was coming. Looking ahead up the valley, we saw an immense wall of water thirty feet high, raging, roaring, rushing toward us.

The engineer reversed his engine and rushed back to the hills at full speed, and we barely escaped the waters. We ran back three hundred yards, and the flood swept by, tearing up tracks, telegraph poles, houses, and trees.

Superintendent Pitcairn was on the train. We all got out and tried to save the floating people. Taking the bell-cord, we formed a line and threw the rope out, thus saving seven persons.

We could have saved more, but many were afraid to let go the debris. It was an awful sight. The immense volume of water was roaring along, whirling over huge rocks, dashing against the banks and leaping high in the air, and this seething flood was strewn with timber, trunks of trees, parts of houses, and hundreds of human beings, cattle, and almost every animal.

The fearful peril of the living was not more awful than the horror of hundreds of distorted, bleeding corpses whirling along the avalanche of death.

We counted 107 people floating by and dead without number. A section of roof came by, on one of which were sitting a woman and a girl.

Other tales by eyewitnesses confirm the fact that the horror has never been excelled by anything of its kind in history.

Indeed, it will never perhaps be known what the real extent of the awful calamity is. Johnstown, with its former population of ten thousand or thereabouts, was almost entirely swept away when the awful floods came, and many of the villages between that point and Nineveh are things of the past so far as life is concerned. Indeed, the whole valley is a veritable Valley of the Shadow of Death.

So great was the crush of the wreckage, debris, and dead bodies at some points along the valley that dynamite had to be used, thus adding to the horror of the scene. Nineveh is twenty-three miles below Johnstown, yet a large number of the bodies found at Nineveh were those of former residents of Johnstown, who had been swept that great distance down the valley to their death. There are incidents where bodies were carried a hundred miles and there deposited.

A relation of some of the real facts, circumstances, and scenes and incidents of the terrible disaster would be considered Munchausenish by the majority of our readers, but some of them were miraculous. Here is one. S. H. Klein, a New Yorker, had a queer experience. He was at the Merchants' Hotel, and he worked like a beaver during the trying times of Friday night and Saturday morning, aiding in the rescue of no less than sixty persons from the floating debris. Among these were the Rev. Mr. Phillips, his wife, and two children. Mr. Phillips is a stalwart man, and when the flood struck his house, he fled to the roof with his family. Presently the house floated, and the sturdy dominie placed his wife and two children on a table. Then he got under the table and, letting it rest with its precious burden on his head, arose to his feet. As the house floated down on the tide, it grazed the hotel building, and Mr. Klein and others assisted in hauling the imperiled parson and his family into an upper window of the hotel.

Here are other incidents: The story of the mishap to the day express train at Conemaugh Bridge is developing slowly through the efforts of the railway authorities to obtain definite information. Of the three hundred passengers on the train, all but eight seem to be accounted for, and it is believed that these eight are lost. They are Bessie Bryan, daughter of Mahlon Bryan of Philadelphia, and her companion, Miss Paulson of Pittsburgh; Mrs. Easley, Rev. Mr. Goodchild, and Robert Hutchinson of Newark, New Jersey; Andrew Leonard; Mrs. J. Smith; and Chris Meisel, manager of the Newark baseball club.

Miss Bryan was a delicate young woman. She was returning from a Pittsburgh wedding with Miss Paulson. They had been preceded the night before by the bridal couple, who were to be guests at the

Bryan home at Germantown. They rode in the Pullman car and did not get out quickly enough. Fearing that they could not reach the hill where the other passengers took refuge, they returned toward the car, but before they had reached it, the waters caught them and carried them away.

Miss Rose Clarke, a beautiful and well-known young lady, the daughter of a very prominent citizen, had a remarkable experience.

"When the water rose," she said,

we were all at home. It drove us from floor to floor, and we had just reached the roof when the house started. It went whirling toward the bridge, struck it, and went down. Mother, my little sister, and I all caught on another roof that was just above the water, but Father and my little brother went down with the house. Father's face was toward us as he sank. He shouted good-bye, and that was the last. Just then my little sister lost her hold, and she followed Father and Brother. Then Mother called out that she was going to drown. I got to her and raised her head out of the water. My head rested on a saw log, and a board protected me from the other timbers. Some rescuers came running down the bridge and saw us. I made them take Mother out first, and meantime I struggled to get out of the timbers, but they closed in on me.

The more I struggled, the tighter they held me. The fire was just behind me, and I could feel its heat. By the time the men had carried Mother to the bank, the fire was so fierce they could hardly get back. When they did reach me, they could not get me out, for my foot was fast between a saw log and a piece of timber. Then they ran for tools. The fire kept sweeping on before the breeze from upstream. I had almost resigned myself to an awful death when some other men braved the fire and reached me. They began chopping and sawing. One blow of an axe cut off a drowned man's hand. The men tied a rope around me. How they got me out finally, I scarcely know. My kneecap was almost cut off. When the current sucked my father down, he caught me by the foot; that is what dragged me so far into the timbers.

Miss Clarke and her mother are both badly injured. Some of the men who rescued the young lady were Slavs.

Miss Mamie Brown was caught in the timbers in almost the same way as Miss Clarke, near the bank. The fire was coming on toward her, and the would-be rescuers had been driven back. Finally John Schmidt braved the dangers and rescued her. Father Trautwein of St. Columbia's Church, who witnessed Schmidt's brave conduct, said if any man is a hero, Schmidt is that man.

As has been written, dynamite had added its horror to the sixty-acre mass of wrecked buildings, railroads, streets, and human beings that lie above the railroad bridge. A half dozen times on the afternoon of June 6, the heavy thunder of the huge cartridges was heard for miles around, and fragments of the debris flew high in the air, while at a distance the crowd looked on in dreadful sorrow at the thought of the additional mangling that the remains of the hundreds of bodies still buried in the mass were bound to undergo. There was little complaint, however, even on the part of those who have relatives or friends buried there, for the work of the past few days has shown how futile was the idea that anything but an explosive could effectually break up and remove the compact mass.

All that hundreds of men have been able to do has amounted to nothing more than a little picking around the edges. Even the dynamite is doing the work slowly. The surface of the mass about where it was used is upheaved and washed about a bit, but the actual progress is, so far as can be seen, very small. It will be a week before the gorge can be opened, even now. Meanwhile a proposition is being discussed not to open it at all but to bury it deep and by filling in to raise the level of the whole city.

There has been an unpleasant feeling between rival committees of citizens, and at a meeting held in Johnstown on Tuesday, the whole matter was settled by the resignation of Chairman Moxham of the old relief committee and the appointment in his place of J. B. Scott of Pittsburgh, who is also chairman of the local relief committee in that city. It is believed that this will be an additional guarantee to the country of fairness and impartiality in the disbursement of the funds.

Gen. Hastings has made an estimate than the number of proven deaths will reach five thousand and that the total will be eight thousand. Besides the bodies which are dug up in this city, scores are brought in daily in wagons and carts from places down the river, where they have been washed ashore. The number of the unknown increases as the passage of time increases the difficulty of identification, and Gen. Hastings's estimate is considered extremely low. The abject destitution is now believed to be confined to Johnstown and the knots of towns immediately surrounding it. South Fork is now in railroad communication with Altoona, and whatever is needed for people there and at Mineral Point and other adjacent places can come in from that direction until railroad and other routes can be opened up the valley from here. The towns are small, and the proportion of deaths smaller than here.

The chief labor of the living is still the burying of the dead. Their sole dependence for support is upon the charity of the country, a charity, be it said, that is proving as ready as the occasion is pressing. The immediate daily necessities of the suffering people are being met by trainloads of provisions and clothing that come in from all directions. The money available is being used to employ the idle in clearing away the debris, exhuming the dead from their hiding places, and generally in making Johnstown, to an extent, an inhabitable place once more for those of its people who have further need of homes above ground. What has been done and can be done with the money already in hand is a trifling beginning, but already the place shows the effects of the gangs of laborers who have been set to pulling down damaged buildings, removing and burning the bodies of animals and other offensive debris, and doing whatever else seemed most immediately necessary for the health and well-being of the place.

From the morgue in the Fourth Ward schoolhouse, 350 bodies have been buried, and more are taken to the Grove Hill Cemetery every hour. They are buried there singly if identified and in rows and narrow trenches, one on top of the other, if not. The scenes at the different relief agencies, where food, clothing, and provisions are given out on the order of Citizens' Committee, are extremely interesting. These are established at the Pennsylvania Railroad depot, at Peters' Hotel, in Adams Street, and in each of the suburbs.

At the depot, where there is a large force of police, the people were kept in files, and the relief articles were given out with some regularity, but at such a place as Kernsville in the suburbs, the relief station was in the upper story of a partly wrecked house.

The yard was filled with boxes and barrels of bread, crackers, biscuits, and bales of blankets. The people crowded outside the yard in the street, and the provisions were handed to them over the fence, while the clothing was thrown to them from the upper windows. There was apparently great destitution in Kernsville.

"I don't care what it is only so long as it will keep me warm," said one woman, whose ragged clothing was still damp this morning.

The stronger women pushed to the front of the fence and tried to grab the pieces of clothing which came from the windows, but the people in the house saw the game and tossed the clothing to those in the rear of the crowd. A man stood on a barrel of flour and yelled out what the piece of clothing was as it came down.

At each yell there was a universal cry of "That's just what I want. My boy is dying. He must have that. Throw me that for my poor wife," and the like of that. Finally the clothing was all gone, and there was some people who didn't get any. They went away, bewailing their misfortune. The fortunate ones were gleeful.

Thousands upon thousands of dollars are being telegraphed here hourly, yes, every minute, for the relief of the bereaved. New York has come to the front nobly with over $200,000, and Brooklyn, Philadelphia, Chicago, and other cities and, indeed, nearly every town and village in the country has sent its quota of relief funds.

A word should be said right here regarding the cause of the disaster. The South Fork Fishing Club is held chiefly responsible. The broken dam shows that it was simply a pile of dirt and rubble dumped across a stream between two hills that formed the banks of the reservoir. When the water began to break through this dam, everything had to give way, causing a torrent sixty feet high to rush onward toward the doomed valley.

The dam was built many years ago to create a reservoir for use as a feeder to the Pennsylvania Canal. The builders placed in the forty-foot space at the bottom, where the creek ran, five huge pipes, each as large as a hogshead. These were covered by an arch of massive masonry and were arranged to be opened or closed by levers in a tower that was built in the center of the dam.

These five big pipes were calculated to be large enough to carry off all surplus water that could ever be poured into the lake above and which could not escape by the regular exit, which was a sluiceway around one corner of the dam at a level of eight or ten feet below the top. This sluiceway was really a new stream, the water passing off through it finding its picturesquely winding course down the hillside and running with the stream again some distance below the dam. The sluiceway and waste gates never failed to do the work for which they were designed, and there is no reason to suppose that they would have failed to do so at the present time and for the future had they been maintained as the builders contemplated.

When the Pennsylvania Canal was abandoned, the dam became useless and was neglected. The tower in which the machinery managing the waste gates is located is said to have fallen into ruin a few years ago.

The lake was then leased by the Pittsburgh Sportsman's Association. Engineer Fulton of the Cambria Iron Company made an inspection of it and pronounced it dangerous. The association set out, they declared, to improve and strengthen it.

They did cut off two feet from the top of the dam and may have strengthened it in some respects, but either because the waste gates were so damaged that to repair them would have been an expensive job or, for the other reason mentioned, that the fish would escape by the waste gates, everyone who lives near says the gates were permanently stopped up. The present appearance of the wreck of the dam indicates the truthfulness of the story. There are remnants of the waste gate masonry, but there is no indication that they have been of any practical use for a long time.

Another awful day has come and gone, and as the work of unearthing the bodies goes bravely on, scenes and incidents have been more heartrending, if possible, than those of the previous days. It is now a pretty well-settled fact that at least twelve thousand souls were washed downward to destruction, desolation, and death. It may be more. The destruction of property is already estimated at over $30,000,000, but the returns are not yet all in by any means.

Up on the hillsides are whole camps of shrieking, crying, groaning, and moaning men, women, and children, nearly naked and almost absolutely without sustenance. Willing hands are aiding and assisting them by all means in their power, but these means are extremely limited.

Thousands upon thousands upon thousands again of dollars from the charitably disposed through the country have been sent here, and the money is being used as best it can. What is more necessary, however, are large quantities of food and clothing.

The readers of this story can best appreciate this fact when it is told that there is not a store of any consequence left in this place or, indeed, anywhere in the vicinity. The committee in charge of the financial part of the work is in despair at the enormous extent of the task before it and today issued an appeal to the official authorities and the financial organizations of the country to designate a commission to take charge of the work.

Disease consequent upon the reaction after the excitement and hardships of the past week threatens to make sad inroads into the portion of the population that still remains alive. The condition of the ruins, filled with dead bodies, menaces a still more serious situation, which is being delayed, providentially, by the continued cool weather. Danger hangs over the unhappy town from another source. The presence of nearly ten thousand laboring men, half of them gathered at random from the idle classes in other parts of the country and divided by race and other prejudices, threatens to lead to rioting and disorder beyond the power of the military now on hand to quell. Liquor has been introduced among these men surreptitiously, and trouble is feared. Very strict regulations are enforced. The whole city is surrounded by a guard of soldiers, and more troops are under orders in Pittsburgh, ready to come here at once if needed. An effort is being made to cut off, as far as possible, the means of entrance to the city, so as to keep away the crowds. The number of passenger trains has been reduced to the lowest possible number, and no tickets to Johnstown are sold except upon a permit from the Relief Committee at Pittsburgh.

The feeling against the Pittsburgh association that owns the lake and dam that caused the calamity grows more intense the more the truth about the dam becomes known. The disclosure of the fact that the dam was simply a heap of dirt with loose stone facings instead of a structure of solid masonry and that the waste gates had been closed up by the association, which was printed in a Pittsburgh paper the other morning, made a sensation here and threatens to bring the matter to a head. Criminal prosecution is freely talked of, but it is thought that it will be difficult to sustain a case; even in courts as prejudiced as those in Cambria County will be against the dam owners. The men are rich and responsible, however, and the liability of civil action is generally believed to be complete. If they should be held liable in civil suits for damages, it is probable that many, if not all of them, will be financially ruined. There is an abundance of evidence that the owners were frequently warned by old residents in the neighborhood of the dam that it was becoming weaker and getting into a more dangerous condition all the time.

One fact alone as to the dam ought to convict the dam owners of negligence. The stone face that went up each side of the dam was not continued across the top. In order to maintain a wagon road there, the top of the dirt heap had merely been leveled off and left in its natural condition. It was a moral certainty that, if the water even rose so high as to go over the top of the dam, it would wash it out. With the water washing over the dirt top of the dam, the rock facing would amount to no more as a source of strength than a sheathing of cardboard. To have covered the top of the dam with a substantial course of stone capping, arched or in some other way arranged, to offer as little resistance as possible to the passage of the water would have spoiled the wagon road, but it might have saved the dam. Better opinion will no doubt prevail, and unless something new transpires later, another scene of devastation will be averted.

En passant, to show the power of the voluminous flood, these incidents of the awful day are related:

The morning of June 6, the wreck of an express train was unearthed. The baggage of Miss Annie Chism of Nashville, Tennessee, was found. She was a missionary on her way to Brazil for the Women's Foreign Missionary Society of the Methodist Church.

Among her effects was a Bible, and in it was a message to be filed at Altoona and addressed to the Methodist concern at No. 20 East Tenth Street, New York, announcing that she was on the train. Her watch, some money, and a Greek Testament were also found. It is evident that many lives were lost on this train, more than at first supposed.

The whole train affair is still a mystery. At least the passengers have not so far been found and located. The body of a nicely dressed lady was found yesterday which was so decomposed as to be unrecognizable. The effects of Miss Chism were sent to Altoona.

There was a small riot at the labor camp one morning on account of a lack of food and of utensils for cooking. Mr. Flinn, who is at the head of the labor bureau, told the men it was impossible to get things down from the railroad but that this would be remedied as soon as possible. He also said that they did not want men who expected to live on the fat of the land and that this was principally a work of charity, even though the men were paid for their work.

A few minutes after this, as Mr. Flinn was drinking some black coffee and eating some hard crackers and cheese, two workmen came up to him and commenced to complain because they did not have soup and meat. This enraged Mr. Flinn, and after telling them that he thought he was used to as good as they were, he ordered the guards to take the men out of town and not permit them to come back again. This seemed to have the desired effect, and there was no more trouble.

It had been known for several days that the Rev. J. A. Ranney and the parents of Mrs. Charles Harly of Delhi, Indiana, were on one of the ill-fated trains overtaken by the flood in Conemaugh Valley, and no tidings could be received from them.

Word comes that Mr. Ranney has arrived home. He telegraphs,

Mrs. Ranney and I were on the train at Conemaugh when the flood came. The occupants of our car rushed for the door, where Mrs. Ranney and I became separated. She was one of the first to jump, and I saw her run and disappear behind the houses in sight. Before I could get out, the deluge was too high, and with a number I remained in the car. Our car was lifted up and dashed against a car loaded with stone and was badly wrecked, but most of the occupants were saved. As far as I know, all who jumped from the car lost their lives. The rest of the train was swept away. I searched for days for Mrs. Ranney and could find no trace of her. I think she perished. The mind cannot conceive the awful sight presented when we first saw the danger. The approaching wall of water looked like Niagara, and huge engines were caught up and whirled away as if they were mere wheelbarrows.

Here is another telegram: "Mrs. Susan Stonebraker with her three children arrived at Camden Station, Baltimore, Maryland, from Johnstown this afternoon and was met by her brothers.

"We lived at Millville, just across the stream from Johnstown," she said.

> When the water rose higher and higher, we sought safety at a neighbor's. Soon after, the water struck us with full force, and I am sure some of the occupants of the house were drowned. Soon after, we all took planks and floated down the stream, as the waters rose so high in the house that we thought it unsafe to remain. I saw babies in cradles floating along, and one floated down as far as Allegheny City, about eighty miles, where it was rescued. Our house was the first to be dashed against the stone bridge, and immediately after, we were swept against it on our boards. I must have seen at least a thousand persons drowned. We stayed on the wreck from 3:30 on Friday afternoon until after 3 on Saturday morning, when we were rescued. My husband, Joseph H. Stonebraker, had several ribs broken and is now in the hospital. Before we were rescued, the wreck took fire, and had we remained a short time longer, we would have been lost.

Word comes from Steubenville, Ohio, to this effect: Mrs. Frank Davis and her two children have arrived home from Johnstown with the body of her husband, who was employed there. Mrs. Davis and her children went to visit him last week and stayed at the house of a friend named Hamilton, where Davis boarded. During Friday water came into the house, and all were busy moving things to the upper floors.

When the deluge came, they were in the third story, and the house was carried against a brick block and was partly broken up but stuck fast.

Davis's foot got crushed in between the timbers, and he was held fast. Every effort was made to release him but to no avail. With one child clinging to her neck and the babe on her shoulders, Mrs. Davis worked desperately, but the fastened foot could not be extricated, and the water continued to rise. How this woman must have suffered! Pangs of the most horrible death couldn't be worse. Men dived down into water to see what held the foot. The water reached Davis's mouth, and he held back his head.

Mrs. Davis laid down her babe in the water and pulled with renewed energy. The water came up to her husband's nose, and while with brave energy she attempted to rescue, she never lost sight of her children, who at times she held above her head to keep them from drowning. Then the roof was taken off the building, the floor lifted up and floated down against another building, where it lodged, and Mrs. Davis and her children were rescued.

Other scenes of a like nature could be told, and as usual in such cases, there was a hero of heroes present, a self-sacrificing young man, who nearly lost his own life in his efforts to save those of his fellows:

Hundreds of lives were saved by this second Paul Revere, by name John G. Parke, and hundreds more would probably have escaped violent death if the warning had been heeded. It is not exaggeration to call young Parke a hero. He is an engineer. He saw that the South Fork dam must go, and jumping into the saddle, he dashed down the valley at terrific speed, shouting out his warning: "The dam! The dam is breaking. Run for your lives!" When he arrived at South Fork station, Parke sent a telegraphic message to Johnstown, two miles below, warning the inhabitants of the town of the coming disaster. He sent his message fully an hour before the flood came. When the water was almost upon him, Parke fled to the mountains.

Too modest to speak of his actions in this regard, young Mr. Parke was prevailed upon to tell what he knew about the breaking of the dam. Said he,

On Thursday night the dam was in perfect condition, and the water was not within seven feet of the top. At that stage the lake is nearly three miles long. It rained very hard Thursday night, I am told, for I slept too soundly myself to hear it, but when I got up Friday morning, I could see there was a flood, for the water was over the drive in front of the clubhouse, and the level of the water in the lake had risen until it was only four feet below the top of the dam. I rode up to the head of the lake and saw that the woods were boiling full of water. South Fork and Muddy Run, which emptied into the lake, were fetching trees, logs, cut timber, and stuff from a sawmill that was up in the woods in that direction. This was about 7:30 o'clock. When I returned, Col. Unger, the president of the club, hired twenty-two Italians, and a number of farmers joined in to work on the dam. Altogether thirty men were at work. A plough was run along the top of the dam, and earth was thrown on the face of the dam to strengthen it. At the same time, a channel was dug on the west end of the dam to make a sluiceway there. There was about three feet of shale rock through which it was possible to cut, but then we struck bedrock that it was impossible to get through without blasting. When we got the channel opened, the water soon scoured down to the bedrock, and a stream thirty feet wide and three feet deep rushed out on that end of the dam, while the weir was letting an enormous quantity on the other end. Notwithstanding these outlets, the water kept rising at the rate of about ten inches an hour.

By 11:30 I had made up my mind it was impossible to save the dam, and getting my horse I galloped down the road to South Fork to warn the people of their danger. The telegraph tower is a mile from the town, and I sent two men there to have messages sent to Johnstown and other points below. I heard that the lady operator fainted when she sent off the news and had to be carried off. The people at South Fork had ample time to get to the high grounds, and they were able to move their furniture, too. In fact, only one person was drowned at South Fork, and he while attempting to fish something from the flood as it rolled by. It was just twelve o'clock when the telegraph messages were sent out, so that the people of Johnstown had over three hours' warning.

As I rode back to the dam, I expected almost every moment to meet the lake coming down on me, but the dam was still intact, although the water had reached the top. At about one o'clock, I walked over the dam. At that time the water was three inches deep on it, and was gradually eating away the earth on the outer face. As the stream rolled down the outer face, it kept wearing down the edge of the embankment, and I saw it was merely a question of time. I then went up to the clubhouse and got dinner, and when I returned I saw a great deal more of the outer edge of the dam had crumbled away. The dam did not give away. At a rough guess, I should say that there was 60,000,000 tons of water in that lake, and the pressure of that mass of water was increased by floods from two streams pouring into it, but the dam would have stood it could the level of the lake have been kept below the top of the dam. But the friction of the water pouring over the top of the dam gradually wore it away from the outer face until the top became so thin that it gave away.

The break took place at three o'clock. It was about ten feet wide at first and shallow, but now that the flood had made a gap, it grew wider with increased rapidity, and the lake went roaring down the valley. That three miles of water was drained out in forty-five minutes. The downfall of those millions of tons was simply irresistible. Stones from the dam and boulders in the riverbed were carried for miles.

Perhaps the most heartless story in the annals of any city has been told today of this unfortunate place. To charge extortionate prices for food, as many of the people in the surrounding villages did when the hungry survivors asked them for bread, was cruel enough. This is an oft-told tale in the presence of such calamities as this, but probably never before did vampires seek to use such a terrible misfortune as this to ruin the souls, to try and lure the orphans of the valley to the dens of vice.

Supt. Hines, the chairman of the Committee on Transportation, is authority for the story that, for the past two days, two women of Pittsburgh have been here offering homes in that city to young girls who have been left without any protectors. Their object was not suspected at first, but subsequently they were recognized, and it became evident that their intention was to take girls away to their own places of iniquity in the Smoky City. It is not known whether any of the unfortunate maidens fell into the trap, as the two women became frightened and left this scene of desolation. Supt. Hines was terribly angered at this exhibition of utter heartlessness and declared after he had tried in vain to find them that, had he laid his hands on them, they would have had a ducking in the Conemaugh before they got away. It is related here that women of the same class have been seen around the depots in Pittsburgh on the arrival of trains from here, waiting to see if they could not gain possession of the poor victims who were going into the city to begin life anew in a strange place.

Today it is reported that a young lad, Eddie Fisher, has committed suicide after spending a week in brooding over the loss of his entire family and that an unknown woman suddenly became insane in the street and had to be removed to a hospital. It is impossible to verify either of these stories, but they are thought to be true, though no information could be had about them at headquarters.

New stories of incidents of the flood are heard every day and probably will continue to be told for weeks to come, but certainly the most touching of any that have yet been narrated is that of the Frohnheiser family. The father was a well-known workman in the Cambria Iron Works and lived with his wife, two little girls, and a son in a cottage, which was washed away. The mother and elder daughter were lost, but the father managed to crawl from the room with the other two children through a rent made by the flood in the roof. He reached down after his boy and told him to come near to him, but the lad answered, "It is no use, Papa. You can't save me; I'm too far away. Save Katie; she is near to you." Now the little girl had her leg broken by being jammed in between some furniture, and she cried, "You can't save me, Papa, for my leg is caught. Save him, or cut my leg off and get me out." The boy also asked the father to give him a pistol and he would shoot himself, but just then the house, which had been floating downstream, suddenly struck high ground and fell over on its side. The father landed unhurt, and the two children were thrown out on the hillside. The boy was unhurt, and the little girl is now in the hospital doing quite well.

In order to prevent the spread of the pestilence which is feared, fires were late last night started among the wreckage. Thus, in order to save valuable remaining lives, it has been deemed necessary to destroy by the other fearful element the festering debris, even if the bodies underneath have to be cremated with it. It is the only manner in which the health of the locality can be sustained.

If Johnstown suffered, Cambria City was almost entirely wiped out. The work of repairing the wreck in this place will be short, as the flood did the most of it. Nowhere in all the fifteen-mile course of the fearful torrent was the surface of the earth swept more clean than in that place. Cambria City was a borough organized separately from Johnstown and lying below it on the opposite side of the river. It began just below the railroad bridge and extended for a mile down the river. The Conemaugh below the bridge makes a long curve from the mountains, and a flat a mile long, with a curving front half a mile wide at its widest point, is left. Cambria City was built upon this flat. There were six hundred houses and about three thousand inhabitants. Most of the houses were small-frame buildings very lightly built. There were a few large stores, a small brick brewery, streetcar lines, electric lights, and other substantial improvements above ground.

The plan of the town in a general way was of four broad streets running across the flat lengthwise, with numerous cross streets at right angles. The first wild dash of the flood, when its advance wave was shattered against the bridge, was turned aside into the Cambria Iron Works, across the river from Cambria City. Passing through these from end to end, the outer half of the flat upon which Cambria City was built lay straight before it. The flood with a front of twenty feet high, bristling with all manner of debris, struck straight across the flat, as though the river's course had always been that way. It cut off the outer two-thirds of the city with a line as true and straight as could have been drawn by a surveyor. On the part over which it swept, there remains standing but one building, the brewery. With this exception, not only the houses and stores but the pavements, sidewalks and curbstones, and the earth beneath for several feet is washed away so that the water mains are laid bare. The pavements were of cinders from the iron works, a bed six inches thick, as hard as stone and with a surface like macadam. Over most of the washed-out portions of the city, not even the broken fragments of these pavements are left. Along the edge of the river, much of the land was made ground built up of these cinders. The mass of them was so great and the surface afforded so little hold for the flood that the land here is two or three feet higher than farther inland, where the ground yielded easier. But even here the water left its mark. Beside the sweeping away of all buildings upon the surface of the land itself, the hard cinder mass is torn, split, and corrugated, as if chiseled and cut by some convulsion of nature.

Of the six hundred houses of Cambria City, nearly four hundred stood upon the part of the flat which the first rush of the flood covered. If all the debris, not only of the houses, but of logs, timber, and other driftwood, that the flood left upon that mile-long shortcut across the bend in the river were piled into a heap, it would not make a mass as large as a single one of all the buildings swept away. There are not half a dozen wheelbarrow loads of earth or sand left upon the surface of the flat. The rush of the water left nothing on top except the heavy rocks and stones, and these were tossed about so thickly that they cover the whole surface, distributed as though some volcano had covered the earth with a shower of rocks.

Aside from the few logs and timbers left by the afterwash of the flood, there is nothing remaining upon the outer edge of the flat, including two of the four long streets of the city, except the brewery mentioned before and a grand piano. The water marks on the brewery walls show that the flood reached twenty feet up its sides, and it stood on a little higher ground than the buildings around it at that. Jacob Greener, the owner, with his family and workmen—nine men and two women in all—were caught in the building by the flood. They took refuge in the attic over the storeroom and were saved. The brewery was completely wrecked and will have to be torn down, but the main walls remained standing. The piano was built by Christie & Son, New York, and was numbered 6,609. Its legs are gone, and its cover is missing. The keys seem a little out of order, and two or three of the wires are broken.

Of the two hundred houses that were not swept away by the shortcut of the flood across the flats, there are not half a dozen that are uninjured. Fully half of them are wrecked completely. The value of those that can be repaired would not pay for the cost of removing the others. As far as property is concerned, it would have been cheaper if the flood had made its clean sweep over the whole of Cambria City. It would surely have done so had not the bridge checked it and turned it aside.

The death rate among these fragile frame buildings was horrible. The borough authorities estimate the loss of life at 1,100. Almost 750 bodies have already been recovered and brought to the morgue. It is not probable that Cambria City will be rebuilt, at least for a long time. The expense of preparing that rocky plain for building would be enormous. There is not a street left or any landmark by which to determine the location of lots, except the water mains through one or two streets. The part of the town still in existence will probably be put in order and maintained, but the broad flat will doubtless remain a rocky desert for a long time to come.

And all the time, all along the valley, the work of recovering the dead goes on with undiminished vigor, and as the workmen become accustomed to the terrible scenes, they apply themselves more diligently to their duty and labor with a system that produces rapid results.

The great number of bodies not identified seems incredible. Some of these bodies have lain in the different morgues for four days. Thousands of people from different parts of the state have seen them, yet they remain unidentified. At Nineveh they are burying all the unidentified dead, but in the morgues in this vicinity, no bodies have been buried unless they were identified. There are at present thirty unidentified bodies at the Fourth Ward schoolhouse.

These bodies have been lying there for the past three days, and in that time at least forty thousand people have viewed them, but no one has identified them, and they have nothing in their clothing to indicate who they are. During the past twenty-four hours, sixty bodies were embalmed and taken from this place. This morning five bodies were brought in.

But to enumerate would be too great a task, when reports of additional bodies being found are constantly coming in from all points along the valley.

Judge Advocate Rogers of Gov. Beaver's staff this morning decided an important question which arose by the discovery of forty barrels of whiskey in a building on Main Street. Adjt.-Gen. Hastings was disposed to confiscate it as a safeguard, according to a section in the military code which prohibited the sale of liquor within the limits of a military camp. Judge Advocate Rogers ruled that it was private property and a licensed dealer had a right to sell liquor. Besides, it was not a military camp but a posse comitatus, the militiamen doing police duty.

Last evening employees of Lutz & Son unearthed ten barrels of beer from the cellar of a building on Main Street. The body of a man was found close beside it. The driver was bringing his capture away when Major Samuel Hastings arrested him. Adjt.-Gen. Hastings knocked in the head of a barrel and let the beer run into the street. Under orders it was all destroyed.

"You will not be paid for the beer," said Gen. Hastings to the owners.

Among the bodies recovered in Kernville yesterday was that of a young woman richly attired, wearing diamond rings and a gold watch marked "J. J. L. to E. J. L." The remains were taken to the chapel on the hill.

It is said that many cases of fever and diphtheria and pneumonia are being concealed from the people here for fear a panic may seize the workers, and if that should happen now, probably no firm or people would attempt to touch the work here perhaps for months. Disinfectants of all kinds are being freely used by the carload, and in addition to this, a score of blazing piles in every direction shows that the purifying element of fire is being applied as rapidly as possible for the safety of the living.

Work was resumed today in the shops of the Cambria Iron Company's mammoth steel mill, and the repairs to the building are being made with remarkable rapidity. The damage to the buildings has been stated, but the machinery was only slightly damaged. The blast furnaces were not hurt at all and will be in operation as soon as a supply of coke can be obtained. There is some coke on hand, but it is too small an amount to begin with. The most serious loss to the firm was the destroyed papers, letters, order books, etc.

The members of secret societies on the Conemaugh Valley fared unusually well. The junior OUAM [Order of United American Mechanics] are very strong here, having a membership of 1,200. Out of this number, only nine lives were lost. Most of them lost their homes, but all have employment and expect to be on their feet again in a short time. The committee from Pittsburgh and Allegheny established headquarters in the upper end of the town and relieved the wants of all who applied. The councils responded, not only very liberally, but promptly.

The Independent Order of Heptasophs had a membership of eighty-five and lost but two. None of their members are in want, and the committee sent to distribute provisions and clothing have returned home. They had more than enough.

The Independent Odd Fellows had a membership of 506 here and out of that number lost 79. The distressed members are being well cared for.

It is not known how many of the Masonic Order are lost, although a prominent Mason says they are few, and the survivors are being royally provided for by the relief committee of that fraternity.

A trap was laid for the crook undertaker who was robbing the bodies in the Fourth Ward morgue. A female was brought in, and before it was dressed for burial, a diamond ring was placed upon one of her fingers, and the pseudo-undertaker was assigned to take charge of the body. He was detected in the act of stealing the jewelry and was promptly arrested by the chief of police, who immediately took him to Ebensburg. The officials refuse to give the name of the man.

About forty bodies were recovered today up to three p.m., but of these only three were recovered at the bridge.

Chalmer L. Dick, the ghouls' nemesis, bid goodbye to this ill-fated town last night. He will hereafter reside in Mount Pleasant.

Already twenty barrels of embalming fluid have been consumed, aggregating eight hundred gallons. It requires from half a pint to a quart for each corpse.

A Masonic relief committee has been organized and solicits aid for distressed Freemasons and their families. Remittances should be made by New York or Pittsburgh drafts to the order of Col. John F. Linton, treasurer, or William F. Myer, secretary. Knights of the Mystic Chain are requested to forward all subscriptions to the Supreme Recording and Corresponding Scribe, Box 321, Pittsburgh.

Fifteen bodies were received at the Fourth Ward morgue, of which seven were unidentified, as follows: James Murray of Philadelphia; William Marshall, Johnstown; Mrs. J. J. Llewellyn, Johnstown; James Dillon, Somerset; Marion Root, Johnstown; Miss Annie McKinstry, Mrs. McKinstry, and Jessie Hipp, Johnstown. At the Pennsylvania Railroad morgue, six bodies were received and two identified as E. M. Thomas and Howard J. Roberts, cashier, First National Bank, Johnstown. At the Presbyterian Church morgue, ten bodies were received and one identified as Sheriff John Ryan of Johnstown.

At 10:30 p.m. forty-seven bodies were discovered in a hole on the site of the Hurlbut House. They are supposed to be the bodies of guests. The number of persons who have so far registered is 20,110. The population of Johnstown and the neighborhood affected by the flood is about 35,000. The registration of 20,110 leaves almost 15,000 to be accounted for. It is not claimed that those who have not registered are dead, for many had left the town before the system of registration began, and it is safe to say that 8,000 people have left.

Among the most interesting relics of the flood is a small gold locket found in the ruins of the Hurlbut House yesterday. The locket contains a small curl of dark brown hair and has engraved on the inside the following remarkable lines: "Lock of George Washington's hair, cut in Philadelphia, while on his way to Yorktown—1781." Mr. Benford, one of the proprietors of the house, says that the locket was the property of his sister, who was lost in the flood, and was presented to her by an old lady in Philadelphia, whose mother had herself cut the hair from the "father of his country," and there is no doubt that the statement is reliable.

Up Stony Creek Gap, above the contractors, the United States Army engineers began work yesterday under command of Capt. Sears, who is here as the personal representative of the secretary of war. The engineers, Capt. Bergland's company from Willett's Point and Lieut. Biddle's company from West Point, arrived last night, having been since Tuesday on the road from New York. Early this morning they went to work to bridge Stony Creek and unloaded and launched their heavy pontoons and strung them across the streams with a rapidity and skill that astonished the natives, who had mistaken them, in their coarse, working uniforms of overall stuff, for a fresh gang of laborers. The engineers, when there are bridges enough laid, may be set at other work about town. They have a camp of their own on the outskirts of the place. There are more constables, watchmen, special policemen, and that sort of thing in Johnstown than in any three cities of its size in the country. Naturally there is great difficulty in equipping them. Badges were easily provided by the clipping out of stars from pieces of tin, but everyone had to look out for himself when it came to clubs. Everything goes, from a broomstick to a baseball bat. The bats are especially popular.

"I'd like to get the job of handling your paper here," said a young fellow to a Pittsburgh newspaperman. "You'll have to get some newsman to do it anyhow, for your old men have gone down, and I and my partner are the only newsmen in Johnstown above ground."

The news-dealing business is not the only one of which something like that is true. There has been great scarcity of cooking utensils since the flood. It not only is very inconvenient to the people but tends to the waste of a great deal of food. The soldiers are growling bitterly over their commissary department. They claim that bread and cheese and coffee is about all they get to eat.

The temporary electric lights have now been strung all along the railroad tracks and through the central part of the ruins, so that the place after dark is really quite brilliant seen from a distance, especially when to the electric display is added the red glow in the mist and smoke of huge bonfires.

Anybody who has been telegraphing to Johnstown this week and getting no answers would understand the reason for the lack of answers if he could see the piles of telegrams that are sent out here by train from Pittsburgh. Four thousand came in one batch on Thursday. Half of them are still undelivered, and yet there is probably no place in the country where the Western Union Company is doing better work than here. The flood destroyed not only the company's offices but the greater part of their wires in this part of the country. The office they established here is in a little shanty with no windows and only one door, which doesn't close, and it handles an amount of outgoing matter daily that would swamp nine-tenths of the city offices in the country. Incoming business is now received in considerable quantities, but for several days so great was the pressure of outgoing business that no attempt was made to receive any dispatches.

The whole effort of the office has been to handle press matter, and how well they have done it is shown by the amount of matter received from there that the daily papers have been publishing every day. The rush of press matter has been slacking a little now, and in a day or two, private messages will probably be going back and forth with reasonable promptness. But there will be no efficient delivery service for a long time. The old messenger boys are all drowned, and the other boys who might make messenger boys are also most of them drowned, so that the raw material for creating a service is very scant. Besides that, nobody knows nowadays where anyone else lives, and it is almost impossible to deliver private messages at all.

The amateur and professional photographers who have overrun the town for the last few days came to grief yesterday. A good many of them were arrested by the soldiers, placed under a guard, taken down to the Stony Creek, and set to lugging logs and timber. Among those arrested were several of the newspaper photographers, and these Gen. Hastings ordered released when he heard of their arrest. The others were made to work for half a day. They were a mad and disgusted lot, and they vowed all sorts of vengeance. It does seem that some notice to the effect that photographers were not permitted in Johnstown should have been posted before the men were arrested. The photographers all had passes in regular form, but the soldiers refused to even look at these. Were not it that Gen. Hastings is a candidate for governor, the reporters expect that they would be the ones to be arrested next.

More sightseers got through the guards at Bolivar last night and came to Johnstown on the last train. Word was telegraphed ahead, and the soldiers met them at the train, put them under arrest, kept them overnight, and this morning they were set to work in clearing up the ruins.

The special detail of workmen who have been at work looking up safes in the ruins and seeing that they were taken care of report that none of the safes have been broken open or otherwise interfered with. The committee on valuables report that quantities of jewelry and money are being turned daily into them by people who have found them in the ruins. Often the people surrendering this stuff are evidently very poor themselves. The committee believes that, as a general thing, the people are dealing very honestly in this matter of treasure trove from the ruins.

Three carloads of coffins were part of the load of one freight train this afternoon. Coffins already are scattered everywhere about the city. Scores of them seem to have been set down and forgotten. They are used as benches and even, it is said, as beds.

One enterprising man has opened a shop for the sale of relics of the disaster and is doing a big business. Half the people here are relic cranks. Everything goes as a relic, from a horseshoe to a two-foot section of iron pipe. Buttons and little things like that that can easily be carried off are the most popular.

Grandma Mary Seter, aged eighty-three years, a well-known character in Johnstown who was in the water until Saturday and who, when rescued, had her right arm so injured that amputation at the shoulder was necessary, is doing finely at the hospital, and the doctors expect to have her around again before long.

There has not been a photographer seen about the place today. The experience of the nine who were arrested and set to work on the ruins yesterday has scared off the rest.

Out of the twenty-five Chinamen in Johnstown, only three escaped the flood. Vice President Frank Thompson of the Pennsylvania Railroad arrived today on his special locomotive, having opened a way through from Harrisburg to Pittsburgh. He is now going to push east over the main line as rapidly as possible. It is not likely that the line will be opened for three or four days yet.

A woman made insane by the loss of her husband and all her children has been wandering about the edge of the gorge this afternoon, moaning and shrieking incessantly. She is one of several women who have been thus affected by their affliction.

7

THE NOME STAMPEDE

BY SAMUEL HALL YOUNG

The discovery of gold in the unforgiving Alaskan wilderness lured thousands of adventurers looking for wealth and fortune on the frontier. It also brought rowdy times and the more unscrupulous types who would do anything to make money. For a preacher, the opportunities were heaven-sent.

It was with the excitement of a veteran soldier going into a fresh battle that I teetered over the springy plank from the Rampart shore to the deck of the Yukon River steamboat. My year's outfit of "grub and duds," as the miners would put it, was aboard. I grasped the hand of Dr. Koonce, with whom I had just floated in an open boat down the Yukon 1,200 miles. A fine fellow—"Kooncie"! We had been camping and fishing and packing and boating together since the first of May, 1899, and it was now the middle of August. He was to stay at the new mining town of Rampart, build a church there, and learn the joyous life of a pioneer missionary.

What a queer mix-up of men on the crowded decks of the steamboat! Wild rumors of a ridiculous sort had reached the ears of gold hunters clear up the two thousand miles of the swift and crooked Yukon to Dawson. Gold! Not snugly reposing in the frozen gravel of deep gulches and canyons cut through the high hills—where respectable and orthodox gold ought to be—but gold on the windswept, stormy, treeless, exposed coast of Seward Peninsula—the tongue that impudent young Alaska sticks out at old Asia. Gold, like yellow cornmeal in the beach sands of Bering Sea, where nobody could lawfully stake a claim but where anybody could go with shovel, pan, and rocker and gather it up. Nuggets aplenty and coarse gold—enticing shallow diggings—in the bed of Anvil Creek and other creeks and runlets in the hills and the flat tundra about Nome.

The reports of the new "strike," often wild and exaggerated, came as a lifesaver to weary and discouraged thousands of Klondikers, who had packed their outfits over the terrible thirty miles of the Chilcoot Pass in the fall of '97 or the spring of '98, sawed the lumber themselves in the "armstrong sawmill," sailed their clumsy boats through the lakes, shot the rapids of the Upper Yukon, spent the summer of '98 and the winter that followed surging here and there on "wildcat" stampedes or putting down "dry" holes on unprofitable lays, and were now eagerly snatching at this new straw, hoping to "strike it" on the Nome beach. From Dawson, Forty Mile, Eagle, Circle, Fort Yukon; from wood camps and prospectors' tents along the Yukon; and now from Rampart, these bearded, battered, sun-blistered men came rushing aboard the steamboat.

I had engaged a stateroom before the steamboat arrived, but when it came, a placard of the company owning the boat menaced us in the office: "All reservations cancelled. Boat overcrowded. No passengers to be taken at Rampart."

Of course there was a mighty howl from the Rampart men, nearly half of whom had packed up to go on the boat. I hurried to the purser, whom I knew, and showed my pass from the manager of the company.

"Can't help it, Doctor," he said in a loud tone, for the benefit of the bystanders. "The boat's past her limit now, and we're liable for big damages if anything happens. We can't take anybody."

Presently he slyly pulled my arm, and I followed him to an inner office of the store. "Get your goods aboard," he directed. "You can spread your blankets on the floor of my office."

While I was checking off my outfit and seeing it onboard, I noticed a lot of the Rampart men, with hand trucks gathered from the various stores, taking their own outfits aboard, ignoring the shipping clerk and dumping their goods wherever they found a place to put them. The officers and deckhands were protesting and swearing, but the men went right along loading their outfits.

Presently the captain pulled the whistle rope and ordered the plank drawn in and the cable cast off from the "deadman." Instantly three men marched to the cable's end, seized the man who was to cast it off, and held him. Then fully fifty men with their packs on their backs filed down the plank. The first mate tried to stop them. He even made a move to draw his pistol, but the foremost man—a big six-footer—threw his arms around him and carried him back against the stairway and held him until the men with their packs were all aboard. It was all done quietly and with the utmost good humor. The men grinned up at the swearing, red-faced captain on the upper deck, and one shouted, "We'll give you a poke of dust, Cap, when we get to Nome."

When all were aboard, somebody on the bank cast off the cable, the swift current caught the boat, the wheel backed, and we swung around and headed down the Yukon, bound for the new strike.

Whiskers were very much in evidence in that closely packed mob of men that stood around on all the decks, stepping on each other's feet, perching on stairways, boxes, pole bunks—anywhere for a resting place. To go from one part of the boat to another was a difficult proposition.

The most evident trait of the crowd was its good nature. The deck-hands, among whom I recognized a lawyer friend from Dawson and a former customs collector from Juneau, were gold seekers like all the rest, and it was, "Hello, Shorty!" "Ah, there, Dutch!" "Where you goin', Jim?" between them and the newcomers. A rollicking, happy-go-lucky crowd, all joyful at being on the way to the new diggings. Even the officers of the boat began to smile, secretly pleased that they had a record-breaking and most profitable load aboard and were free from blame for overloading because they could not help it.

As for me, I was well content, even to be hustled and jostled and elbow-punched by this horde of scraggly-bearded men of the north-western wilderness. This was my parish, my home, and these were my comrades, my chums, my brothers. I was just as sunburned and weather-beaten as they were and felt the same tingling of nerves, the same leap of the blood at the call of fresh adventure.

I was dressed in the same sort of rough woolen mackinaw clothes and soft flannel underwear as the men around me. I had left my cler-ical suit and white shirts and collars behind for three reasons: First, for the sake of economy. These strong, loose garments did not cost a third as much as broadcloth and would wear twice as well. Besides, it would cost a dollar and a half to have a white shirt laundered in interior Alaska (which, at that time, was twice the original cost of the shirt), and twenty-five cents to do up a collar, the cost price of which "outside" was three for a quarter. I could wash my flannel shirts myself. Second, for comfort's sake. The soft wool of these garments was so much warmer and more pliable than a "Prince Albert" suit, and a starched collar would sear one's neck like fire when it was "sixty below." My chief reason, however, was that I wished to create no artificial barriers between my parishioners and myself. I wished to stand on the same social level. I desired these men to feel that I was one of them and could camp and "rustle," carry a pack, live on rabbits, and rough it generally as deftly and cheerfully as they—live the same outdoor life and endure the same so-called hardships.

The viewpoint of these "sourdoughs" was shown in a funny way at our first landing place after leaving Rampart, which was the little town of Tanana. When the boat tied up, the whistle gave three sharp hoots, showing that the stay would be very short. As soon as the plank was ashore, a man ran up it, and when he reached the deck, he called loudly, "Is there a preacher aboard? Is there a preacher aboard?"

A grizzled old miner who did not know me pointed to the only man on the steamboat who wore a Prince Albert coat and white shirt and collar and drawled, "Wa-al, that there feller, he's either a preacher or a gambler; I don't know which."

The "dressed-up" man proved to be a gambler. I made myself known to the anxious man from the village, followed him ashore, and married him to a woman who was waiting in the company's office.

That was one voyage of mingled discomfort and pleasure. Discomforts and hardships are as you make them and take them. There were a few of that company who grumbled and swore at being crowded, at being obliged to stand up all day, to lie on the floor or on the piles of cordwood at night, besides being compelled to fairly fight for their meals or to get their food from their own kits. But the majority of these men had been camping and roughing it for two years. Many of them had packed heavy loads over the Chilcoot Pass in the great Klondike Stampede, had made their own boats and navigated hundreds of miles of unknown and dangerous rivers, had encountered and overcome thousands of untried experiences. To all of them, these little discomforts were trifles to be dismissed with a smile or joke, and they had contempt for any man who fussed or complained.

One of the cheeriest of the crowd aboard the steamboat was a newsboy twelve or thirteen years old. His name was Joe; I never knew his surname. He had had a very wonderful time. The year before—the summer of 1898—he was selling papers in Seattle. He heard of the high prices paid for newspapers and magazines at the camps of the Northwest. He bought three or four hundred copies of the *Seattle P.I.* (*Post-Intelligencer*) and *Times*. He paid two and a half and three cents apiece for them, the selling price at Seattle being five cents. Then he got five or six hundred back numbers of these papers, from a day to a week old, for nothing. He also got, mostly by gift from those who had read them, three or four hundred of the cheaper magazines, some new, some a month or two old. For his whole stock, he paid scarcely fifteen dollars.

Joe smuggled himself and his papers aboard a steamboat bound for Skagway and worked his passage as cabin boy, waiter, and general roustabout. At Juneau and Skagway, he sold about one-fourth of his papers and magazines—the papers for twenty-five cents each and the ten-cent magazines for fifty cents. He could have sold out but, hearing that he could get double these prices at Dawson and down the Yukon, held on to his stock.

He formed a partnership with an old "sourdough" miner, who helped him get his papers over the Chilcoot Pass and down the Yukon to Dawson. At the great Klondike camp, he quickly sold out his papers at a dollar each and the magazines at a dollar and a half to two and a half.

Joe spent the winter of 1898–1899 at Dawson selling the two papers published in that city and running a general newsstand, in which he sold the reading matter he had sold before but gathered up again from the buyers. Sometimes he sold the same magazine four or five times.

When the Nome stampede began, Joe got into the good graces of the manager of the steamboat company and got free passage down the Yukon. He shared my wolf robe on the floor of the purser's room, and we became great chums. The boy was so bright and quick and at the same time so polite and accommodating that he made friends everywhere. He was a Sunday-school boy and distributed my little red hymnbooks when I held service in the social hall of the steamboat on Sunday, and his clear soprano sounded sweetly above the bass notes of the men.

"Joe," I asked him one day, "how much money have you made during the last year and a half?"

"Well," he replied, "I sent two thousand dollars out home from Dawson before I started down here, and with what I am making on this trip and what I hope to make at Nome, I think I'll have five thousand dollars clear when I land at Seattle the last of October."

"That's a dangerous amount of money for a small boy to have," I warned him. "Have you lost any of it?"

Joe grinned. "No, I dassent. Some card sharps tried to get me to gamble at Dawson. They said I could double my money. But my partner [the old miner] said he'd lick me half to death if I ever went near the green tables. I didn't want to, anyhow. Everybody helps me take care of my money."

"What are you going to do with it?"

"Why, give it all to mother, of course. She'll use it for me and my sister. I'm going to school as soon as I get home. Mother works in a store, but I guess this money'll give her a rest. She needs it."

A word more about little Joe before I leave him. He made good at Nome in September and sailed for Seattle the last of October. The last I heard of him, four or five years later, he was making his way through the University of Washington and still managing newspaper routes in Seattle. His is a case of exceptional good fortune, and yet I know of a number of boys who have made remarkable sums selling papers in Alaska. It is a boy's land of opportunity as well as a man's.

Our voyage to St. Michael was a tedious one—down the long stretches of the Lower Yukon, worming through the sandbars and muddy shallows of the interminable delta, waiting through weary hours for tide and wind to be just right before venturing out on Bering Sea. Hurrying at last under full steam through the choppy sea, with the waves washing the lower deck and producing panic, uproar, and swearing among the men packed upon it—we came to the harbor of St. Michael on the windswept, treeless, mossy shore of Norton Sound.

I was still to work my way through a tangle of delays and adventures before I could reach my goal—the great new camp at Nome, 130 miles from St. Michael.

I had first to get my outfit together on the wharf, counting the boxes and war bags, pursuing the missing ones to other outfits, and proving my claim to them. In the confusion this was a hard job, but I only lost two or three of my boxes. I piled my goods in a corner of the big warehouse of the North American Trading and Transportation Co. and set up my tent on the beach, for I was near the end of my money and could not pay the high prices charged at the hotels. I got into my camp kit and did my own cooking, protecting my food as best I could against the thievish Eskimo dogs.

Then began a search, which lasted a week, for means of getting to Nome. The gold hunters were putting off every day in whale boats, Eskimo oomiaks, and small sloops and schooners but these craft were too small and uncertain for me to risk passage in them. My caution proved wise, for five or six of these small boats, after setting out, were never heard of again.

While I was waiting, the U.S. revenue cutter, *Bear*, came into the harbor, and aboard her was Sheldon Jackson, superintendent of education for Alaska, the noted pioneer missionary. He was just returning from a tour of the native schools and reindeer stations. (He was the man who had introduced the reindeer into Alaska from Siberia to supply the wants of the Eskimo.)

"Hurry on to Nome," he counseled me. "You were never needed more in all your life."

At length there limped into the harbor a little tub-like side-wheel steamboat belonging to the Alaska Exploration Company, whose wharf was a mile and a half distant up the harbor. There was no way of getting my goods across the swampy tundra of St. Michael Island to the wharf. On the beach I found an abandoned old rowboat with open seams. I procured pieces of boards, some oakum, and pitch and set to work to repair the old boat. The steamboat was to sail for Nome the next forenoon. I worked all night. I made a pair of clumsy oars out of boards. Then I carried my goods to the leaky boat and rowed them to the dock. It took three trips to transfer my outfit, and while I was rowing back and forth, somebody carried off my most valuable warbag, containing most of my footwear and underclothes—one hundred dollars' worth.

I was a tired man when I stumbled down the steep stairs into the dark and stuffy hold of the little steamboat and much more tired when, after two and a half days of seasickness, bobbing up and down in the choppy seas like a man on a bucking bronco, I pulled up the stairs again and let myself down the rope ladder into the dory which was to take the passengers ashore at Nome.

"You can only take what you can carry on your back," announced the captain. "There's a storm coming up, and I've got to hurry to the lee of Sledge Island, twenty miles away. You'll get your outfits when I come back. Lucky we're not all down in Davy Jones's locker."

I strapped my pack-sack, containing my wolf robe and a pair of blankets, on my back, glad to get ashore on any terms. The dory wallowed heavily in the waves, the strong wind driving it toward the sandy beach. Boats have to anchor from one to two miles offshore at Nome. When we reached the beach, a big wave lifted the dory and swung it sideways. The keel struck the sand, and she turned over, dumping us all out, the comber overwhelming us and rolling us over and over like barrels. Drenched and battered, we crawled to land.

A heavy rain was falling as I staggered up the beach with my water-soaked blankets on my back, looking for a lodging house. The beach was lined with tents, placed without regard to order or the convenience of anybody except the owner of each tent. A few straggling board shacks were stuck here and there on the swampy tundra. Two or three large, low store buildings represented the various pioneer trading companies. The one street, which ran parallel to the beach, was full of mud. The buildings most in evidence were saloons, generally with dance hall attachments. The absence of trees; the leaden, weeping sky; the mud; the swampy tundra; the want of all light and beauty made this reception the dreariest of all my experiences in the new mining camps.

But I long ago learned that nothing is so bad but that it might be worse. I had not at that time seen Edmund Vance Cook's sturdy lines, but the spirit of them was in my heart:

> Did you tackle the trouble that came your way
> With a resolute heart and cheerful,
> Or hide your face from the light of day

With a craven heart and fearful?

Oh, a trouble's a ton or a trouble's an ounce,

Or a trouble is what you make it;

And it isn't the fact that you're hurt that counts,

But only, how did you take it!

I soon found a sign written in charcoal on the lid of a paper box—Lodging. I entered the rough building and found a cheery Irish woman named McGrath. There was no furniture in the house except two or three cheap chairs and a homemade board table.

"Shure, ye can," she answered in reply to my question about spending the night there. "Ye'll spread yer robe an' blankets on the flure, an' it'll only cost ye a dollar an' four bits. Ye'll plaze pay in advance."

I took stock of the contents of my pocketbook. There was just five dollars and a quarter left of the thousand dollars with which I had started from home on the first of May. It was now the first of September, and no more money was due me until the next spring. My food and tent were on the steamboat and would not be likely to come ashore for many days. It was Sunday evening, and a whole week must elapse before I could take up a collection.

I paid my landlady and she put my blankets by her stove to dry. I paid another dollar and a half for a supper of beans and flapjacks—the first food I had tasted for three days. I slept soundly that night on the floor, without a care or anxiety. The next morning I paid another dollar and a half for breakfast and could not resist the temptation of purchasing a Seattle paper (only three weeks old—what a luxury!). I had just twenty-five cents left—and I was a stranger in this strange corner of the earth!

I could not help laughing at my predicament as I entered the Alaska Exploration Company's store. A bearded man standing by the stove bade me "good morning."

"You seem to be pleased about something," he said. "Have you struck it rich?"

"Well, yes!" I replied. "A rich joke on me," and I told him of the fix I was in.

"What? You are Dr. Young?" he exclaimed, shaking me heartily by the hand. "Why, I'm a Presbyterian elder from San Francisco."

The man's name was Fickus, a carpenter, who had come to Nome to build the store and warehouses of one of the big companies. He had held the first religious meetings in the new camp and had found quite a circle of Christian people.

He offered to lend me money, but I refused to take it. "No," I said, "let us wait and see what happens."

Something happened very quickly. While we were talking, a young man entered the store and came up to me.

"I understand that you are a minister," he said.

"Yes," I replied. "What can I do for you?"

"You can marry me to the best woman in Alaska."

"Is she here?" I asked, with a triumphant smile at Fickus.

"Oh, yes; she came on the last boat from Seattle."

"When do you wish the ceremony to take place?" I inquired.

"Right now," he replied. "You can't tie the knot too quickly to suit me."

I followed the eager young man, married him to a nice-looking girl who was waiting in a nearby cabin, received a wedding fee of twenty dollars, and returned to my newly found friend with the assurance that my wants were supplied until my outfit would come ashore.

This was my introduction to the second great gold camp of the Northwest—the raw, crazy, confused stampede of Nome.

8

HOW THE *MERRIMAC* WAS SUNK IN CUBA

BY RUPERT S. HOLLAND

The Spanish fleet was mounting an assault in the Cuban harbor of Santiago. It would be an easy sail into the Caribbean for a surprise attack on the Americans. Or so they thought. A heroic crew on a secret and audacious mission and an iconic old ship would change Spanish plans.

In the small hours of the morning of June 3, 1898, the *Merrimac*, a vessel that had once been a collier in the United States Navy, slipped away from the warships of the American fleet that lay off the coast of Cuba and headed toward the harbor of Santiago. The moon was almost full, and there was scarcely a cloud in the sky. To the northwest lay the *Brooklyn*, her great mass almost white in the reflected light. On the northeast the *Texas* loomed dark and warlike, and farther away lay a ring of other ships, dim and ghostly in the distance.

Ahead was the coast of Cuba, with an outline of mountains rising in a half circle beyond the harbor. Five miles across the water, Morro Castle guarded the entrance to the harbor, in which lay a fleet of the Spanish admiral Cervera.

To steer directly for Morro Castle would be to keep the *Merrimac* full in the moon's path, and to avoid this she stood to the eastward of the course and stole along at a slow rate of speed. The small crew onboard, a commander and seven men, were stripped to their underclothes and wore life preservers and revolver belts. Each man had taken his life in his hand when he volunteered for this night's work. They wanted to sink the *Merrimac* at a narrow point in the harbor and bottle up the Spanish fleet beyond it.

As they neared the great looming fortress of the Morro, it was impossible to keep the ship hidden; the sentries on the castle must see the dark object now and wonder what she intended. The *Merrimac* gave up its oblique course and steered straight ahead. The order "Full speed!" went from Lieutenant Hobson, a naval constructor in command, to the engineer. Foam dashed over the bows, and the long shape shot for the harbor entrance, regardless of what the enemy might think or do. Soon the Morro stood up high above them, the moon clearly revealing the great central battery that crowned the fortress top.

The Spanish guns were only five hundred yards away, and yet the enemy had given no sign of having seen the *Merrimac*. Then suddenly a light flashed from near the water's edge on the left side of the entrance, and a roar followed. The *Merrimac* did not quiver. The shot must have fallen astern. Again there was a flash, and this time the crew could hear the splash of water as the projectile struck back of them. Through their night glasses, they saw a picket boat with rapid-fire guns lying close in the shadows of the shore. Her guns had probably been aimed at the *Merrimac*'s rudder, but so far they had missed their aim. With a rapid-fire gun to reply, the *Merrimac* might have demolished the other boat in half a minute, but she had no such equipment. She would have to pass within a ship's length of this picket. There was nothing to do but pay no heed to her aim at the *Merrimac*'s rudder and steer for the high wall off Morro Castle, where the deepwater channel ran close inshore. "A touch of port helm!" was the order. "A touch of port helm, sir," came the answer, and the vessel stood toward the wall.

There came a crash from the port side. "The western battery has opened on us, sir!" reported the man on the bridge to Hobson. "Very well; pay no attention to it," was the answer. The commander knew he must take the *Merrimac* at least another ship's length forward and wondered if the enemy would give him that much grace. A shot crossed the bridge and struck. No one was hurt. They had almost reached the point where they were to stop. Another moment or two, and over the engine telegraph went the order, "Stop!" The engineer obeyed. The *Merrimac* slowed off Morro rock.

A high rocket shot across the channel entrance. From each side came the firing of batteries. Hobson and his men were too busy to heed them. The *Merrimac*, still swinging under her own headway, brought her bow within thirty feet of the rock before she righted. Another ship's length, and she would be at the point where her commander had planned to take her; then the steering gear stopped working, and she was left at the mercy of the current.

The ship must be sunk before the current could carry her out of the course. This was done by exploding torpedoes on the outside of the vessel. Hobson gave the order, and the first torpedo went off, blowing out the collision bulkhead. There was no reply from the second or third torpedoes. Hobson crossed the bridge and shouted, "Fire all torpedoes!" In the roar of the Spanish batteries, his voice could hardly be heard.

Meantime the guns on the shores back of the harbor were pouring their shot at the black target in the moonlight, and the din was terrific. Word came to Hobson that some of the torpedoes could not be fired, as their cells had been broken. The order was given to fire the others, and the fifth exploded promptly, but the remaining ones had been shattered by Spanish fire and were useless. The commander knew that under these circumstances it would take some time for the *Merrimac* to sink.

The important point was to keep the ship in the center of the harbor, but the stern anchor had already been cut away. Hobson watched the bow move against the shoreline. There was nothing to do but wait and see where the tide would swing them.

The crew now gathered on deck. One of them, Kelly, had been dazed by an exploding shell. When he had picked himself up, he started down the engine-room hatch but found the water rising. Then he remembered the *Merrimac*'s purpose and tried to reach the torpedo of which he had charge. The torpedo was useless, and he headed back to the deck, climbing up on all fours. It was a strange sight to see him stealing up, and Hobson and some of the others drew their revolvers, thinking for the moment that he must be an enemy who had boarded the ship. Fortunately they recognized him almost immediately.

The tide was bearing them to the center of the channel when there came a blasting noise and shock. A mine had exploded beneath them. "Lads, they're helping us!" cried the commander. But the mine did not break the deck, and the ship only settled a little lower. For a moment it seemed as if the coal might have closed the breach made by the explosion, but just as the crew feared that they were to be carried past the point chosen for sinking the current from the opposite shore caught them, and the Merrimac settled crosswise. It was now only a matter of time before she would sink in the harbor.

The crew could now turn their attention to themselves. Hobson said to them,

> We will remain here, lads, till the moon sets. When it is dark, we will go down the after hatch to the coal, where her stern will be left out of water. We will remain inside all day and tonight at ebb tide try to make our way to the squadron. If the enemy comes onboard, we will remain quiet until he finds us and will repel him. If he then turns artillery on the place where we are, we will swim out to points farther forward.

He started toward the bow to reconnoiter but was persuaded not to expose himself to the enemy's fire. One of the men discovered a break in the bulwarks that gave a good view, and Hobson stood there. The moon was bright, though now low, and the muzzles of the Spanish guns were very near them. The crew, however, remained safely hidden behind the rail. From all sides came the firing, and the Americans, lying full length on the Merrimac's deck, felt the continual shock of projectiles striking around them. Some of the crew suggested that they should take to the small boat, but the commander knew that this would be certain destruction and ordered them to remain. Presently a shot struck the boiler, and a rush of steam came up the deck near where they lay. A canteen was passed from hand to hand. Hobson, having no pockets, carried some tourniquets around his left arm and a roll of antiseptic lint in his left hand, ready in case any of his crew was wounded.

Looking through the hole in the bulwarks, the commander saw that the Merrimac was again moving. Sunk deep though she was, the tide was carrying her on and might bear her some distance. There seemed to be no way in which they could make her sink where she was. Two more mines exploded but missed the ship, and as she floated on, it became evident that they could not block the channel completely. But shortly the Merrimac gave a lurch forward and settled to the port side. Now the Spanish *Reina Mercedes* was near at hand, and the *Pluton* was coming close inboard, but their guns and torpedoes did not hasten the sinking of the collier. She plunged again and settled in the channel.

A rush of water came up the gangway, and the crew were thrown against the bulwarks and then into the sea. The life preservers helped to keep them afloat, but when they looked for the lifeboat, they found that it had been carried away. A catamaran was the largest piece of floating wreckage, and they swam to this. The firing had now stopped. The wreckage began to drift away, and the crew were left swimming about the catamaran, apparently unseen by the enemy. The men were ordered to cling to this rude craft, their bodies in the water, their heads hidden by the boards, and to keep quiet, as Spanish boats were passing close to them. All the crew were safe, and Hobson expected that in time some Spanish officers would come out to reconnoiter the channel. He knew that his men could not swim against the tide to the harbor entrance, and even had they been able to do so, it would have been too dangerous a risk, as the banks were now lined with soldiers and the water patrolled by small boats. Their hope lay in surrendering before they were fired upon.

The moon had now nearly set, and the shadow of the high banks fell across the water. Boats rowed by Spanish sailors pulled close to the catamaran, but acting under orders from their commander, the crew of the *Merrimac* kept well out of sight. The sun rose, and a new day came. Soon the crew could see the line of distant mountains and the steep slopes leading to Morro Castle. A Spanish torpedo destroyer was heading up the harbor, and a bugle at one of the batteries could be heard across the waters. Still the Americans clung to the catamaran, although their teeth were chattering, and they had to work their arms and legs to keep warm.

Presently one of the men said, "A steam launch is heading for us, sir!" The commander looked about and saw a large launch, the curtains aft drawn down, coming from around a point of land straight toward the catamaran. As it drew near, the launch swerved to the left. When it was about thirty yards away, Hobson hailed it. The boat instantly stopped and began to back, while some riflemen appeared on the deck and took position for firing. No shot followed, however. Hobson called out again, asking whether there were any officers on the boat and adding that if there were he was ready to surrender himself and his American sailors as prisoners of war. The curtain at the stern was lowered, a Spanish officer gave an order, and the rifles dropped. The American commander swam to the launch and climbed onboard, being helped up by the Spanish officer, who turned out later to be no other than Admiral Cervera himself. Hobson surrendered for himself and his crew. The launch then drew close to the catamaran, and the sailors clinging to it were pulled onboard. Although the Spaniards knew that the *Merrimac*'s men had bottled up their warships in the harbor, they could not help praising their bravery.

The Spanish launch took them to the *Reina Mercedes*. There the men were given dry clothes and food. Although all were scratched and bruised, only one was wounded, and his wound, though painful, was not serious. The American officer was invited to join the Spaniards at breakfast and was treated with as much courtesy as if he had been an honored guest. Afterward Hobson wrote a note to Admiral Sampson, who was in command of the American fleet. The note read, "Sir: I have the honor to report that the *Merrimac* is sunk in the channel. No loss, only bruises. We are prisoners of war, being well cared for." He asked that this should be sent under a flag of truce. Later in the day, the Americans were taken from the warship in a launch and carried across the harbor to Morro Castle. This course brought them within a short distance of where the *Merrimac* had sunk, and as Hobson noted the position, he concluded that the plan had only partly succeeded and that the channel was not completely blocked.

Landing at a small wharf, the Americans were marched up a steep hill that led to the Morro from the rear. The fortress stood out like one the medieval castles of Europe, commanding a wide view of sea and shore. The road brought them to the bridge that crossed the moat. They marched under the portcullis and entered a vaulted passage. The American officer was shown into the guard room, while the crew were led on. A few minutes later Admiral Cervera came into the guard room and held out his hand to Hobson. The admiral said that he would have liked to send the American's note under a flag of truce to his fleet but that this had been refused by the general in command. He added, however, that some word should be sent to inform their friends of the safe escape of the *Merrimac*'s men. Hobson was then led to a cell in the tower of the castle. As the jailer stopped to unlock the door, Hobson had a view of the sea and made out the line of the American battleships moving in two columns. He was told to enter the cell, which was a bare and ill-looking place, but a few minutes later, a Spanish captain arrived with apologies, saying that he hoped soon to provide the Americans with better quarters.

A little later furniture was brought to the cell and food, cigars, cigarettes, and a bottle of brandy provided for the American officer. In fact, he and his men fared as well as the Spanish officers and soldiers themselves. The governor of the fortress sent a note to ask what he could do to improve Hobson's comfort. Officers of all ranks called to shake hands with him and express their admiration for his courage.

That first night in the castle, after the sentries had made their rounds, Hobson climbed up on his cot-bed and looked through a small window at the top of the cell. The full moon showed a steep slope from the fortress to the water, then the wide sweep of the harbor, with a picket boat on duty as it had been the night before and beyond the boat the great Spanish warships and still farther off the batteries of Socapa. It was hard to believe that, only twenty-four hours before, the center of that quiet moonlit water had been ablaze with fire aimed at the small collier Hobson had commanded. As he studied the situation, he decided that the *Merrimac* probably blocked the channel. The enemy would hesitate a long time before they would try to take their fleet past the sunken vessel, and that delay would give Admiral Sampson time to gather his ships. Even if the channel were not entirely blocked, the Spanish ships could only leave the harbor in single line and with the most skillful steering. Therefore, he concluded that his perilous expedition had been successful.

Next morning a Spanish officer brought him news that a flag of truce had been carried to Admiral Sampson with word of the crew's escape and that the messengers had been given a box for Hobson and bags of clothes, some money, and other articles for him and his crew. The men, now dressed again in the uniform of American marines, were treated as prisoners of war and lived almost as comfortably as their captors.

While Hobson was having his coffee on the morning of June 6th, he heard the whiz and crash of an exploding shell, then another, and another and knew that a general bombardment of the fortress had begun. He hastily examined the cell to see what protection it would offer from bricks and mortar falling from the walls and roof. At the first shot, the sentry on guard had bolted the door and left. The American pulled the table and washstand in front of the door and stood the galvanized iron box that had been sent him against the end of the table; this he thought would catch splinters and stones, which would probably be more dangerous than actual shells. He lay down under the protection of this cover. He knew that the gunners of the American fleet were good shots and figured that they could easily demolish all that part of the Morro in which his cell was situated. One shell after another against the walls of the fortress made the whole structure tremble, and it seemed as if part of the walls would be blown away. Fortunately, however, the firing soon turned in another direction, and Hobson could come from his shelter and, standing on his cot-bed, look through the window at the battle. Several times he took shelter again under the table and several times returned to watch the cannonade. The shells screamed through the air, plowed through shrubs and earthworks, knocked bricks and mortar from the Morro, and set fire to some of the Spanish ships. But no serious damage was done, and the bombardment ended in a stand-off between the two sides.

The American officer had no desire to pass through such a cannonade again, and he wrote to the Spanish governor to ask that his crew and himself be transferred to safer quarters. Next day an officer arrived with orders to take all the prisoners to the city of Santiago. So, after a four days' stay in Morro Castle, the little party set out on an inland march, guarded by some thirty Spanish soldiers. It was not far to Santiago, and there the Americans were housed in the regular army barracks. These quarters were much better than those in the fortress, and the British consul secured many comforts and delicacies for the Americans.

The men of the *Merrimac* stayed in Santiago during the siege of that city. On July 5th arrangements were made to exchange Hobson and his men. In the afternoon they were blindfolded and guided out of the city. Half a mile or more beyond the entrenchments, they were told that they might remove the handkerchiefs and found themselves facing their own troops on a distant ridge. Soon they were being welcomed by their own men, who told them of the recent victories won by fleet and army. Not long afterward they reached their ships and were received onboard the *New York* by the officers and men who had watched them set out on their dangerous mission on that moonlit night of June 3d. They gave a royal welcome to the small crew who had brought the collier into the very heart of the Spanish lines and sunk her, taking their chances of escape. They were the heroes of a desperate adventure, from which every man returned unharmed.

9

BEHEADED

BY DANIEL COLLINS

*Daniel Collins thought the trip from Wiscasset to Cuba would be quick
and uneventful. An unmarked reef, a shipwreck, and an indecisive captain were the first indications that things would not be normal. But
that was only the beginning.*

On the 28th of November, 1824, I sailed from Wiscasset (Maine) for
Matanzas, in the island of Cuba, onboard the brig *Betsey*, laden with
lumber; our officers and crew consisting of seven: Ellis Hilton of Wiscasset, master; Joshua Merry of Edgecomb, first mate; Daniel Collins
of Wiscasset, second mate; Charles Manuel (a Portuguese), Seth Russell, and Benjamin Bridge, seamen; and Detrey Jeome, cook. On the
18th of December, we passed the Berry Islands and early next morning came to anchor within a league of Orange Key, on the Bahama
Banks. It was the morning of the Sabbath, so calm and clear that even
the lengthened billows of the Gulf Stream seemed sleeping around us,

and the most untutored son of Neptune could not but remember that it was a holy day, consecrated to devotion and rest. Here we continued until noon, when a fresh breeze from the north invited us to weigh anchor and unfurl our sails, which, swelling with a fair wind, were as buoyant as our own spirits at the increasing prospect of reaching our port of destination.

Our course was west-southwest that afternoon and night. At four o'clock next morning, by order of Capt. Hilton, who had been sick most of the passage out and was now unable to appear on deck during the night, we kept her away one point, steering southwest by west, calculating the current easterly at three knots, which he supposed would clear us of the Double Headed Shot Keys.

About sunset, a dark and stormy night approaching, I suggested to our captain the propriety of shortening sail, to which he would not assent, presuming we might get into Matanzas the next day. The night was so dark that we could not discover objects distinctly beyond the length of the vessel, and the wind blew more than a usual wholesale breeze, which drove her, heavy-laden as she was, at the rate of nine knots, calculating ourselves more than six leagues to the windward of the Double Headed Shot Keys. At half past two o'clock, I was relieved at the helm, and after casting a glance over the lee side and discovering no alteration in the appearance of the water, I observed to my shipmate at the helm, "There is no fear of you"—went below and turned in with my clothes on. No one was below at this time except the captain, who stood at the foot of the companion way viewing the appearance of the weather.

I had been in my berth about half an hour when I felt a tremendous shock, which covered me with the muskets that were overhead, boxes, barrels, and other cabin articles, the water pouring into my berth through the quarter. I cleared myself by a violent effort, ran for the companion way—it was gone—turned—leaped through the skylight, and was on deck in an instant. We were in the hollow of a sea, and I could just discern over our main peak the dark top of the rock, which we had struck, stem on, then going at the rate of nine knots. This rock, which some of our crew supposed to be a wreck, was concealed from the helmsman by the mainsail. Two of the crew were at the pumps—the deck load, which consisted of boards, scantlings, and oars piled on each side as high as their heads—the other two people were probably on the quarter deck. It was a careless watch for a dark night, even at our supposed distance from the keys, but we were now in no situation to complain. A part of our stern and the yawl at the davits had gone together. I ran forward to clear the anchors in order to prevent her from ranging ahead on another rock, which I could perceive among the surf, but a greater part of the bows were gone and with them the anchors. The water was already groaning under the deck. She arose for the last time on the crest of another sea nearly to the top of the rock, quivering like a bird under its death wound. Our captain and crew were around the longboat, endeavoring to cut the leashings and right her, while I secured a compass, an axe, a bucket, and several oars. The next sea we descended, she struck; opened fore and aft; the masts and spars, with all sails standing, thundering against the rock; and the lumber from below deck cracking and crashing in every direction.

We were all launched overboard on the lumber that adhered together, clinging hold of the longboat as the seaman's last ark of refuge and endeavoring to right her, which we did in a few moments but not without the misfortune of splitting a plank in her bottom. We all sprang in, bearing with us nothing but the sea clothes we had on, the few articles before named, and some fragments of the boat's leashings. The captain's dog, which a few moments before had been leaping from plank to plank after the cat, with as determined an enmity as though the pursuit had been through a farmyard, followed us, a companion by no means unwelcome to those who, without provision or water, might have been compelled to depend on this faithful animal for the preservation of their lives.

A new difficulty now presented itself: Our boat leaked so fast that three hands, two with hats and one with the bucket, were unable to free her, but with the aid of the only knife we had saved and the fragments of the leashings, I filled some of the seams, which helped to free her but not so effectually as to relieve a single hand from bailing.

About a league from the rock, we hung on our oars, watching the sea that ran mountains high until daylight, when we pulled up under its lee but could discover neither freshwater nor a particle of provisions, except a few pieces of floating bread that we dared not eat. Fragments of boards and spars were floating here and there, but the only article either of convenience or comfort we could preserve was a large blanket, which was converted into a sail and set, and being compelled by the violence of the sea, we put her away before the wind, steering south half-east—a course that must have carried us far east of our intended track, had it not been for the strong westerly current in St. Nicholas's Channel.

The rock on which we were wrecked and from which we took our departure in the boat proved to be one of the northeast range of the Double Headed Shot Keys.

We steered the above course all that day, bailing and rowing without a moment's cessation and approaching, as was then supposed, the island of Cuba, the coast of which, except the entrance of Matanzas and Havana, was unknown to us. We knew, however, that the whole coast was lined with dangerous shoals and keys, though totally ignorant of the situation of those east of Point Yeacos. A hundred times during the day were our eyes directed to every point of the compass in search of a sail but in vain—we were too far to the eastward of the usual track to Matanzas.

As night approached the danger of our situation increased. We had all been fatigued—some of us much bruised—by the disasters of the preceding night, and our toils during the day, as may well be conceived, were not much relieved by an incessant rowing and bailing without a particle of food to assuage our hunger or one drop of freshwater to cool our parched tongues. Anxiety was depicted in every visage, and our spirits were clouding like the heavens over them. Capt. Hilton, whose sickness and debility had been increased by fatigue and hunger, could no longer smother the feelings that were struggling within. The quivering lip, the dim eye, the pallid cheek, all told us, as plainly as human expression could tell, that the last ray of that hope which had supported him during the day was now fading away before the coming night. I had seen much more of rough service and weather than anyone onboard and, having been blessed with an excellent constitution, made it my duty to encourage the rest by representing our approach to the island as certain and safe; this seemed to stimulate increased exertion at the oars, and the breeze continuing fair, we made good headway.

About midnight, Capt. Hilton's oar touched something which he supposed bottom but which the blade of the oar discovered to be a shark that followed us next morning. Deeming us, therefore, over some dangerous shoal, he gave full vent to his feelings by observing that, if even we were to escape these dangerous shoals, our distance from the island was so great that we could never endure hunger, thirst, and the fatigue of bailing long enough to reach it. I endeavored to convince him that we must reach the land by another night in the direction we were steering. The disheartened crew soon caught the contagious and fatal despair which the captain had incautiously diffused among them.

In vain did I expostulate with him on the necessity of continuing our exertions at the oars—he burst into tears, kneeled down in the bottom of the boat, and implored Divine protection. It is true our hold on life was a frail one. In an open boat, that from leaking and the violence of the sea we could scarcely keep above water—without food, drink, or clothing sufficient to defend us from the cold and rain of a December norther—in an irregular and rapid current that prevented any correct calculation of our course—on an unknown and dangerous coast without a chart to guide us.

In a state of mind bordering on that insanity which is sometimes caused by hunger, thirst, and despair united, we passed a most perilous night. At the very first dawn of light, every eye was again in search of a sail. A small, dark speck on the ocean was descried ahead, about five leagues distant! The joyful sound of land ran through our nerves like an electric shock and gave new life to the oars. The wind being fair, the aid of our sail, which was equal to two additional oars, gave us such headway that, as the rays of the rising sun sported over the tops of the waves and fell on the small spot of land ahead, we found ourselves nearing one of the Cuba Keys.

The land we first discovered was a little island of about three acres that arose above the surrounding key, as high as the tops of the mangroves. The name of this key—the largest of its group—was of so sacred an import that one would have supposed it had been a refuge no less from the storms of persecution than those of the element around it.

Cruz del Padre, or the Cross of our Father, situated in west longitude 80°5' and north latitude 23°11'—is about twenty-seven leagues east by north from Matanzas. It is a long, narrow key, of whose size we could not accurately judge. Around its north side, about a league distant from the shore, was a semicircular reef, over which the sea broke as far as the eye extended. It was a tremendous battery in a storm, and were I approaching it in an American squadron, I should fear its ground tier more than all the cabanas of the Morro. But hunger and thirst are powerful antidotes to fear. We therefore boldly approached it with confidence in that Divine interposition which had been recently so signally displayed toward us. Availing ourselves of the deepest water and the swell of a sea, we were hurried on the top of a breaker that shook our longboat like an aspen leaf and nearly filled her with water, but in a moment she was floating on a beautiful bay that presented to the eye "the smooth surface of a summer's sea."

The northern boundary of this bay was formed by the reef, making the inner part of a crescent—the southern, by two long lines of mangroves on each side and a small beach of beautiful white pipe clay that formed the front of the little island in the center. The distance across was about three miles, two of which we had already passed, directly for the beach, a few rods from which, as we had previously discovered, were two huts inhabited by fishermen, whom we could now see passing in and out. When at the above distance from the reef, our attention was suddenly arrested by the appearance of two wrecks of vessels, of too large a size, one would have supposed, to have beaten over the reef. As the water grew shoaler, I could see an even pipe clay bottom, on which our boat grounded a hundred yards from the shore. One of the inhabitants came off in a flat-bottom'd log canoe about twenty-five feet long and two and a half wide, hailed us in Spanish, demanding who we were, and was answered by Manuel, our Portuguese.

As this Spaniard, who was the head fisherman, came alongside, he was recognized by Capt. Hilton as the same of whom he had purchased some sugars the voyage before at Matanzas.

The two huts we have named were formed of the planks and cabin boards of wrecks, about seven feet high and ten by fifteen on the ground, with thatched roofs. At the northeast corner was a group of old weather-beaten trees, the only ones above the height of a mangrove on the island, on which the fishermen hung their nets. In front of the beach was a turtle troll about fifteen feet square surrounded by a frame, from which were suspended a great number of wooden hooks, on which their fish were hung and partially preserved by drying in the sea breeze. It was about eight o'clock in the morning when we were conducted into one of the huts, and as we had had neither food nor drink for nearly two days and nights, some refreshment, consisting of turtle and other fish, hot coffee, &c., was immediately provided.

After our refreshment some sails were spread on the ground, on which we were invited to repose. My shipmates readily accepted the invitation, but I had seen too much of Spanish infidelity under the cloak of hospitality to omit an anchor watch, even in our present snug harbor.

There were five fishermen, all stout, well-built Spaniards, the master of whom was over six feet and had much the appearance of an American Indian. My companions were soon in a "dead sleep," and when the fishermen had left the hut, I walked out to explore our new habitation. The two huts were so near that a gutter only separated them, which caught the water from the roofs of each and conducted it into a hogshead bedded in the sand, from which other casks were filled against a drought; the freshwater thus obtained being all the island furnished. West of the beach was a small bay, in the center of which was an island about a mile in circumference. At the head of this bay, a creek made up several rods into the mangroves, which served as a harbor for a small fishing vessel of about twelve tons, decked over, in which they carried their fish to Matanzas and elsewhere about the island of Cuba. East of the beach was a cove that extended about a quarter of a mile into the bushes, forming a kind of basin at its head, which was as still as a millpond. This basin was surrounded by thick mangroves and completely concealed from everything without by the jutting out of a point at its entrance.

A more lonely place I never saw. Around its borders a "solitary guest," you might see the flamingo strutting in all the pride of its crimson plumage, as erect and nearly as high as a British soldier. The bottom of this cove was like that of the bay.

The mangroves are very thick, their trunks covered with oyster shells that adhere to them like barnacles to a vessel's bottom, which annoy those who attempt to pass among them by tearing their clothes and wounding the flesh as high up as the hips.

Among the bushes were concealed two clinker-built boats, remarkably well constructed for rowing, with their bottoms greased or soaped; in one of which, I found a handkerchief filled with limes: I took one and brought it into the house; this displeased the fishermen, who afterward told Manuel that the boats and limes belonged to some people at a small distance who would return in a few days. There were also two yawls moored in front of the huts that appeared to have belonged to American vessels.

~~~~~~

When I returned to the hut, my shipmates were yet asleep, and we did not awake them until supper was prepared, which was much the same with our breakfast, except the addition of plantain. After supper we all sat around the table, devising means to get to Matanzas. Through Manuel, Capt. Hilton offered the master fisherman our longboat and forty dollars in cash on our arrival at Matanzas, which was accepted, and we were to sail in their small schooner as soon as the weather would permit. About eight or nine o'clock, we all turned in, but my suspicions would not allow me to sleep, for when all was silent, I could hear the Spaniards conversing with each other in a low tone, on which I spake to Manuel with the hope that he might understand the subject of their consultation, but he, like his companions, was too sound asleep to be easily awakened.

A lamp of fish oil had been dimly burning for two or three hours, when the master fisherman arose and extinguished it. About this time an old dog belonging to the fishermen commenced a most hideous howling without that was occasionally answered by our dog within. Supposing some boat might be approaching, I went out but could discover no living being in motion. It was a starlit night, the wind blowing fresh with a few flying scuds. When I returned into the hut, I sat down between two barrels of bread, against one of which I leaned my head, prepared to give an early warning of any foul play that might befall us, but the night passed without any incident to interrupt the slumbers of my weary messmates.

Early in the morning, they turned out, and we went down to the cove before described in order to bathe. While we were clothing ourselves on the shore at the head of the cove, we discovered, at high-water mark, a number of human skeletons—except the skulls—bleached and partly decayed. The bones of the fingers, hands, and ribs were entire. To me this was no very pleasant discovery, and I observed to Mr. Merry that "we might all be murdered in such a place without the possibility of its being known," but the bones were, at the time, supposed to have belonged to seamen that might have been shipwrecked on the reef near this part of the key.

After breakfast we finished loading the little schooner and returned to the huts to bring down some small stores. As we were all standing before the huts, the master fisherman was seen pointing to the eastward and laughing with his companions. On looking in the direction he was pointing, I discovered the object of his amusement to be a small vessel just doubling an easterly point of the key, about seven miles distant within the reef and bearing away for us. I had too often seen the grin of a Spaniard accompanied with the stab of his stiletto to pass the circumstance unnoticed. By my request Manuel inquired of the Spaniards what vessel it was and received for answer that "it was the king's cutter in search of pirates." This answer satisfied us, and in a short time, we were all hands, the master fisherman and three of his crew, onboard our vessel. As soon as we were ready to weigh anchor, observing the Spaniard intent on watching the "cutter" and delaying unnecessarily to get underway, I began to hoist the foresail, on which he, for the first time, sang out to me in broken English, "No foresail, no foresail." By this time the sail was within three quarters of a mile of us. As I stood on the forecastle watching her, I saw one of her people forward, pointing at us what I supposed a spyglass, but in an instant the report of a musket and whistle of a bullet by my ears convinced me of my mistake. This was followed by the discharge of at least twenty blunderbusses and muskets, from which the balls flew like hailstones, lodging in various parts of our schooner, one of which pierced my trousers and another Mr. Merry's jacket, without any essential injury.

At the commencement of the firing, the four fishermen concealed themselves below deck, out of danger, and our Portuguese, attempting to follow their example, was forced back. I remained on the forecastle watching the vessel until the whistling of six or seven bullets by my ears warned me of my danger. At first I settled down on my knees, still anxious to ascertain the cause of this unprovoked outrage, until they approached within two or three hundred feet of us, when I prostrated myself on the deck, soon after which the master fisherman arose, waved his hat at them, and the firing ceased. About forty or fifty feet abreast of us, she dropped anchor and gave orders for the canoe at our stern to come alongside, which one of our fishermen obeyed, and brought onboard of us their captain and three men. The supposed cutter was an open boat of about thirty-five feet keel, painted red inside and black without, except a streak of white about two inches wide, calculated for rowing or sailing—prepared with long sweeps and carrying a jib, foresail, mainsail, and squaresail. She was manned by ten Spaniards, each armed with a blunderbuss or musket, a machete, long knife, and pair of pistols. They were all dressed with neat jackets and trousers and wore palm-leaf hats. Their beards were very long and appeared as though they had not been shaved for eight or nine months.

One of them had an extremely savage appearance, having received a blow, probably from a cutlass, across his face that had knocked in all his front teeth and cut off a part of his upper lip, the scar extending some distance beyond the angles of the mouth—three of the fingers of his left hand, with a part of the little finger, were cut off, and the thumb was badly scarred. He was tall, well proportioned, and appeared to have some authority over the others. The captain was stout and so corpulent that I should not underrate his weight at 260 pounds. He reminded me strongly of a Guinea captain I had formerly seen. He was shaved after the manner of the Turks, the beard of his upper lip being very long—was richly dressed—armed with a machete and knife on one side and a pair of pistols on the other, besides which, he wore a dirk within his vest. After examining our papers, which had been accidentally saved by Capt. Hilton, he took out of a net purse two doubloons and presented them to the master fisherman in presence of all hands. This we at first supposed to be intended as some compensation for the injury done by firing at us. The account of our shipwreck, sufferings, and providential escape to the island was now related to him by Manuel, which he noticed by a slight shrug of the shoulders, without changing a single muscle of his face. He had a savage jeer in his look during the recital of our misfortunes that would have robbed misery of her ordinary claims to compassion and denied the unhappy sufferer even a solitary expression of sympathy.

After he had ascertained who we were, he returned to his own boat with three of his men, leaving one onboard of us as a kind of prize master. Our master fisherman, who also accompanied him, was greeted by all onboard the armed vessel in a manner that denoted him to have been an old acquaintance. We could see them passing to each other a long, white jug, which, after they had all drank, they shook at us, saying in broken English, "Anglois, vill you have some Aquedente?" to which we made no reply. When they had apparently consulted among themselves about half an hour, they sent two men with the jug onboard of us, from which we all drank sparingly in order to avoid offense, and they returned to their own vessel, took in two more men, and proceeded to the huts, which they entered and went around several times, then came down to our longboat, and examined her carefully. After this they came off to our vessel with the two canoes, one of which went to the armed boat, and brought onboard of us all but the captain and two of his men. Our little crew had thus far been the anxious spectators of these mysterious maneuvers.

There were circumstances which at one time encouraged the belief that we were in the hands of friends and at another that these pretended friends were calmly preparing for a "foul and most unnatural murder." Capt. Hilton was unwilling yet to yield his confidence in the treacherous Spaniard, who, I did not doubt, had already received the price of our blood. In this state of painful suspense, vibrating between hope and fear, we remained, until the master fisherman threw on the deck a ball of cord made of tough, strong bark, about the size of a man's thumb, from which they cut seven pieces of about nine feet each—went to Capt. Hilton and attempted to take off his overcoat but were prevented by a signal from their captain. They now commenced binding his arms behind him just above the elbows with one of the pieces of cord, which they passed several times round and drew so tight that he groaned out in all the bitterness of his anguish.

My fears that they were pirates were now confirmed, and when I saw them, without temptation or provocation, cruelly torturing one whom shipwreck had thrown among them, a penniless sailor reduced by sickness to an almost helpless condition, and entreating with all the tenderness of a penitent that they would not cut him off in the blossom of his sins and before he had reached the meridian of life—reminding them of the wife and parents he left behind, I burst into tears and arose involuntarily as if to sell my life at the dearest rate but was shoved back by one of the pirates, who gave me a severe blow on the breast with the muzzle of his cocked blunderbuss. A scene of woe ensued which would have tried the stoutest heart, and it appeared to me that even they endeavored to divert their minds from it by a constant singing and laughing so loud as to drown the sound of our lamentations. After they had told Manuel they should carry us to Matanzas as prisoners of war, they proceeded to pinion our arms as they had Capt. Hilton's, so tight as to produce excruciating pain.

We were now completely in their power, and they rolled us about with as much indifference as though we had been incapable of feeling, tumbling us into the canoes without mercy. They threw me with such force that I struck the back of my neck against the seat of the canoe and broke it. Capt. Hilton, Mr. Merry, Bridge, and the cook were in one canoe; Russell, Manuel, and myself, in the other. For the first time, they now informed us that they were about to cut our throats, which information they accompanied with the most appalling signs by drawing their knives across their throats, imitating stabbing, and various other tortures. Four pirates accompanied the other canoe and three ours, besides the four fishermen, two to manage each canoe. We were thus carried alongside the piratical schooner, when all their firearms were passed onboard of her; the arm chest, which was in the stern sheets and covered with a tarpaulin, opened, several long knives and machetes taken out, their keen edges examined with the greatest scrutiny, and passed onboard the canoes for the expressed purpose of murdering us all.

The seven pirates and four fishermen, as before, now proceeded with us toward the beach until the water was about three feet deep, when they all got out, the two fishermen to each canoe, hauling us along, and the pirates walking by the side of us, one to each of our crew, torturing us all the way by drawing their knives across our throats, grasping the same, and pushing us back under the water, which had been taken in by rocking the canoes. While some of us were in the most humiliating manner beseeching of them to spare our lives and others with uplifted eyes were again supplicating that Divine mercy which had preserved them from the fury of the elements, they were singing and laughing and occasionally telling us in broken English that "Americans were very good beef for their knives." Thus they proceeded with us nearly a mile from the vessel, which we were now losing sight of by doubling a point at the entrance of the cove before described, and when within a few rods of its head, where we had before seen the human bones, the canoes were hauled abreast of each other, from twelve to twenty feet apart, preparatory to our execution.

The stillness of death was now around us—for the very floodgates of feeling had been burst asunder and exhausted grief at its fountain. It was a beautiful morning—not a cloud to obscure the rays of the sun— and the clear, blue sky presented a scene too pure for deeds of darkness. But the lonely sheet of water, on which side by side we lay, presented that hopeless prospect which is more ably described by another.

We had scarcely passed the last parting look at each other, when the work of death commenced.

They seized Captain Hilton by the hair—bent his head and shoulders over the gunwale, and I could distinctly hear them chopping the bone of the neck. They then wrung his neck, separated the head from the body by a slight draw of the sword, and let it drop into the water; there was a dying shriek—a convulsive struggle—and all I could discern was the arms dangling over the side of the canoe and the ragged stump pouring out the blood like a torrent.

There was an imploring look in the innocent and youthful face of Mr. Merry that would have appealed to the heart of anyone but a pirate. As he arose on his knees in the posture of a penitent, supplicating for mercy even on the verge of eternity, he was prostrated with a blow of the cutlass, his bowels gushing out of the wound. They then pierced him through the breast in several places with a long-pointed knife and cut his throat from ear to ear.

The captain's dog, repulsed in his repeated attempts to rescue his master, sat whining beside his lifeless body, looking up to these bloodhounds in human shape, as if to tell them that even brutal cruelty would be glutted with the blood of two innocent, unoffending victims.

Bridge and the cook, they pierced through the breast, as they had Merry, in several places with their knives and then split their heads open with their cutlasses. Their dying groans had scarcely ceased, and I was improving the moment of life that yet remained, when I heard the blow behind me—the blood and brains that flew all over my head and shoulders warned me that poor old Russell had shared the fate of the others; and as I turned my head to catch the eye of my executioner, I saw the head of Russell severed in two nearly its whole length, with a single blow of the cutlass and even without the decency of removing his cap. At the sound of the blow, Manuel, who sat before me, leaped overboard, and four of the pirates were in full chase after him. In what manner he loosed his hands, I am unable to say—his escape, I shall hereafter explain. My eyes were fixed on my supposed executioner, watching the signal of my death—he was on my right and partly behind me—my head, which was covered with a firm tarpaulin hat, was turned in a direction that brought my shoulders fore and aft the canoe—the blow came—it divided the top of my hat, struck my head so severely as to stun me, and glanced off my left shoulder, taking the skin and some flesh in its way, and divided my pinion cord on the arm. I was so severely stunned that I did not leap from the canoe but pitched over the left side and was just arising from the water, not yet my length from her, as a pirate threw his knife which struck me but did not retard my flight an instant, and I leaped forward through the water, expecting a blow from behind at every step.

The shrieks of the dying had ceased—the scene of horrid butchery in the canoes was now over—Manuel and I were in the water about knee deep—two of the pirates after me, and all the rest, with the fishermen, except one pirate, after Manuel. We ran in different directions, I, toward the mouth of the cove, making nearly a semicircle in my track to keep them over my shoulder, which brought me back again toward the canoes, and as the remaining pirate came out in order to cut me off, I was obliged to run between the canoes so near the last pirate that he made a pass at me and fell, which gave me the start. At the first of our race, I was after Manuel, with pirates before and behind. My object was to gain the bushes as soon as possible, supposing their cutlasses would be an obstacle, which I had the good fortune to prove. I lost sight of Manuel just as I entered the bushes; he was up to his breast in water and the pirates near him. When I entered the bushes, one of the pirates was within ten feet of me and continued striking, hoping to reach me, and all of them yelling in the most savage manner during the whole distance. The most of the way, the water and mud was nearly up to my hips—the mangroves were very thick, covered, as I before observed, with oyster shells up to high water mark. It was about noon when I entered these bushes, my course westerly, the pirates after me, repeatedly in view, one of them frequently within three rods of me. Had it been on cleared land, I should soon have been overtaken by them, but the bushes were so large and thick as frequently to entangle their swords. I was barefoot, and had I worn shoes, they would soon have been lost in the mud. My feet and legs were so badly cut with the oyster shells that the blood flowed freely; add to this, my head was very painful and swollen, and my shoulder smarted severely. In this manner and direction, I ran till the sun about an hour high, when I lost sight of the pirates and paused for a moment; pulled off my jacket (the cord being yet on my right arm, which I slipped off), in which I rolled my hat; and taking it under my arm, I settled down on my knees, which brought the water up to my chin, in order to secrete myself. In this way I crept till nearly sunset, when, to my astonishment, I discovered the ocean, and just as the sun was setting, I crawled out to the border of the island. I looked round and saw a very large bush of mangroves, the highest near, among the roots of which I concealed myself. When the sun was setting, I could distinctly hear the splashing of water and cracking of bushes and the pirates hallooing to each other, which increased my apprehensions, supposing they might discover my track through the muddy water. I was almost exhausted from a severe pain in my side caused by running so long, though I had determined not to yield to them until I fell under the blow of their cutlass. Soon after the sun was down, their noise ceased, and I crept up to the top of the tall mangrove, put on my hat and jacket, where I sat all night, until the sun rose the next morning, that I might discover if they had come round the island to intercept my passage.

As I ran through the bushes, I disturbed numberless birds, among which was the flamingo, who was extremely bold, flying around me with such a noise that I feared it would betray me by serving as a guide to my pursuers.

When the sun had arisen without a cloud, I could discover nothing to increase my apprehension. I descended the mangrove and proceeded to the border of the key—looked across the water before me, where lay another key, which I judged two and a half or three miles distant. Here I stripped myself to my shirt, the sleeves of which I tore off, and with my trousers threw them into the sea. I then tied my jacket, which was of broadcloth, by means of the cord that was on my arm, slung it over my neck, and put my hat on to protect my wounded head from the sun. In this plight I committed myself to the sea, first supplicating on my knees a Divine blessing on my undertaking but doubting whether I should ever reach the opposite key. Being, however, an excellent swimmer, having before swum nearly two miles on a wager, I reached the opposite key without any other injury than the galling my neck with the cord and with much less fatigue than I could have supposed. This key was much of the description of the last but smaller. I made but little pause, continuing my course southwesterly across it, which was, I should suppose, about three miles, and as I had not hurried, owing to my fatigue, when I arrived at its border, it was about the middle of the afternoon. At about two miles distance, I descried another key, to which I swam, slinging my jacket as before. When I arrived at this, which was the third key, it was a little before sunset. I proceeded into the bushes about three-fourths of a mile, it being a small key, and came out nearly to its margin, where I passed the night, leaning against a bunch of mangroves, with the water up to my hips. Such had been my fatigue and mental excitement that, even in this unpleasant situation, I slept soundly, until I was disturbed by a vision of the horrible scene in the canoes—the images of Capt. Hilton and Mr. Merry, mangled as when I last saw them, came before my eyes, and in my fancied attempt to rescue them, I awoke but could not convince myself it was a dream until I grasped my own flesh. Again I slept interruptedly until daylight. Being excessively hungry, for this was the third day since I had taken a single particle of food or drink, I plucked some of the greenest of the leaves; this relieved my hunger but increased my thirst. About sunrise I departed from this key, wading with the water at times up to my neck for nearly a mile, when it grew deeper.

The next and fourth key, being about another mile distant, I swam to. This day I kept on about the same course, southwesterly, and crossed three more small keys about a mile distant from each other. I had now arrived at the seventh and last key; on this I passed the night, having prepared a kind of flake of old roots, on which I slept soundly, for the first time out of water since I left Cruz del Padre. Between daylight and sunrise, having eaten of the green leaves as before and having been refreshed by sleep, I departed from the last key, by this time so weak that I could scarcely walk. The water was not so deep, but I could wade until within half a mile of what afterward proved to be Cuba but of which I was ignorant at the time.

While I was crossing this last passage, I had to contend with a strong current, probably from the mouth of the very river I afterward forded, and when but a few rods from the shore, a shark approached within a rod, but to my great joy, he turned and left me.

I had now swum about nine miles beside the distance I had traveled through mud and water, and the hunger and thirst I had endured, having tasted neither food nor drink except a few salt leaves of mangroves during my flight. And to add to my sufferings, my almost-naked body was covered with mosquitoes, attracted by the blood and sores produced by my escape from Cruz del Padre.

~~~~~~

Observing that this shore varied a little from those I had passed, I followed it in an easterly direction, which was reversing my former course, for nearly two miles, when I came to a large yawl with her foremast standing. As I set me down on her gunwale, the thought struck my mind that this boat, like our own, might have preserved some unfortunate crew from the fury of the storm in order to offer them up to the pitiless pirate, who, perhaps, had not suffered a solitary individual to escape and say that the vengeance of man on these encrimsoned shores had sacrificed those whom the mercy of God had spared amid the dangers of his "mighty deep." While I was employed by these reflections, the gnawings of hunger were suddenly aroused by the appearance of two crawfish under the stern sheets, one of which I caught and devoured with such greediness that it was very soon rejected, and although I at first thought I could have eaten a dozen of them, the exhaustion produced by my efforts to vomit destroyed all relish for the other.

I again proceeded on my old course, southwesterly, until about the middle of the afternoon, when I approached dry land and set me down on a windfall to contemplate my situation, to a description of which I might well have adapted the language of Job: "My flesh is clothed with worms and clods of dust; my skin is broken and become loathsome." Near the roots of this tree, as I sat viewing some holes formed by land crabs, I observed water issuing from one of them. A more grateful and unexpected sight the Israelites could not have witnessed at the smitten rock, for I soon found the water proceeded from a boiling spring, and without it, I am sure I could not have survived another day, for it will be recollected that this was the first freshwater I had tasted since the morning my shipmates were murdered. But pure as it was, my parched stomach would not retain it, until after repeated trials I succeeded in quenching my thirst. I again proceeded southwesterly, the land gradually elevating, until there suddenly opened upon me an immense plain, where the eye could reach over thousands of acres without the obstruction of a tree, covered with cattle of every age and description, some of which came snuffing around, so near that, in my crippled condition, I feared they might board me. But a swing of my hat set them capering and snorting in every direction. The number and variety of wild cattle collected on these plains is immense. I should think I saw more than five hundred hogs, chiefly of a dark color, and more than half that number of horses, principally white; bulls and cows with calves by their sides; goats; mules; &c.

I traveled on my course with as much rapidity as my feeble and exhausted condition would allow until dusk, when I arrived at the bank of a small river; here I reposed uninterruptedly until daylight next morning. When I first attempted to arise, my limbs refused their duty, and I was compelled to seize hold of a bush that was near in order to raise myself upon my feet. This is not strange when we consider the fatigue and hunger I had endured, the wounds all over my limbs, and the numbness produced by sleeping without a covering, exposed to the dampness that arises from a freshwater river in a climate like that of Cuba.

I paused on the bank a few moments observing the current in order to ascertain the direction of its source, toward which I proceeded, traveling on the bank until noon, when I entered a beautiful lime grove, the fruit of which completely strewed the ground. After I had devoured as many of these, rind and all, as satisfied the cravings of hunger, I filled my jacket pockets, fearing I might not again meet with such a timely supply.

By this time I had discovered a winding footpath formed by droves of wild cattle, but in vain did I search for the impression of a human footstep. This path I followed until it led to a fording place in the river, where I paused, dreading the effect of freshwater on my sores, some of which had begun to scab over. But my situation would not admit delay; I therefore forded the river, which had been so swollen by recent rains that I was compelled to wade up to my armpits. This produced the apprehended effect, for I had no sooner reached the opposite shore than my sores began to bleed afresh and smart severely. My supply of limes recruited my strength sufficiently to pursue my path until sunset, when I again halted and set me down on a log.

The only article of clothing I had to cover my nakedness was my jacket, for the body of my shirt I had left on one of the keys, fearing that the blood stains upon it might bring on me some unjust suspicion. My numerous sores, owing to the alternate influence of heat and freshwater, had now become so offensive as to occasion a violent retching that nearly overcame the feeble powers of my stomach, and had it not been for my providential supply of limes, that afterward, in some degree corrected their fetor, I must have laid me down by this log, a mass of corruption, and given my body up a prey to the birds and wild beasts of the forest. The reader will not think this an exaggeration, for while I was sitting here, the numerous turkey buzzards that were roosting over my head, attracted by my offensive smell, alighted within a few feet of me and began to attack each other with as much ferocity as if they were already contending for their prey. I arose, as if to convince them that I yet possessed the power of motion, though I doubted within myself whether they would not have possession of me before the setting of another sun. But onward I traveled as far and as fast as my feeble condition would permit, until it was too dark to follow the path, when I laid down and passed a restless night, annoyed, as usual, with mosquitoes. In the morning I arose feeble and dejected, and in my prayers, which I had daily addressed to Him whose mercy seat had so often covered me from the tempest and whose "pillar of cloud by day and pillar of fire by night" had not yet forsaken me in the wilderness, I desired that I might meet this day (the sixth of my miraculous escape) some being to whom I could relate my sufferings and the murder of my companions as an appeal to my country (bound as she is to protect the humblest of her citizens) to arise in the majesty of her naval power and stay the hands of those who are coloring these barbarous shores with the blood of her enterprising seamen.

My life glass appeared to be nearly up, and I now began to yield all hopes of being relieved. My feet and limbs began to swell from the inflammation of the sores, and my limes, the only sustenance I had, although they preserved life, began to create gnawing pains in my stomach and bowels. I however wandered on, following the intricate windings of the path, until the middle of the forenoon, when I discovered, directly in the way, several husks of corn and, soon after, some small sticks like bean poles that had evidently been sharpened at one end by some human hand. This discovery, trifling as it may appear, renewed my spirits and strength to such a degree that I made very little pause until about sunset, when I espied in the path, not a great distance ahead, a man on horseback, surrounded by nearly twenty dogs! Fearing he might not observe me, I raised my hat upon my walking stick as a signal for him to approach. The quick-scented dogs were soon on the start, and when I saw that they resembled bloodhounds, I had serious apprehensions for my safety, but a call from their master, which they obeyed with prompt discipline, put my fears to rest. The man was a negro, mounted on a kind of mat made of the palm leaf and generally used for saddles by the plantation slaves on this island. When within a few rods of me, he dismounted, approached with his drawn sword (machete), and paused in apparent astonishment, I pointing to the sores on me, fearing from his attitude he might mistake me for some highway robber. He now began to address me in Spanish, of which I knew only enough to make him understand I had been shipwrecked, on which he made signs for me to mount the horse. This I attempted but was unable to do, until he assisted me. He then pointed in the direction of the path for me to go on, he following the horse with his sword in his hand.

After traveling nearly three miles, I discovered a number of lights about half a mile distant, and when we came up with them, we halted near a large bamboo grove, where, with his aid, I dismounted and, by a signal from him, sat down until he went to a hut and returned with a shirt and pair of trousers, with which he covered my nakedness. He now took me by the hand and led me into a large house occupied by his master, the owner of the plantation. A bench was brought me, on which I seated myself, and the master of the house, a gray-headed Spaniard, probably turned of seventy, came toward me with an air of kindness, understanding from the black I had been shipwrecked. As the old man was examining my sores, he discovered on my arm a handsome impression of the Crucifix that had been pricked in with indelible ink in the East Indies some years before, which he kissed with apparent rapture, saying to me, "Anglois very much of the Christian," supposing me to be a Roman Catholic. This drew around me all the members of the family, who kneeled in succession, kissing the image and manifesting their sensibility by tears at the sufferings which they perceived by my sores and emaciated appearance I must have endured. I was then conducted by an old lady, whom I took to be his wife, into another apartment, in the corner of which, was a kind of grate where a fire was kindled on the ground. Here a table was spread that groaned under all the luxuries which abound on the plantations of this island, but it was perhaps fortunate for me that my throat was so raw and inflamed I could swallow nothing but some soft-boiled rice and coffee. After this refreshment, the kind old Spaniard stripped me, dipped a clean linen cloth into pure virgin honey, and rubbed it over my sores. He then pointed to the bed, which had been prepared for me in the same room. I gave him to understand by signs that I should besmear his clean sheets, but this was negatived by a shake of the head, so without further ceremony I turned in—it was the softest pillow I ever did or expect to lay my head on—yet it was rest, not sleep.

The old man had ordered a servant to attend me during the night, fearing the little food I had taken, after so long an abstinence, might produce some serious illness. Every time I groaned or turned, this servant would run to me with a bowl of strong hot coffee, which I could not refuse without disobeying his master's orders. Early in the morning, before I arose, the old planter came to my bedside, examined my pulse and tongue, and brought me a quart bowl of fresh tamarinds, more than half of which he compelled me to eat in order to prepare my stomach for the after reception of food and prevent those symptoms of inflammation, which his intimate knowledge of the healing art had enabled him to discover.

10

AN ILL-FATED ROBBERY

BY GEORGE HUNTINGTON

The James and Younger brothers knew what they were doing, and they always did it well. After all, they'd been robbing banks for a long time, and no one had been able to catch them. A well-planned heist of a small bank in the quiet town of Northfield, Minnesota, would be a walk in the park. Or so they thought.

In the latter part of August 1876, a mysterious company of men made their appearance in southern Minnesota and proceeded to visit various cities and villages in that part of the state. There were certainly eight of them and possibly nine, some of them hard, vicious-looking fellows, from whom people instinctively shrank; others gentlemanly, handsome, and even imposing in personal appearance. They traveled on horseback and rode like men accustomed to live in the saddle. They had the finest of horses and equipment, part of it brought with them, the rest purchased after they entered the state. They had plenty of money and spent it lavishly.

In their progress from place to place, they did not go like an organized band but wandered here and there, sometimes two by two, sometimes four or five together. When several of them visited a town together, they went to different hotels and avoided all appearance of collusion or of common design. Often they avoided towns and sought entertainment at the houses of farmers or other citizens, where they found no difficulty in making themselves agreeable and in giving a plausible account of themselves. Wherever they went, they attracted more or less attention, excited the curiosity of the inquisitive and occasionally the suspicions of the wary, but upon most people they made the impression of well-bred respectability.

They passed for civil engineers looking up railway routes, for capitalists in search of land, for stockmen dealing in horses and cattle. Their outfit and mode of travel made either of these suppositions reasonable, and their smooth courtesy, affability, and apparent frankness were accepted in lieu of credentials of character. That they were not all that they pretended to be many people suspected, but that they were a band of outlaws, or rather a combination of three bands, comprising the most notorious desperadoes in the country, laying their plans for a great robbery, no one suspected. Still less did they themselves suspect that their career of crime was so near its close or that they were making deliberate plans for their own destruction.

Of course, they passed under assumed names, introducing themselves as J. C. King, Jack Ward, etc. It is now known that the band consisted of the following men: Jesse James and his brother Frank; Thomas C. Younger (commonly known as Cole Younger) and his brothers James and Robert; Clel Miller; William Stiles, alias Chadwell; and Charles Pitts, alias George Wells. Some persons maintain that there was a ninth man, but he has never been identified and is commonly believed to be mythical. The eight whose names are given were all men of criminal antecedents and some of them with a record for deeds of the most revolting atrocity, though several of them were connected with highly respectable families.

In prospecting for a favorable opening, they visited a number of places, going as far north as St. Paul and Minneapolis and as far east as Red Wing. In each place they made a careful study of the chances for successful operations in their line and of routes of escape, visiting the banks on one pretext or another and familiarizing themselves with all facts that had any bearing on their scheme. They took special pains to make themselves acquainted with such features of the country as would aid or hinder them in going and coming on their intended raid; as, for instance, the location of lakes, streams, swamps, or forests on the one hand and that of roads, bridges, and fords on the other.

The situation and the resources of villages, the extent of country population, and the nationality and character of the people also interested them. With the aid of maps, printed statements, and minute inquiries, they succeeded in gaining a large amount of information without betraying their purpose—information which they found exceedingly convenient at a later day. They also had the advantage of being to a certain extent personally conducted. Stiles, one of their number, had formerly lived in Rice County and was therefore able to act as a sort of guide for the expedition, if indeed he was not, as some think, its instigator. Their reliance upon him, however, proved in the end, as we shall see, a source of danger rather than of safety.

Finding nothing to their mind in the great cities, they turned their attention to a group of country towns lying farther south, including St. Peter, Mankato, Lake Crystal, Madelia, St. James, Garden City, Janesville, Cordova, Waterville, Millersburg, Cannon City, and Northfield. These, again, divide themselves into two smaller groups, having direct or indirect relation to the two points of attack selected by the robbers and all of them being on or near a diagonal line, extending about thirty or forty miles southwest and about forty or fifty miles northeast of Mankato.

Having completed their preliminary survey, they prepared for their grand exploit. Their first project was the robbery of one or more of the banks of Mankato, a thriving town at the great bend of the Minnesota River. Five of the band appeared in Mankato on Saturday, September 2nd, and, as usual, created a sensation with their fine horses and horsemanship. They made purchases at some of the stores and paid a visit to the First National Bank, where they got change for a fifty-dollar bill. According to their custom, they stayed at different hotels; at least four of them did, while the fifth sought some other resort not identified. On Sunday night two of them were known to be at a notorious resort on the opposite side of the river, a rendezvous of the lowest criminals, where, as is believed, they were in consultation with confederates with reference to their intended raid and subsequent escape.

Meantime, Jesse James had been recognized by a man who knew him by sight, and the fact was reported to the police, who shadowed the men until midnight, and put some of the bank people on their guard against possible burglaries, though no one anticipated an open attack by daylight.

On Monday, the 4th, the robbers mounted their horses and rode forth to their intended attack. Their plan was to make it about noon, when the bank force would be reduced and the streets would be most free of citizens. They had already arrived opposite the First National Bank, when they noticed a number of citizens on the sidewalk and saw one of them apparently calling another's attention to the approaching horsemen. The robbers, fearing that they were suspected and watched, deferred the attack till a later hour. On returning, however, they saw the same citizens again, seeming, as before, to be keeping close watch upon the strangers. Convinced now that their purpose was discovered and that the citizens were prepared for them, the robbers abandoned their project and left Mankato as speedily as possible.

The truth was that they were at that moment the object of no suspicion whatever. The regular weekly meeting of the board of trade and some repairs on an adjoining building had called together the unusual number of persons whom the robbers observed, and the man who was supposed to be directing his companion's attention to the bandits was simply remarking upon the fine quality of their horses. No doubt, however, the presence of so large a number of spectators would have seriously embarrassed the gang in beginning operations. As it was, they sensed just as good a purpose in repelling the attack as if they had been a company of armed militia on duty.

Abandoning Mankato, the robbers now moved upon Northfield as directly as roads and available stopping places would permit. Monday night found them in Janesville, eighteen miles east of Mankato; Tuesday night in Cordova, about the same distance north of Janesville; Wednesday night in Millersburg, northeast of Cordova. The rest of the band spent the same Wednesday night in Cannon City. Millersburg is eleven miles west of Northfield, Cannon City ten miles south.

Northfield is a quiet but enterprising little city in the heart of a rich and well-cultivated agricultural region which is tributary to it. It has good railroad facilities, and the Cannon River, flowing through the town, affords power for its mills and adds a picturesque feature to its scenery. A bridge crosses the river in the center of the town, connecting its eastern and its western divisions and leading, on the eastern side, into an open space known as Bridge Square, where many of the stores are to be found. On the eastern side of the square runs Division Street, the principal business street of the city, along the foot of a bluff some fifty feet in height; ascended by various streets; and crowned with residences, churches, and educational buildings. Prominent among the public edifices are those of Carleton College in the northeastern part of the city, while St. Olaf surmounts a high eminence in the northwestern. An observant stranger entering the city for the first time could hardly fail to get the impression of intelligence, thrift, and commercial enterprise. This was precisely the impression made upon the robbers, and it was this impression which led them to select Northfield as a field of operations.

Ten or twelve days before the final attempt upon the bank, two members of the band had visited the town for a preliminary survey. They conversed with citizens, as their custom was, making inquiries about roads, etc., particularly about the route to Mankato, and awakened the suspicion of at least one or two of the citizens as to the truth of their pretension. They found a bank doing a large business and presumably carrying a large volume of cash, and they saw the people quiet and industrious and presumably neither prepared nor disposed to meet force with force. What plans they then formed for the subsequent raid, it is impossible to say, but it is certain that they were no sooner foiled in Mankato than they started for Northfield.

As we have already seen, the two divisions of the band spent the night of Wednesday, September 6th, in neighboring villages, within easy reach of their next day's destination. Early on the morning of Thursday, the 7th, they took up their march along the roads converging upon Northfield, meeting in the woods west of the town. In the course of the forenoon, some of them appeared upon the streets and in the stores, where two of them were recognized as the same two that had made the previous visit of inspection already referred to. They all wore linen dusters, a garment much more common with the traveler in those days than in our own and one that seemed entirely suitable for the sultry weather then prevailing, while it served to conceal the pistols and cartridge belts with which the robbers were so liberally supplied. Five of the men dined together at a restaurant on the west side of the river, waiting contentedly for their dinner to be cooked, conversing with the proprietor on politics and other indifferent subjects, and, after they had finished their meal, still delaying unaccountably, probably to give time for the arrival of the rest of their accomplices. Finally, they remounted their horses and rode over the bridge.

It is difficult and, so far as the present writer is concerned, impossible, after the most painstaking study of all available sources of information, to determine the exact order of events at the opening of the attack. No one observer followed all the preliminary movement of the robbers. One person noticed one thing and another, and each depended more or less upon hearsay for items not within his personal knowledge. The similarity of dress already referred to made it difficult to distinguish the robbers from one another, while the wild excitement which soon ensued gave little opportunity for careful observation. With no attempt to reconcile conflicting statements, therefore, which happily differ only in unimportant details, this narrative will confine itself to those facts upon which all witnesses agree.

The center of operations was the corner of Bridge Square and Division Street. On this corner stood a two-story stone building known as the Scriver Block. Its upper story was used for offices and was reached by an outside stairway on Division Street. The larger part of the lower story was occupied by two stores ranging north and south and having their front entrances on the northern Bridge Square side. At the extreme southern end of the building and having its entrance on the eastern, or Division Street side, was the object of attack, the First National Bank. On the western side of the block ran a narrow alley, affording rear entrances to the stores and the bank. West of the alley and fronting on the square were two hardware stores, whose respective proprietors were leading actors in the scene that followed—J. S. Allen and A. R. Manning. On the eastern side of Division Street, opposite the Scriver Block, were a hotel and a number of stores, in front of one of which stood a young man who was also to have a prominent part in the coming affray—Mr. H. M. Wheeler, then at home on a vacation from his medical studies in Michigan University.

As has been previously stated, the robber band comprised three subdivisions—the two James brothers, the three Younger brothers, and three odd ones—Miller, Pitts, and Stiles. In their active operations, another threefold division was adopted, each of the squads containing one of the Younger brothers and one of the odd ones, and two of them containing one of the James brothers. That is, there were two trios and one couple. Of these, one trio was detailed to commit the robbery, while the couple cooperated with them on Division Street and the other trio acted as a rear guard on Bridge Square, the direction in which the band intended to retreat.

It was about two o'clock in the afternoon that the first trio, consisting of Pitts, Bob Younger, and, it is believed, one of the James brothers, came over the bridge and, crossing the square from northwest to southeast, dismounted in front of the bank, throwing their bridle reins over some hitching posts beside the street. They then sauntered to the corner and lounged upon some dry-goods boxes in front of the store (Lee and Hitchcock's), assuming an air of indifference and whittling the boxes, like the most commonplace loafers. Presently the two horsemen constituting the second detail entered Division Street from the south and rode toward the bank. They were

Cole Younger and Clel Miller. Upon their approach the three men at the corner walked back to the door of the bank and went in. Miller, dismounting in front of the door, left his horse unhitched, went to the door, and looked in and then, closing it, walked back and forth before it. Younger dismounted in the middle of the street, where he made a pretense of tightening his saddle girth.

By this time the attention of several citizens had been attracted to the maneuvers of the robbers. Word had been brought that nine men on horseback had been seen coming out of the woods southwest of the city, and the presence of so many strange horsemen on the street began to awaken uneasiness. Yet when some expressed these fears, they were laughed at by others and assured that the men were merely cattle buyers on a legitimate business tour.

Among those whose suspicions had been especially aroused were Dr. Wheeler and Mr. J. S. Allen, already referred to. Dr. Wheeler was sitting under an awning in front of his father's store on the east side of Division Street when the men entered the street, and as their actions seemed to him to indicate some mischievous intent, he rose and moved along the sidewalk till he was opposite them. Mr. Allen was on the other side of the street, and when he saw the three men enter the bank, he attempted to follow them in. He was instantly seized by Miller, who had been placed there for that purpose and who, drawing his revolver and pouring forth a volley of oaths, ordered Allen to stand back and warned him on peril of his life not to utter a word. Allen jerked away from the ruffian's grasp and ran back to and around the corner toward his store, shouting in a voice that resounded blocks away, "Get your guns, boys! They're robbing the bank!" At the same time, Dr. Wheeler had stepped into the street and was shouting, "Robbery! Robbery!" his alarm being at once justified and intensified by the round of pistol shots within the bank.

Upon this, Miller and Younger sprang into their saddles, ordering Wheeler back with oaths and threats and firing one or two shots over his head to intimidate him and to give notice to their confederates that their game was discovered. Then the two robbers began riding up and down Division Street at their utmost speed, shooting right and left, with horrible oaths calling upon everyone they saw to "get in"—an order that was obeyed with pretty general promptness and unanimity. At the same time, the three men near the bridge took up the same tactics and came dashing across the square, shooting and shouting like their comrades, whom they joined on Division Street. Wherever they saw a head out of doors or at a window, they sent a shower of balls. The air was filled with the sounds of the fray, the incessant *bang, bang* of the heavy revolvers; the whistling of bullets; the crashing of glass; and the chorus of wild yells and imprecations. The first intention of the robbers was not to kill anyone but to strike terror into the mind of the people and, by driving everybody from the streets, to give the men in the bank time to work, to prevent any attempt at interference, and to secure themselves an unobstructed line of retreat. Strange to say, during this part of the affray, though the robbers kept up a constant fusillade from their revolvers, but one person was shot—a Scandinavian who could not understand English and who was fatally wounded while persistently remaining on the street.

Meantime, a very different scene was enacted within the bank, where the first trio of robbers were dealing with a trio of bank employees as resolute as themselves. These were Mr. A. E. Bunker, teller; Mr. J. L. Heywood, bookkeeper; and Mr. F. J. Wilcox, assistant bookkeeper. The cashier, Mr. G. M. Phillips, being out of the state, Mr. Heywood was acting cashier. The bank was at the time occupying temporary quarters, not arranged with reference to emergencies of this kind. A counter, constructed somewhat like an ordinary office or store counter, extended across two sides between the lobby and the interior of the room. This was surmounted for nearly its entire length by a high railing containing glass panels, but in the angle between the two sections of the counter, there was an open space, entirely unprotected, wide enough for a man to pass through.

When the three robbers entered the bank, the employees were busy at their tasks and had no suspicion of approaching danger. Mr. Bunker, the teller, hearing footsteps in the lobby and supposing that some customer had entered, turned from his work to wait upon him, coming to the open space before referred to. There three revolvers were pointing at him, and he was peremptorily ordered to throw up his hands. His first impression was that one of his friends was playing a practical joke upon him. Before he had time to comprehend the situation, the three robbers had climbed over the counter and, covering him and his associates with their revolvers, commanded them to hold up their hands.

"We're going to rob this bank," said one of the men. "Don't any of you holler. We've got forty men outside." Then, with a flourish of his revolver, he pointed to Heywood and said, "Are you the cashier?"

"No," replied Heywood.

The same question was put to Bunker and to Wilcox, each of whom made the same reply.

"You are the cashier," said the robber, turning upon Heywood, who was sitting at the cashier's desk and who appeared to be the oldest of the employees. "Open that safe—quick, or I'll blow your head off."

A second robber—Pitts—then ran to the vault and stepped inside, whereupon Heywood, who had risen to his feet, followed him and attempted to close the door. He was instantly dragged back, and the two robbers, thrusting their revolvers in his face, said, "Open that safe now, or you haven't but a minute to live," accompanying their threats with oaths.

"There is a time lock on," Heywood replied, "and it cannot be opened now."

"That's a lie!" retorted the robbers, again repeatedly demanding, with threats and profanity, that the safe be opened and dragging Heywood roughly about the room.

Finally, seeming to realize what desperate men he was dealing with, Heywood shouted, "Murder! Murder!" Whereupon one of the robbers struck him a terrible blow on the head with a revolver, felling him to the floor. Pitts then drew a knife from his pocket and, opening it, said, "Let's cut his—throat," and made a feint of doing so, inflicting a slight wound on Heywood's neck as he lay helpless upon the floor. The two men then dragged him from where he lay at the rear of his desk back to the door of the vault, still demanding that he open the safe. Occasionally also they turned from him to Bunker and Wilcox, pointing their revolvers at them and calling on them to "unlock that safe." To this demand the young men answered that they could not unlock the safe. The statement was true, though in a sense quite different from that in which the robbers understood it. The reason that they could not unlock it was that it was unlocked already. The door was closed and the bolts were shot into place, but the combination dial was not turned. This was one of the humors of the situation but one which those in the secret were not in a position to enjoy. As a last resort for coercing Heywood, who was still lying on the floor in but a partially conscious condition, Pitts placed his revolver close to Heywood's head and fired. The bullet passed into the vault and through a tin box containing jewelry and papers left by some customer for safe keeping. This was the first shot fired in the bank, and its futility well foretokened the failure of the whole effort.

While Bunker and Wilcox received occasional attention from Heywood's assailants, their special custodian was Bob Younger. As Bunker had his pen in his hand when first ordered to hold up his hands, it remained for a time poised in the air. When he made an effort to lay it down, Younger, noticing the movement and thinking it an attempt to reach a weapon, sprang at Bunker and, thrusting his revolver into his face, said, "Hear, put up your hands and keep 'em up, or I'll kill you!" Then, to hold his prisoners more completely under his control, he compelled them both to get down on their knees under the counter. All the robbers were very much excited and increasingly so as they found themselves baffled and resisted. Younger would point his pistol first at one of the young men and then at the other, turning from time to time to search among the papers on the desk or to open a drawer in quest of valuables.

While still on his knees, Bunker remembered a revolver kept on a shelf under the teller's window and edged toward the place in hope of reaching it. Turning his head that way while Younger's back was toward him, his movement was instantly detected by Pitts, who leaped before him and, seizing the pistol, put it in his own pocket, remarking, "You needn't try to get hold of that. You couldn't do anything with that little derringer, anyway." It is no doubt fortunate that Bunker did not succeed in reaching the weapon, as he would almost certainly have been shot down by the robbers before he could use it. The pistol was found upon Pitts at the time of his capture and death.

Bunker now rose to his feet, intending to make some effort to escape or to give an alarm. As he did so, Younger turned to him and said, "Where's the money outside the safe? Where's the cashier's till?" Bunker showed him a partitioned box on the counter containing some small change and fractional currency but did not call his attention to a drawer beneath the counter containing $3,000 in bills. Again ordering Bunker to get down on his knees and keep his hands up, Younger drew from under his coat a grain sack, which he began to fill from the box.

Presently he turned again to Bunker, and finding him on his feet, he said with a wicked look and with an outburst of horrible profanity, "There's more money than that out here. Where's that cashier's till? And what in—are you standing up for? I told you to keep down." Seizing Bunker and forcing him to the floor, Younger pressed the muzzle of his revolver against Bunker's temple and said, "Show me where that money is, you—or I'll kill you!" Receiving no answer, he left Bunker and renewed his search for the money.

Bunker once more regained his feet, and taking advantage of a moment when the robber's face was turned, he dashed past Wilcox into and through the directors' room, to the rear door, then closed with blinds fastened on the inside. His intention was to enter the rear of Manning's hardware store on the other side of the alley and give the alarm. He knew nothing yet of what was going on in the street, and he believed Heywood to be dead from the effect of the pistol shot apparently aimed at his head.

The first of the robbers to notice the escape was Pitts, whose eyes seemed to be everywhere at once and who was then with Heywood in front of the vault. Before he had time to shoot, however, Bunker was out of his range around the corner of the vault and making for the door. With a mad yell, Pitts bounded after the fugitive and, coming in sight of him, fired as he ran, the ball whizzing past Bunker's ear and through the blind in front of him. Bunker threw his weight against the blinds, bursting them open; plunged down a flight of outside steps; and had nearly reached the rear entrance of the next building when he was again fired upon by Pitts. This time the ball hit its mark, passing through the right shoulder near the joint, barely missing the subclavian artery, and coming out just below the collarbone. As he felt the sting and shock of the wound, he stumbled, but keeping his feet and not knowing how badly he might be wounded, he ran on across a vacant lot and around to a surgeon's office in the next block. Pitts gave up the chase and returned to his companions in the bank but only to hear one of their confederates on the outside shout, "The game is up! Better get out, boys. They're killing all our men." Hearing this, the three robbers sprang through the teller's window and rushed into the street. As the last one climbed over the counter, he turned toward poor Heywood, who had gotten upon his feet and was staggering toward his desk, and deliberately shot him through the head. The act was without provocation or excuse and was afterward denounced by others of the gang as "a fool act," though others still made an absurd attempt to justify it on the ground of self-defense. It was a piece of cowardly revenge on the part of a ruffian who was made desperate by defeat and who, as was evident throughout the entire scene in the bank, was badly under the influence of liquor.

The battle in the street was now at its height, and the spirit in which it was waged on the part of the citizens showed how grossly the robbers had mistaken the mettle of the people with whom they had to deal. The community was taken by surprise and at a great disadvantage. It was at the height of the prairie chicken season, and a majority of the men who had guns were away in the field. The excellent hunting in the neighborhood had drawn many sportsmen from the larger cities, accustoming the people to the presence of strangers, while they had no reason to expect a hostile invasion. When the mounted bandits on Bridge Square and Division Street began riding and shooting, the first impression was that of surprise. Some thought it the reckless fun of drunken scapegraces. Some took the riders to be the attachés of a traveling show advertising their performance. When the bullets began to fly about people's ears and the character of the invaders became evident, everybody was stunned and dazed, and there was a general scramble for shelter. But the next moment, there was an equally prompt rally of brave men to repel the attack.

Dr. Wheeler, who had been one of the first to give the alarm and who had been driven from the street by the imprecations and bullets of the robbers, hastened to the drugstore, where he usually kept his gun. Remembering as he went that he had left it at the house, he did not slacken his pace but kept on through the store, heading first for the house of a neighbor, where he hoped a weapon might be found, but on second thought turning into the Dampier Hotel, close at hand, where he remembered to have seen one. There, instead of the fowling piece he looked for, he found an old army carbine, for which, with the help of Mr. Dampier, the clerk, three cartridges were discovered in another part of the house. All this was so quickly done that he was at a second-story chamber window with his gun loaded in time for the beginning of the fight.

Meantime Mr. Allen, who had also sounded so prompt and vigorous an alarm, ran to his store, where he had a number of guns, and, loading them with such ammunition as came to his hand, gave them to anybody who would take them. One of them was taken by Mr. Elias Stacy, who used it to good purpose in the battle that followed.

As Mr. Allen went to his own store, he had passed that of Mr. Manning, to whom he shouted his warning concerning the robbers. Up to this time, Manning had no suspicion of what was going on. One of the robbers had been in the store in the forenoon, looking about and pretending he wanted to buy a gun. He was a genteel, well-dressed fellow, and Manning supposed him to be some stranger who had come to Northfield to hunt, though he did not believe that he wanted any gun and thought there was something wrong about him. Even when the three horsemen dashed through the square so noisily and belligerently, he thought little of it. But when he heard Allen's shout and made out the words "robbing the bank," he recalled what he had seen, and the meaning of it all flashed upon his mind. Abruptly leaving the customer he was serving, he rushed for a weapon, thinking hard and fast. Pistols? No; they would be of little account. His shotgun? Yes— no; he had left all his loaded cartridges at home. His breach-loading rifle! That was the thing, and here it was in the window, and there in a pigeonhole of his desk were the cartridges, where they had been carelessly thrown months before. All this came to him without an instant's loss of time. He forgot nothing, and he made no mistakes. Stripping the rifle of its cover and seizing a handful of cartridges, he hurried to the scene of battle, loading as he ran.

The scene on the street is indescribable. People had not only made haste to get out of the way of the leaden hailstorm that had burst forth but had also taken measures to protect themselves and their property against the raiders, whose intention was believed to be not only to rob the bank but to pillage the entire town. Stores and offices were hastily closed. The postmaster, Capt. H. S. French, who chanced to have an exceptionally heavy registered mail on hand that day, hastened to lock it in the safe and close the office. Jewelers and others who had valuable and portable stock pursued a similar course. The news of the invasion, emphasized by the sound of the shooting, spread swiftly through the town. Warning was sent to the public school and to Carleton College to keep the students off the streets. The general impression was that the town was in possession of a horde of robbers, numbering nobody knew how many and coming nobody knew whence, and bent on ruthless plunder, nobody knew to what extent.

The scene of the actual conflict was that part of Division Street on which the bank faced and scarcely a full block in length. Here the five mounted robbers went riding back and forth, up one side of the street and down the other, doing their utmost with voice and arms to keep up the reign of terror which they had begun. The citizens whom they had driven in were looking for weapons, and the bolder ones were coming back, some armed and some unarmed, around the margin of the field. Capt. French, having made Uncle Sam's property as secure as possible, stood in front of the locked door, wondering where he could soonest find a gun. Justice Streater and ex-policeman Elias Hobbs stepped out into the square, empty-handed but undaunted and determined to do something by way of resistance to the invasion. A few were so fortunate as to have not only the courage but the means for an armed defense. Mr. Stacy, already referred to, came out with a fowling piece and, confronting Miller, just as the latter was mounting his horse, fired at his head. The fine bird shot marked the robber's face, and the force of the charge knocked him back from the saddle but inflicted no serious wound. There was a poetic justice in the incident, as it was Allen, whom Miller had seized and threatened at the bank, who owned and loaded the gun and sent it out in the hands of his neighbor to draw first blood from the very man that had assaulted its owner.

Later on in the battle, Messrs. J. B. Hyde, Ross Phillips, and James Gregg also did their best with similar weapons, and it was not their fault that the shotguns they used upon the bandits were inadequate to the occasion. Mr. Hobbs, who had no weapon at all, fell back upon more primitive methods and, at the height of the fray, came on shouting, "Stone 'em! Stone 'em!" and suiting the action to the word and choosing not "smooth stones from the brook" but big and formidable missiles more fit for the hand of Goliath than for the sling of David, hurled rocks and curses at the enemy and not without effect. Col. Streater also joined in this mode of warfare, which, if not the most effective, certainly evinced as high a degree of courage as they could have shown in the use of the most approved weapon. Other citizens, too, took a hand in the affair, as opportunity offered, and some of them had narrow escape from the bullets with which the robbers responded to their attentions.

But while there was no lack of good intentions on the part of others, it was the two men with rifles, Manning and Wheeler, who were able to do real execution upon the enemy and finally to put them to rout. We go back, therefore, to the moment when Manning came running from his store with the rifle in his hand. Taking in the situation at a glance and intent only upon getting at the robbers, he stepped out into the open street and, amid a shower of bullets, coolly looked for his game. Before him stood the horses of the men who were still in the bank, and over the heads of the horses, he saw the heads of two men, upon whom he instantly drew a bead. The men ducked behind the horse, whereupon Manning, without lowering his gun, changed his aim and shot the nearest horse, rightly judging that this would cripple the band almost as effectually as shooting the men. He then dropped back around the corner to reload, but finding to his chagrin that the breach lever would not throw out the empty shell, he was obliged to go back to the store and get a ramrod with which to dislodge it, thus losing valuable time. The interruption proved a good thing for him, however, moderating his excitement and rashness and preparing him to do better execution. Soon he was at the corner again. Peering around the corner, he saw one of the robbers between the horses and the bank door and fired at him. The ball grazed the edge of a post, deflecting it slightly, but it found Cole Younger, wounding him in a vulnerable though not vital place. Again Manning dropped back to reload. The shell gave him no trouble this time, and he was quickly at his post once more. As he looked cautiously around the corner, he saw Stiles sitting on his horse, some seventy-five or eighty yards away, apparently doing sentry duty in that part of the street. Manning took deliberate aim at him—so deliberate as to excite the impatience and call forth the protests of some who were near him—and fired, shooting the man through the heart. Manning, as before, stepped back to reload; the robber fell from his saddle, dead; and the horse ran to a livery stable around the corner.

While these things were going on, Dr. Wheeler was not idle. His first shot was at the head of Jim Younger, who was riding by. The gun carried high, and the ball struck the ground beyond him. Younger looked first at the spot where it struck and then turned to see where it came from but did not discover the sharpshooter at the window above him. Wheeler's next shot was at Clel Miller, whom Stacy had already peppered with bird shot. The bullet passed through his body almost precisely as Pitts's bullet had passed through Bunker's, but in this case the great artery was severed, and almost instant death ensued. Wheeler's third and last cartridge had fallen upon the floor, bursting the paper of which it was made and spilling the powder. Hurrying in search of more, he met his friend Dampier coming with a fresh supply.

The robbers were now badly demoralized. Their shooting had been wild and fruitless. They had lost two men and a horse killed; a third man was wounded; two riderless horses had escaped from them, and an armed force had cut off their proposed line of retreat. It was at this juncture that Cole Younger rode to the door of the bank and shouted to the men inside to come out, which they made all haste to do. Two of the men mounted their horses, which still stood before the door. There was no horse for Bob Younger, and he was compelled to fight on foot.

By this time Manning and Wheeler had both reloaded and returned to their places. As Manning showed himself, ready to renew the battle, Bob Younger came running toward him down the sidewalk. Manning raised his rifle to shoot at the approaching robber, and at the same instant, Younger drew his revolver to shoot Manning. In the effort to get out of each other's range, Younger dodged under the outside stairway of the Scriver Block, while Manning stood at the corner beyond it. The stairs were thus between them, and neither of them could get a shot at the other without exposing himself to the fire of his adversary. For a time they kept up a game of hide and seek, each trying in vain to catch the other off his guard and get the first shot. At this point Wheeler, though he could but imperfectly see Younger's body beneath the stair, took a shot at him. The ball struck the robber's elbow, shattering the bone. He then coolly changed his pistol to his left hand and continued his efforts to shoot Manning.

It then occurred to Manning that, by running around through the store, he might reach the street on the other side of the robber and so drive him from his hiding place. This plan he instantly put in execution. At the same moment, Wheeler was engaged in reloading his gun. But the robbers had their plans, too, and took advantage of this momentary lull to make their escape. Bob Younger sprang from his hiding place and ran up Division Street, where he mounted behind his brother Cole, and the entire band—or at least what was left of it—turned and fled. Wheeler returned to his window, and Manning emerged upon the sidewalk only to find that their game had flown. Even then there was an excellent chance for long-range shooting, but the intervening distance was immediately filled with people, making it impossible to shoot without endangering innocent lives.

This battle between desperadoes and peaceful citizens has well been cited as proof that the prowess, courage, and dead-shot skill at arms commonly ascribed to the border ruffian are largely imaginary. On the one side was a band of heavily armed and thoroughly trained and organized banditti, carrying out a carefully made plan in their own line of business after weeks of preparation. On the other side was a quiet, law-abiding community, unused to scenes of violence, taken utterly by surprise and at a fearful disadvantage, with no adequate means of defense except two long-disused rifles in out-of-the-way places and one of them on the retired army list. Yet the banditti were beaten at their own game, and their courage lasted only while the odds were in their favor. As to marksmanship, they were vastly outdone by their citizen opponents. Excepting the cold-blooded murder of a defenseless spectator, they did not in the entire fight fire one effective shot. It is said that at least thirty shots were fired at Manning alone, yet he escaped without a scratch.

In the bank, heroism of another order had displayed itself. Without the excitement of open battle or the stimulus of numbers and without the slightest means or opportunity for defense, the three unarmed young men balked the three armed ruffians who held them in their power, meeting threats and violence with passive resistance and, in the face of death itself, refusing to yield one jot to the demands of their assailants.

The brunt of this unequal contest fell upon poor Heywood. How he met it has been already related. Threatened, assaulted, dragged about, brutally struck down, menaced with the knife, ostensibly shot at, he could not be persuaded or bullied into surrendering his trust or becoming the accomplice of robbers. It is interesting to know that, before this ordeal came to him, he had been led to ask himself what he would do in such an emergency and had made up his mind that he would under no circumstances give up the property of his employers. His steadfast resistance to the robbers' demands, therefore, was not due to a hesitating policy or to the mere obstinate impulse of the moment but was the result of a deliberate purpose and conviction of duty. The fatal cost of his fidelity was something which he could not have failed to take account of all along as the most probable end of a struggle with such desperate men as he was dealing with. At a time when we hear so often that persons in similar circumstances have been compelled to unlock vaults or to open safes at the dictation of robbers, there is a wholesome tonic in the example of a man who proved that there is not in the whole world of criminal force a power that can overcome one brave man who chooses at all hazards to do his duty.

The battle was over. So swift had been its movement, so rapidly had its events followed one another, that it was done before people beyond its immediate vicinity knew that it had begun. From its opening to its closing shot, it had occupied but seven minutes. But it had been as decisive as it was brief. The object of the attack had failed. The funds of the bank were intact. Six of the robbers were in flight, two of them wounded. In front of the bank lay the dead horse, the first victim of the fight. Nearby was the body of Clel Miller, and a half block away, on the other side of the street, that of Stiles. Of the three deaths, that of the horse alone moved the pity of the spectators. On every hand were shattered windows, the work of the vicious revolvers, while hitching posts, doors, window frames, and storefronts were scored with bullets. Heywood lay on the bank floor, where he had fallen at the post of duty. Bunker was in the hands of the surgeons. All the bells of the town had been set ringing. People came hurrying to the scene from every direction. Excited preparations were making to pursue the escaping robbers.

The scenes that followed showed that there were heroines as well as heroes in the community. While the first wild rumors of the affair were rife and it was believed that scores of marauders had invaded the town and that general pillage might be expected, ladies went to the public school and to the girls' dormitory of Carleton College to give warning of the impending danger. One of the teachers in the public school was the wife of Mr. Bunker, the wounded teller. From different sources she received information first that he was wounded and then that he was killed. Crediting the least-alarming statement, she first made arrangements for the care of her pupils and then started to find her husband. Fortunately she met a friend with a carriage, who took her to the doctor's office where Mr. Bunker was receiving surgical care. Mrs. Heywood's first intimation of her husband's death was received by accident and in a painfully abrupt manner. Being at her house on the west side of the river at a considerable distance from the scene of the tragedy, she chanced to hear one neighbor shout the news to another across the street. President Strong of Carleton College had already started at the request of friends to break the intelligence to her, when he learned that his errand was needless. The body was placed in a carriage and supported in the arms of President Strong, while it was driven to the Heywood residence. Mrs. Heywood showed herself worthy to be the wife of such a man. She bore the awful blow with the greatest calmness, and when she heard how he met his death, she said, "I would not have had him do otherwise."

The dead robbers received attentions of quite another sort. The two bodies were placed in an empty granary, where they remained during the night. The news of the raid had been telegraphed all over the country, and the evening trains brought crowds of curious people, eager to see and hear everything pertaining to the affair. The next day the number of visitors was so largely increased and the desire to see the dead bandits was so great that the bodies were brought out into the open square, which was soon packed with people. Among the visitors from other towns were sheriffs, police officers, and private citizens who had come to join in the pursuit of the escaped robbers.

That afternoon the county coroner, Dr. Waugh of Faribault, held an inquest on the three bodies, and a verdict was found according to the facts: "That J. L. Heywood came to his death by a pistol shot fired by an unknown man who was attempting to rob the First National Bank of Northfield"; "That the two unknown men came to their death by the discharge of firearms in the hands of our citizen in self-defense and in protecting the property of the First National Bank of Northfield."

The grief and indignation over the death of Mr. Heywood were intense. He was a man greatly respected in the community, was prominent in church and business life, and at the time of his death was the city treasurer and also the treasurer of Carleton College. On Sunday, the 10th of September, two funeral services in honor of the murdered man were held in Northfield. In the morning came the public service in High School Hall, the largest auditorium in the city. The place was packed, notwithstanding the excessive rain and mud then prevailing. The introductory exercises were conducted by the Rev. Messrs. Gossard and Utter, the pastors of the Methodist and the Baptist churches, and the funeral address was delivered by the Rev. D. L. Leonard, pastor of the Congregational Church, the regular church services of the day being omitted. The admirable address of Mr. Leonard has been preserved in a neat pamphlet entitled, "Funeral Discourse on Joseph Lee Heywood," published by Johnson and Smith, Minneapolis, and is a valuable contribution to the literature of this subject. As much of its biographical and historical matter is substantially covered by the present narrative, it need not be reproduced, but some extracts relating to Mr. Heywood's personal character may properly be quoted, as showing the estimation in which he was held by one who not only knew him well but was voicing the sentiments of the community to which and for which he spoke.

> Mr. Heywood was, beyond most men, modest and timid. He shrank from the public gaze, and considering his high gifts and his standing in the community, he was retiring almost to a fault. He set a low estimate upon himself. He would not own to himself, did not even seem to know, that he was lovable and well-beloved.

He courted no praise and sought no reward. Honors must come to him unsought if they came at all. He would be easily content to toil on, out of sight and with service unrecognized, but in every transaction he must be conscientious through and through and do each hour to the full the duties of the hour.

Yes, something such a one as this walked our streets, worshipped in our assemblies, and bore his share of our public burdens for ten years. And so dull is human appreciation that had he ended his days after the ordinary fashion of humanity, it is to be feared his worth had never been widely known. But not so now, since, as I may almost say, in the sight of thousands, he has been translated that he should not see death and was caught up from earth to heaven in a chariot of fire. Surely we cannot forget that spectacle to our dying day. The glory of his departure will cast back a halo of glory over all his career. We shall reread the record, as he made it, with sharpened vision. Besides, some of the virtues in which he excelled, such as integrity, moral courage, steadfastness in pursuing the right, in the tragic circumstances attending the close of his life, found their supreme test not only but their sublime climax as well. The charm lies in the perfect harmony existing between the acts of the last hour and the conduct of all the life that went before.

And sure am I that we all, in moments when we are most calm and rational and when the noblest in us finds voice, discover the conviction possessing us that there was something most fitting, something surpassingly beautiful, in such an exit after such a career—such a sunset after such a day.

For, for what, I pray you, was man made but to do his duty? To be brave and true, reckless of results? And what is life worth, I wonder, if to be preserved only at the price of cowardice and faithlessness? . . . Surely to him that is gone, life as the purchase of dishonor would have been an intolerable burden. . . . Whoso consents to stand on duty, in the army, on the railway train, in the banking house or store, must do it with open eyes, ready to take the consequences, fully determined, whatever befall, to play the man. . . . When so many are corrupt and venal, are base and criminal in the discharge of public duties, the spectacle of such a life as we have looked upon is worth far more to society than we can well reckon up. And if, as a result of last Thursday's events, those just entering upon life and we all shall be warned of the evil and curse of transgression and be reminded of the surpassing beauty of honor and faithfulness and in addition shall catch an enthusiasm of integrity, it will go no small way to compensate for the terrible shock that came to this city and for the agony that has fallen upon so many hearts. . . . We know today that public and private worth are still extant and that the old cardinal virtues are still held in honor. We need no lantern to find a man.

In the afternoon President Strong, assisted by other clergymen, conducted the funeral service proper at Mr. Heywood's late residence and paid an equally cordial testimony to the character of the man and to the high quality of heroism which he had displayed. Dr. Strong was able to speak from the point of view of personal friendship and from that of official relation, having been Mr. Heywood's pastor at Faribault in former years and having been more recently associated with him in connection with the college. It was in a casual conversation which they had held but a few days before the tragedy that Mr. Heywood dropped the remark which showed that he had already decided how he would meet such an ordeal if it ever came to him. The president had been inspecting the new time lock which had just been placed upon the door of the vault. The circumstance recalled to his mind the famous St. Albans bank raid, which had especially interested him through his personal acquaintance with the victimized cashier. Having spoken of the course pursued by the raiders in that case, he said, in mere playfulness, to Mr. Heywood, "Now if robbers should come in here and order you to open this vault, would you do it?" With a quiet smile and in his own modest way, Mr. Heywood answered, "I think not." Neither of them dreamed how soon and with what tragical emphasis he would be called to test that resolution.

Mr. Heywood was buried in the Northfield cemetery at the southern extremity of the city, where his remains still rest and where an unpretentious monument marks his grave.

In an obscure corner of the same cemetery, at night, with neither mourner nor funeral rites, two boxes were buried, supposed to contain the bodies of the dead robbers. No one took the trouble to ascertain the genuineness of the proceeding or to guard the grave from desecration. That the bodies of criminals belong to anatomical science is a prevalent opinion. That these criminals were not too good for such a purpose was readily conceded. That they somehow found their way to a certain medical college and that one of them was subsequently rescued from its fate by friends are said to be facts of history.

While the excitement over the tragedy was at its height and the inquests and the funeral services over the dead were in progress, the escaped robbers were not forgotten.

They had left Northfield by what is known as the Dundas Road, leading to the town of that name, three miles to the south. Their original plan had been to go westward, over the route by which they had come, and to stop at the telegraph office on their way and destroy the instruments, in order that the news of the raid might not be spread till they were out of reach in the great forest tract lying in that direction. But, as they afterward said, finding it "too hot" for them in that part of the town, they were glad to escape by any route they could find, while the telegraph was publishing their deeds and their descriptions in every direction. Dundas being the nearest place at which they could cross the Cannon River, they made all possible speed toward it, six men on five horses. They rode abreast, like a squad of cavalry, taking the whole road, and compelling everyone they met to take the ditch. Meeting a farmer with a good span of horses, they stopped him and helped themselves to one of the horses, for the use of Bob Younger, who had been riding behind his brother Cole. A little farther on they "borrowed" a saddle for him of another farmer, representing themselves to be officers of the law in pursuit of horse thieves, a pretense which they made much use of during their flight. As soon as possible, they got back into their former route, where they were once more on somewhat familiar ground. The death of Miller had deprived them of the guide upon whose knowledge of the country they had depended. The loss of their trained and high-bred saddle horses was perhaps a still more serious calamity, a loss which they were not able to make good with any of the farm horses stolen one after another. Their rush at full speed through Dundas caused a sensation, but owing to the absence of the telegraph operator, the news of the raid had not been received, and they were not molested. Millersburg, where some of them had spent the previous night, was reached about half past four. They were recognized by the landlord who had entertained them, but they were still in advance of the news of their crime and far in advance of their pursuers. They rode hard, sparing neither themselves nor their beasts, although Bob Younger's arm was causing him much suffering. His horse fell under him, breaking the saddle girth, and was abandoned in disgust, Younger again mounting behind one of his companions. Another horse was seized in a similar manner, regardless of the protests of his owner, but the animal balked so obstinately that he, too, had to be abandoned. Thus began a dreary two weeks' flight, which grew more and more dismal day by day, as the fugitives skulked from place to place, now riding, now walking, now hiding in a region where, as they too well knew, every man's hand was against them. Nature and providence seemed to be against them, too. A cold, drizzling rain set in the day after the raid and continued almost incessantly for two weeks. The way of the transgressor was hard, and it grew harder at every step.

The pursuers were after them. Before the robber cavalcade was out of sight of the scene of their raid, almost before the smoke of the battle had passed away, men were running for their guns and horses to join in the chase. The first movements were made under intense excitement and were necessarily irresponsible and futile. But more deliberate measures were soon taken. Mr. J. T. Ames called for volunteers for a systematic pursuit and telegraphed to the state capital for aid. Sheriffs, detectives, chiefs of police, and scores of private citizens promptly responded. As soon as practicable, a small army of pursuers was organized, and systematic plans for their transportation and sustenance were perfected.

Three times on Thursday afternoon, advanced detachments of this force encountered the fugitives. First a couple of volunteer scouts mounted, by a singular coincidence, on the horses of the dead robbers came within sight of the band as they were seizing the farmer's horse on the Dundas Road. But as the robbers were six to the scouts' two, the latter did not venture an attack but contented themselves with trailing their game until reinforcements should arrive. Again, at Shieldsville, fifteen miles west of Northfield, a squad of Faribault men had arrived in advance of the pursued by taking a shorter road. But not knowing how close at hand the bandits were, they had gone within doors, leaving their guns outside, when the raiders suddenly appeared before the door, from which they did not permit their unarmed pursuer to issue but coolly watered their horses at an adjacent pump, shot a defiant volley of bullets into it, and went on their way. The outwitted scouts quickly regained their guns and, being reinforced by a dozen or more local recruits, hastened after the robbers. The band was overtaken in a ravine about four miles west of Shieldsville, where the two forces exchanged some long-range shots without effect on either side, and the robbers escaped into the thick woods beyond.

While these preliminary contests were taking place, the more systematic campaign was arranged and inaugurated. Before Thursday night two hundred men were in the field, and on Friday, five hundred. Other hundreds still joined the chase later on, swelling the number at one time to at least a thousand. It is impossible to give a list of those engaged or to do justice to the zeal, the determination, and the endurance that they showed. Among those who were prominently engaged, either in organizing the forces or in conducting operations in the field, may be mentioned Mayor Solomon P. Stewart of Northfield; Sheriff Ara Barton and George N. Baxter, Esq., of Faribault; Chiefs of Police King of St. Paul and Munger of Minneapolis; Detectives Hoy and Brissette; and many others. Of the men under them, several were experienced officers, and not a few were veteran soldiers. There were also, of course, in so large and hastily mustered a force, very many who had no fitness for the service, either in personal qualities or in equipment, and no conception of the requirements of such a campaign. They came armed with small pistols and old fowling pieces of various degrees of uselessness and utterly without either judgment or courage. Their presence was a source of weakness to the force. Their foolish indiscretions embarrassed and defeated the best-laid plans, and their failure at critical moments and places to do what they had been depended upon to do made them worse than useless—worse than enemies. Many went into the service from mercenary motives. Large rewards for the capture of the robbers dead or alive were offered by the Northfield bank, the governor of the state, and the railway companies, and this inducement drew into the ranks of the pursuers much poor material. These statements need to be made, not so much by way of censure upon the inefficient as in justice to the better members of the force and as an explanation of some of the vexatious delays and failures of the campaign. For, while it constantly suffered from the presence of these mercenaries and blunderers, it did not lack, from its first day to its last, a nucleus of brave, keen-witted, coolheaded, determined men, whom nothing could daunt or discourage. And the best of them were not too capable for the work. Two objects were to be accomplished—the retreat of the fugitives was to be cut off, and they were to be hunted down and captured. To secure the first, picket lines were thrown out in advance of them, covering every route which they could possibly take and especially guarding roads, bridges, and fords. To secure the second, scouting parties were put upon their trail to follow them from place to place and to explore the country far and near in search of them. It was no holiday excursion. They were in a vast forest tract known as the Big Woods, broken here and there by clearings and by settlements great and small but embracing also wide area of uncut timber, full of dense thickets and ravines and abounding in lakes, streams, and swamps. The weather made difficult trailing, as tracks and other signs were soon obliterated, and the nature and extent of the ground to be covered rendered it impossible to keep the picket line strong at all points. The rain and the mud, the dripping forests, the swollen streams, the softened fields multiplied the hardships of the pursuers. Their very numbers caused confusion. They were for the most part unable to recognize with any certainty either the robbers or one another or to tell whether some squad of horsemen in the distance were friends or foe. The bandits were shrewd enough to take advantage of this doubt. It was their favorite trick to pass themselves off as a sheriff's posse in pursuit of the bank robbers. Under this subterfuge they inquired their way of unsuspecting people, obtained provisions, secured information about the position and movements of their pursuers, and repeatedly supplied themselves with fresh horses. But this is in advance of our story.

We left the robbers in their Thursday night's hiding place in the woods beyond Shieldsville. Thence on Friday they moved first westward and then southwestward in the direction of Waterville. Coming to a ford of the Little Cannon River, guarded by three men poorly armed, they were fired upon and turned back into the woods. Finding shortly afterward that the guard had withdrawn, they returned to the ford, crossed over, and disappeared in the forest beyond. Thus the picket line which had been so laboriously posted was broken at its weakest point.

The news of the escape was immediately carried to those in command, a new picket line was thrown out in advance of the robbers, and the pursuer pressed the more eagerly after them. The whole region was now aroused. The telegraph was kept constantly busy, flashing items of fact and a good many items of fiction to and from the field of operations. The railways did good service in transporting men to accessible points, but the flight and the pursuit were chiefly out of the range of towns, telegraphs, or railways in the heart of the forest.

Pushing on into the township of Elysian, the robbers found themselves in a labyrinth of lakes and swamps, where it seemed easy to prevent their escape. At an isolated farm, they exchanged two of their exhausted horses for fresh ones, against the owner's protest. In the evening they made a similar exchange in an out-of-the-way pasture without consulting the owner. Late Friday night they went into camp between Elysian and Gentian Lake. The stolen horses were now turned loose, and all returned to their masters. The remaining horses were tied to trees; a sort of tent was made by spreading blankets over some bushes, and under this the fugitives spent the rainy night.

On Saturday morning they abandoned their horses altogether; tied their blankets about their bodies with the bridles; and, though already lame and disabled, continued their journey on foot. The horses were found three days later, one of them still tied to the tree, the other two having gnawed off their halters and escaped. The robbers now proceeded more circumspectly. The dash and daring of their previous course were exchanged for the stealth and caution more befitting their condition. They went no farther on Saturday than to find a hiding place on an island in the middle of the swamp, where they encamped for the day. After dark they took up their journey, marched slowly all night, and at daylight on Sunday morning again halted near the village of Marysburg, whose church bell they could hear from their camp in the woods. Passing around Marysburg, they next encamped four miles south of that village, so slow was their progress and so short their marches. Nine miles west of this camp and within two or three miles of Mankato, they found a deserted farmhouse in the woods, where they spent Monday night, Tuesday, and Tuesday night, having advanced less than fifty miles in five days.

Even at this rate, they had distanced their pursuers, who did not suspect that they had abandoned their horses and who, confident that no mounted cavalcade had passed their lines, were still searching the swamps and bottoms about Elysian. This delusion was painfully dispelled on Tuesday morning by the discovery of the half-starved horses and the deserted camp. The robbers had stolen away on foot and had at least a three days' start. This was regarded as evidence of the hopelessness of the chase. The fugitives were no doubt far away, and in what direction no one could conjecture. A large proportion of the pursuers, including many of the most efficient leaders, therefore gave up the hunt and returned to their homes. Even some authentic reports from persons who had caught glimpses of the robbers near Mankato were scouted as absurdly incredible.

Soon, however, further news was received which could not be disputed and which at once aroused fresh interest in the chase. On Tuesday the robbers, it seemed, had invited themselves to breakfast at the house of a German farmer. On Wednesday morning they had captured another farmer's hired man in the woods and, after binding him, extorting information from him, threatening to kill him, and finally swearing him to secrecy, had let him go. Believing that a bad promise was better broken than kept, he had immediately reported the incident to his employer, who hastened with the news to Mankato, whence the telegraph sent it everywhere. Excitement was at once renewed. The disbanded forces hurried back, and hundreds of fresh recruits joined in the chase. A thousand men were soon on the ground, and a new campaign was organized under the direction of Gen. Pope of Mankato. Again patrols and searching parties were sent out, and every possible avenue of escape was guarded night and day. But again the fugitives escaped, not so much by virtue of their own cunning as through favorable accidents and the inefficiency of the guards on duty. Part of them crossed the railroad bridge over the Blue Earth River during Wednesday night. Two others mounted on a stolen horse passed the picket line near Lake Crystal on Thursday night. These last were challenged, fired upon, and probably wounded by a brave young fellow named Richard Roberts, whose sleeping companions had left him to hold the pass alone. The horse threw his riders and ran away, and they escaped in the darkness to the adjacent field, one of them leaving his hat behind him.

The band had now divided, Pitts and the three Youngers forming one division, and the two Jameses, the other. It is believed to have been the James brothers whom Roberts fired upon. Continuing their flight, they stole a fine span of gray, on which they mounted bareback. This capture was a most fortunate one for them and enabled them to make rapid progress and to assume again the role of officers in pursuit of criminals. They had no difficulty in getting food and information from unsuspecting people, who found only too late how they had been imposed upon. The two men went almost due west during the next forty-eight hours, traveling day and night at the utmost practicable speed and making eighty miles with scarcely a halt. On Sunday, September 17th, they crossed the Minnesota line into what is now South Dakota. That evening they took the liberty of exchanging their over-driven grays for a span of blacks, one of which proved to be blind in one eye and the other in both. Not finding these satisfactory, they exchanged them in turn in the small hours of Monday morning for another span of grays. They now turned southward, passed through Sioux Falls, exchanged salutations with the driver of the Yankton stage and clothes with a Sioux City doctor, and quietly pursued their flight by a route and to a destination best known to themselves.

They had not been permitted to make this escape without interference. No sooner was it known that they had gone through the picket line than scouts were sent out in every direction to overtake or intercept them. The best men in the field took up the trail. The most comprehensive measures were adopted for their capture. But owing perhaps to the unexpected celerity of their movements, so different from the previous methods of the gang, and to unforeseen slips and miscalculations, they succeeded in eluding their pursuers, most of whom abandoned the chase at the Dakota line.

This episode had entirely diverted attention from the rest of the band, as it was not then known that a division had taken place, and when the two horsemen were finally lost track of, the general supposition was that the whole band had escaped. Some persons, indeed, believed that the four unaccounted for were still in the neighborhood in which they had last been seen. The disreputable house near Mankato, already referred to as the place where two of the robbers were known to have been on the night of September 3d, was searched, and many suspicious characters in various places were arrested and investigated. This vigilance resulted in securing some criminals, including two notorious horse thieves, but it discovered no clue to the bank robbers.

The mortification of the pursuers was intense, and the denunciations heaped upon some of them and the ridicule upon all was a bitter reward for their two weeks of hard service. The failure of their campaign could not be denied. The only consolation they had was in reflecting that they had done their best and in joining in the general laugh at their own expense. The robber hunt was the great joke of the season.

Thursdays were notable days in the robber calendar. On Thursday, September 7th, the attack upon the bank was made. On Thursday, the 14th, the trail of the main band was found and lost in the Minnesota valley beyond Mankato, and on the evening of that day, the two horsemen went off on their tangent, drawing almost the entire force of the pursuers after them. On Thursday, the 21st, the public was again electrified by the news that the remaining four, who had also been supposed to have escaped, were yet in the state and had been located in the neighborhood of Madelia.

Madelia is a small village in Watonwan County and on the Waton-wan River, about twenty-four miles southwest of Mankato. One of the principal features of the surrounding country is a chain of pictur-esque lakes lying a few miles north of the town, while about five miles southwest of the lakes ran the north fork of the Watonwan River, des-tined to be as famous in the closing scenes of the raid as the Cannon had been at its beginning.

Madelia was one of the towns visited by the robbers in their prelim-inary survey. About two weeks before the robbery, Cole Younger and one other of the band spent a Sunday at the Flanders House in that place. They asked many questions of the landlord, Col. Vought, and excited some curiosity in the community. Younger expressed his admi-ration of the adjacent lake region, with whose geography he seemed to have made himself familiar. When the bank raid occurred a few days later, Col. Vought immediately understood who his guests had been and did not doubt that Younger's interest in the topography of the neighborhood had reference to a line of retreat. And when guards were being placed throughout the region to intercept the robbers in their flight, Col. Vought advised guarding a certain bridge between two of these lakes, at a point of which Younger had made special men-tion and by which anyone acquainted with the region would be sure to pass. This counsel was followed, and Col. Vought himself, with two others, guarded the bridge for two nights.

A few rods from this bridge lived a Norwegian farmer named Suborn, with his wife and his son Oscar, an intelligent and active lad about seventeen years of age. As the men kept watch at the bridge in the evening, Oscar would come down and sit with them, talking of the robbers and the robbery and forming in his mind a pretty distinct idea of the appearance and the tactics of the outlaws. He repeat-edly expressed the wish that he might meet them and have a shot at them with his father's old gun. When the band was supposed to have escaped and the guards were withdrawn, Col. Vought charged Oscar to keep a sharp lookout and, if he saw any fellows that he thought might be the robbers, to come into Madelia and tell the colonel. This the boy promised to do.

On the morning of September 21st, while Oscar and his father were milking the cows, two men walked by, bidding Oscar a civil good morning as they passed. Something in their appearance instantly convinced the boy that they were the bandits, and he ran to his father and said, "There goes the robbers." His father scouted the idea and bade him go on with his milking. But the conviction grew upon the boy as he milked, and he soon set down his pail and ran to look after the men, making inquiries of the neighbors and freely expressing his views concerning them. When he returned to the house, he learned that the men he had seen and two others had been there asking for food and saying that they were fishermen. Oscar insisted that they were the robbers and, after many objections on his father's part, finally got permission to take a horse and go and tell people what he had seen.

He instantly started for Madelia, seven or eight miles away, urging the old farm horse to the top of his speed and shouting to everybody he passed, "Look out! The robbers are about!" but finding nobody to believe him. A short distance from Madelia, the horse fell down, throwing the excited rider into the mud, but he was soon up and away again faster than ever.

Entering Madelia, he rode straight to the Flanders House, according to his promise to Col. Vought. The latter was standing on the porch of the hotel when the messenger dashed up, boy and horse equally out of breath and both of them covered with mud. A few questions sufficed to convince the colonel that the boy knew what he was talking about, and he immediately seized his gun, mounted his horse, and started for the Suborn farm. Sheriff Glispin had come up during the conversation with Oscar and also joined in the chase. Dr. Overholt, W. R. Estes, and S. J. Severson did the same. These five went in company. C. A. Pomeroy heard the news and hastened after them. G. A. Bradford and Capt. W. W. Murphy followed hard and reached the field in time for effective service. From St. James, a neighboring town to which the telegraph had carried the news came G. S. Thompson and B. M. Rice, most of their neighbors being too incredulous or too indifferent to join them. In the immediate vicinity of the robbers, all was excitement, and people were gathering in greater and greater numbers as the facts became known.

The first detachment from Madelia had no difficulty in learning where the robbers were and lost no time in reaching the locality. The band was soon descried, making its way on foot through what is known as Hanska Slough. Sheriff Glispin called upon them to halt, and as they paid no attention to his demand, he and his men fired upon them.

The robbers ran until they were out of sight behind a knoll and, before their pursuers came up with them, had crossed Lake Hanska, a considerable body of water. The Madelia men, finding some difficulty in getting their horses through the water, separated, part of them going upstream and part down in search of crossings. Reaching the other side, Col. Vought and Dr. Overholt again caught sight of the robbers, and the doctor fired at them, with so good an aim as to hit the stick with which Cole Younger was walking. Sheriff Glispin and his two companions now came up from the other direction. Seeing that the robbers were making for a herd of horse on an adjacent farm, the Madelia men intercepted the movement and for their pains received a volley from the enemy's revolvers, the bullets flying thick about the heads of the pursuers, though at pretty long range, and one of them grazing Glispin's horse.

Thus foiled, the bandits went down to the riverbank opposite the house of Andrew Anderson and, telling him that they were in pursuit of the bank robbers, ordered him to bring his horses over to them. The old ruse did not work. Instead of putting his horses at the service of the band, the shrewd farmer ran them off in the opposite direction. Foiled again, the men went up the river to a ford, crossed over, and came down through the Anderson farm to a granary, where they seemed about to make a stand, but changing their plan, they made one more effort to supply themselves with horses. Mr. Horace Thompson and his son of St. Paul were hunting in the neighborhood and had two livery teams belonging to Col. Vought of Madelia. Spying these horses, the robbers made a rush for them, but the Thompsons promptly exchanged their light charges for wire cartridges loaded with goose shot and prepared to give the freebooters a warm reception. The freebooters did not care to risk the encounter and, turning back, took refuge in the brush in the river bottom. Mr. Thompson proposed to some of those present to go in after them and hunt them out, but the armed force then present was not thought to be strong enough for such a movement.

The robbers were now hemmed in upon all sides. On the south was a high bluff, curving slightly outward to enclose the low bottom land at its base. On the north was the Watonwan River, washing the bluff on the left, then swinging away from it in a double curve, and then back toward the bluff again. A rude triangle was thus enclosed, some five acres in extent, nearly level, open in some places, but for the most part covered with an almost impenetrable growth of willows, box elders, wild plums, and grapevines.

The robbers having been driven to cover in these thickets, the next effort was to prevent their escape. A considerable number of people had by this time collected, some on one side at the river and some on the other. Glispin and Vought went down to the lower end of the ravine and posted guards on the bluffs to watch that point. Meantime Capt. Murphy had arrived and at once took similar precautions on the other side of the river. But they had no intention of waiting for the robbers to come out or to give them a chance to escape, as they had so often done, under cover of darkness. Capt. Murphy, having made his picket line secure on the north side of the river, came around to the south side, where some of his Madelia neighbors and other resolute men were gathered, and proposed that they go into the brush and rout out the bandits. A number seemed willing to join him in this attempt, but the list was much reduced when they heard his startling instructions as to the method of procedure. Moreover, some of the best men on the ground had been assigned to guard duty and were not available for this service. In a few minutes, however, six brave fellows stood by his side, ready to go wherever he would lead them.

The roll of this Spartan band of seven is as follows: Capt. W. W. Murphy, Sheriff James Glispin, Col. T. L. Vought, B. M. Rice, G. A. Bradford, C. A. Pomeroy, S. J. Severson. Capt. Murphy formed his men in line, four paces apart, ordering them to advance rapidly but in line, to keep their arms ready, observe the front well, and the instant the bandits were discovered concentrate the fire of the whole line upon them.

They advanced promptly across the eastern side of the triangle, from the bluff to the river, and then, turning to the left, followed the river's course, with the line at right angles with it. They had advanced some fifty or sixty yards in this direction, when they discovered the robbers, crouching and almost concealed in a thicket of vine-covered willows and plumtrees. At the same instant, one of the robbers fired. It was the signal for a general fusillade on both sides. Firing was rapid and at close range, the two forces being not more than thirty feet apart at the center of the line and all heavily armed. The battle was sharp but brief. Again, as in the Northfield fight, the palm of marksmanship was with the citizens and not with the professional crack shots. Mr. Bradford had his wrist grazed by a ball as he raised his rifle for his first shot. Another ball grazed Mr. Severson. Another still struck Capt. Murphy in the side and, glancing on a brier-root pipe in his pocket, lodged in his pistolbelt. With these exceptions not a man in the party was touched. Of the robbers, on the other hand, Bob Younger was wounded in the breast, his brother James had five wounds, Cole had eleven, and Pitts was dead, having been hit five times. When Capt. Murphy ordered firing to cease and called upon the robbers to surrender, Bob Younger was the only one who could respond. "I surrender," said he. "They are all down but me." As he rose to his feet, at the command of his captors, the movement was not understood by the guards on the bluff, and they fired at him, wounding him slightly, but Capt. Murphy immediately checked the untimely attack.

The arms of the robbers were taken from them, and they were placed in a wagon and taken to Madelia in the custody of the sheriff, escorted by their captors as bodyguard and by a miscellaneous company of those who had been directly or indirectly connected with the engagement. A mile from town, they met another company of people who had come by special train from other towns where the news of the reappearance of the robbers had been received. The visitors found themselves too late to take part in the capture, the honor of which belonged solely to local heroes, but they could join in the general rejoicing and help to swell the triumphal procession. As the returning throng entered Madelia, it was received with great demonstrations of joy, to which the wounded bandits responded by waving their hats.

The chagrin and exasperation which followed the escape of the two Jameses were changed to exultation over the victory in the Watonwan bottom—a victory well worthy to close the campaign so bravely begun in the streets of Northfield. Whatever blunders had been made, whatever hardships and disappointments had been endured, the final result was fairly satisfactory. Of the eight desperados who rode forth so confidently on their career of plunder, three were dead, three were prisoners, and the other two were in ignominious retreat—one of them wounded. They had wasted a month in fruitless effort, lost their splendid horses and equipment, spent much money and gained none, suffered unutterable hardship, and achieved nothing but two brutal and profitless murders.

Arrived in Madelia, the captured men were taken to the Flanders House, where Cole Younger and his now-dead comrade Pitts had played the role of gentlemen travelers a month before. Younger had recognized Col. Vought and saluted him as "landlord" when they met as captor and captive on the bloody field of the Watonwan. He also recognized Mr. G. S. Thompson, who was doing guard duty at the time of the capture, and reminded him of a visit which Pitts and himself had made to Thompson's store in St. James during the same preliminary tour.

The Flanders House was made for the time being a hospital and a prison. Guards were posted within and without, and every precaution was taken to prevent either the escape of the prisoners or any unlawful attack upon them. The men were wet, weakened by fatigue and exposure, nearly famished, and shockingly wounded. They received such attention as humanity dictated. Their wounds were dressed, their wet garments were exchanged for dry ones, their hunger was appeased, and they were placed in comfortable beds.

They appreciated this treatment most gratefully. They had hardly expected less than being lynched or torn in pieces by the infuriated people, and they repeatedly expressed their admiration both of the bravery of their captors and of the magnanimity of those who had them so absolutely at their mercy. It was indeed rumored that a train-load of lynchers was on the way, bent on summary vengeance, but the officers of the law and the people of Madelia were prepared to resist such an attempt to the utmost, and it never was made.

Sightseers and lion hunters came by hundreds from every direction. On the day following the capture, the hotel was besieged by an eager throng that filled its halls and corridors and the adjacent street and kept a continuous stream of visitors filing through the room where the robbers were confined. Reporters, photographers, and detectives were there, each intent on his own professional ends, and every type of sentiment was represented, from open vindictiveness to morbid sympathy and admiration for criminal audacity.

The prisoners talked freely on certain subjects and with shrewd reserve upon others. They claimed to be the victims of circumstances rather than of their own inclinations. They talked pathetically of their family and their antecedents, advised young men to shun bad ways, and requested the prayers of pious women. Being allowed an opportunity to confer together, they agreed to admit their own identity but refused to divulge that of their companions, either the dead or the living. They denied that the two who escaped were the James brothers but would give no further information concerning them. The work of identification was effected, however, without their aid. Chief of Police McDonough of St. Louis and other officers and citizens were able of their own knowledge, with the aid of collateral testimony and of rogues-gallery pictures, to identify the two killed at Northfield as Clel Miller and Bill Stiles and the one killed in the capture as Charley Pitts, alias George Wells. Little doubt was entertained, also, that the ones who escaped were Jesse and Frank James, who about that time reappeared in their old haunts in Missouri.

On Saturday, September 23d, the prisoners were delivered to Sheriff Barton of Rice County, by whom they were taken to Faribault and safely lodged in the county jail a few miles from the scene of their crime.

Here, again, they were visited by multitudes of people of all sorts and conditions and received many attentions, pleasant and unpleasant, as the reward of bad notoriety. Here also they were menaced with a threatened lynching, this time a dead-in-earnest affair prevented only by the vigilance and determination of the officers of the law, aided by the citizens of Faribault. So strongly was the jail guarded and so strict was the discipline maintained in its defense that, when a member of the city police one night approached the guard, making some motion that was deemed suspicious and imprudently neglecting to respond to the challenge of the guard, he was fired upon and killed.

The 9th of November, just nine weeks after the attack upon the Northfield bank, was another fateful Thursday in the robber calendar. On that day they were arraigned for trial before the Rice County District Court at Faribault, Judge Samuel Lord presiding and G. N. Baxter, Esq., being the prosecuting officer. On the previous day, the sister and the aunt of the three prisoners had arrived to attend them during the ordeal. The refinement and respectability of these ladies served to emphasize yet more strongly the social standing from which the men had fallen and the needlessness of the disgrace which they had brought upon themselves and their friends.

The arraignment presented one of the most dramatic scenes in connection with the crime. The prisoners, in expectation of the summons, had prepared themselves to make the best possible appearance in public. The three were shackled together, Cole in the middle, with Bob on the right and Jim on the left. The sheriff, chief of police, and his lieutenant walked by their side, an armed guard marched before them and another behind them. The robbers somewhat distrusted the temper of the crowd that filled the streets, and there were some mut-terings of a threatening nature but no overt acts of hostility. At the courthouse the guard opened to the right and left to admit the sheriff and his prisoners and prevent the entrance of improper persons.

Four indictments had been found against the prisoners by the grand jury. The first charged them with being accessory to the mur-der of Heywood; the second with attacking Bunker with intent to do great bodily harm; the third with robbing the First National Bank of Northfield. The fourth charged Cole Younger as principal and his brothers as accessories with the murder of Nicholas Gustavson, the Swede whom the robbers shot for remaining on the street when ordered to leave. These indictments having been read, the prisoners were, at the request of their counsel, allowed two days to decide how they would plead. It was a question of peculiar difficulty. On the one hand, to plead guilty was to renounce all hope of eluding justice through the loopholes of legal technicality. On the other hand, to plead not guilty was to ensure the severest penalty in case of convic-tion. For the laws of Minnesota were then such that if a murderer pleaded guilty, capital punishment could not be inflicted upon him. This law, designed to prevent long and needless trials in a certain class of case, afforded these criminals an advantage which the public bitterly begrudged them but of which, in view of the practical cer-tainty of conviction, they decided to avail themselves.

Accordingly, being again arraigned in court on the following Sat-urday, they pleaded guilty to all the indictments. Whereupon Judge Lord pronounced upon them the severest penalty then allowed by the law—imprisonment for life.

A few days later, Sheriff Barton, with the aid of a strong guard, conducted the robbers to Stillwater, and the state prison, the goal of so many a criminal career, closed its doors upon them. Though commonly regarded as but the second-best place for them, it has thus far safely held them, except in the case of one of them, whose sentence had expired under the great statute of limitation. Robert died in prison, September 16th, 1889. Many attempts have been made to secure pardons for the others, but thus far no governor has been found willing to accede to such a request.

11

KIT CARSON ON THE FRONTIER

BY EDWARD S. ELLIS

The legendary scout shrugged off challenges that would send most men whimpering back to civilization. There were very few things that could flap the unflappable adventurer. But sometimes even Kit Carson would start to worry if he'd make it back alive.

Carson gathered the horses together and set out on his return. The distance was considerable, and he was compelled to encamp more than once on the road while he was continually exposed to attack from Indians, but with that remarkable skill and foresight which distinguished him when a boy, he reached home without the slightest mishap and turned over the recovered animals to their owner. Some days later, several trappers entered camp with the statement that a large body of hunters were on Snake River, a fortnight's journey distant. Captain Lee at once set out with his men and found the company, who gave them a warm welcome. They purchased all the supplies Captain Lee had for sale, and then, as Carson's engagement with the captain was ended, he attached himself to the other body.

He remained, however, only a few weeks, for he saw there were so many that they could never take enough peltries to bring much money to the individual members. He decided to do as he had done before—arrange an expedition of his own. He had but to make known his intentions, when he had more applicants than he could accept. He selected three, who it is needless to say had no superiors in the whole party. The little company then turned the heads of their horses toward Laramie River.

At that day, the section abounded with beaver, and although the summer is not the time when their fur is in the best condition, the party trapped on the stream and its tributaries until cold weather set in. They met with far greater success than could have come to them had they stayed with the principal company of trappers. But they had no wish to spend the winter alone in the mountains, and gathering their stock together, they set out to rejoin their old companions.

One day, after they had gone into camp, Carson, leaving his horse in charge of his friends, set out on foot to hunt some game for their evening meal. They had seen no signs of Indians, though they never forgot to be on their guard against them. Game was not very abundant, and Carson was obliged to go a long ways before he caught sight of some elk grazing on the side of a hill. Well aware of the difficulty of getting within gunshot of the timid animals, the hunter advanced by a circuitous course toward a clump of trees, which would give him the needed shelter, but while creeping toward the point he had fixed upon as the one from which to fire, the creatures scented danger and began moving off. This compelled him to fire at long range, but he was successful and brought down the finest of the group.

The smoke was curling upward from the rifle of Carson, when he was startled by a tremendous crashing beside him, and turning his head, he saw two enormous grizzly bears making for him at full speed. They were infuriated at this invasion of their home and were evidently resolved on teaching the hunter better manners by making their supper upon him.

Carson had no time to reload his gun: Had it been given him, he would have made short work of one of the brutes at least, but as it was, he was deprived of even that privilege. Fortunate indeed would he be if he could escape their fury.

The grizzly bear is the most dreaded animal found on this continent. He does not seem to feel the slightest fear of the hunter, no matter whether armed or not, and while other beasts are disposed to give man a wide berth, old "Ephraim," as the frontiersmen call him, always seems eager to attack him. His tenacity of life is extraordinary. Unless pierced in the head or heart, he will continue his struggles after a dozen or score of rifle balls have been buried in his body. So terrible is the grizzly bear that an Indian can be given no higher honor than the privilege of wearing a necklace made from his claws—that distinction being permitted only to those who have slain one of the animals in single-handed combat.

No one understood the nature of these beasts better than Kit Carson, and he knew that, if either of the animals once got his claws upon him, there would not be the faintest chance of escape. The only thing, therefore, that could be done was to run.

There were not wanting men who were fleeter of foot than Carson, but few could have overtaken him when he made for the trees on which all his hopes depended. Like the blockade runner closely pursued by the man of war, he threw overboard all the cargo that could impede his speed. His long, heavy rifle was flung aside, and the short legs of the trapper doubled under him with amazing quickness as he strove as never before to reach the grove.

Fortunately the latter was not far off, and though the fierce beasts gained rapidly upon him, Carson arrived among the timber a few steps in advance. He had no time even to select the tree, else he would have chosen a different one, but making a flying leap, he grasped the lowermost limb and swung upward at the moment the foremost grizzly was beneath him. So close in truth was his pursuer that the hunter distinctly felt the sweeping blow of his paw aimed at the leg, which whisked beyond his reach just in the nick of time.

But the danger was not over by any means. The enthusiastic style in which the bears entered into the proceedings proved they did not mean that any trifles should stop them. They were able to climb the tree which supported Carson, and he did not lose sight of the fact. Whipping out his hunting knife, he hurriedly cut off a short thick branch and trimmed it into a shape that would have made a most excellent shillelagh for a native of the Green Isle.

He had hardly done so, when the heads of the bruins were thrust upward almost against his feet. Carson grasped the club with both hands and raising it above his shoulders brought it down with all his might upon the nose of the foremost. The brute sniffed with pain, threw up his head, and drew back a few inches—just enough to place the other nose in front. At that instant, a resounding whack landed on the rubber snout, and the second bear must have felt a twinge all through his body.

Though each blow caused the recipient to recoil, yet he instantly returned, so that Carson was kept busy pounding the noses as if he was an old-fashioned farmer threshing wheat with a flail.

It was a question with Carson which would last the longer—the club or the snouts, but in the hope of getting beyond their reach, he climbed to the topmost bough, where he crouched into the smallest possible space. It was idle, however, to hope they would overlook him, for they pushed on up the tree, which swayed with their weight.

The nose of the grizzly bear is one of the most sensitive portions of his body, and the vigorous thumps which the hunter brought down upon them brought tears of pain to their eyes. But while they suffered, they were roused to fury by the repeated rebuffs and seemed all the more set on crunching the flesh and bones of the insignificant creature who defied them.

It must have been exasperating beyond imagination to the gigantic beasts, who feared neither man nor animal to find themselves repeatedly baffled by a miserable being whom they could rend to pieces with one blow of their paws, provided they could approach nigh enough to reach him.

They came up again and again; they would draw back so as to avoid those stinging strokes, sniff, growl, and push upward, more eager than ever to clutch the poor fellow, who was compressing himself between the limb and the trunk and raining his blows with the persistency of a pugilist.

They were finally forced to desist for a few minutes in order to give their snouts time to regain their tone. The bulky creatures looked at each other and seemed to say, "That's a mighty queer customer up there; he doesn't fight fairly, but we'll fetch him yet."

Once more and for the last time, they returned to the charge, but the plucky scout was awaiting them, and his club whizzed through the air like the piston rod of a steam engine. The grizzlies found it more than they could stand, and tumbling back to solid earth, they gave up the contract in disgust. Carson tarried where he was until they were beyond sight, when he descended and hastily caught up and reloaded his rifle, having escaped, as he always declared, by the narrowest chance of all his life.

The day was drawing to a close when Carson set out for camp, which was not reached until after dark. His companions did not feel any special alarm over his continued absence, for the good reason that they were confident he could take care of himself no matter in what labyrinth of peril he might become involved.

It was too late to send for the carcass of the elk, and more than likely it had already been devoured by wolves. So the trappers made their breakfast on one of the beavers found in their traps and went into camp to await the arrival of the main body of trappers, which Carson was confident would come that way. Some days later they put in an appearance, and the company proceeded to the general rendezvous on Green River, where were found assembled the principal trappers of the Rocky Mountains. There were fully two hundred divided into two camps. What a history could have been written from the thrilling experiences of such a body of men!

They had gathered at the rendezvous to buy what supplies they needed and to dispose of their peltries. It was several weeks before the negotiations were over, when the assemblage broke up into smaller companies, which started for their destinations hundreds of miles apart.

Carson joined a party numbering about fifty who intended to trap near the headwaters of the Missouri. Hundreds of beavers had been taken in that section, but poor success went with the large band of which Carson was a member. That was bad enough, but they were in a neighborhood which, it may be said, was the very heart of the Blackfoot country, and those hostiles were never more active and vigilant in their warfare against the invaders.

The Blackfeet, or Satsika today, are the most westerly tribe of the Algonquin family of Indians, extending from the Hudson Bay to the Missouri and Yellowstone. They number over twelve thousand warriors about equally divided between Montana and British America. They have always been a daring and warlike people, and the early explorers of the Far West probably met with more trouble from them than from any other tribe on the continent.

Carson and his companions ran into difficulty at once. The Blackfeet seemed to swarm through the woods and sent in their treacherous shots from the most unexpected quarters. Whoever made the round of the traps in the morning was almost certain to be fired upon. Matters became so bad that after a time the trappers decided to leave the country. Accordingly, they made their way to the Big Snake River, where they went into quarters for the winter. Even there they were not safe from molestation at the hands of their old enemies, the Blackfeet.

One night, when there was no moon or stars, a band of warriors stole into camp and ran off about twenty of the best horses. This outrage touched the hunters in the most sensitive part of their nature, and the truth no sooner became known than they unanimously agreed that the animals not only should be recovered but the audacious aggressors should be chastised.

Twelve men were selected for the most difficult and dangerous task, and need we give the name of the youth who was made the leader?

With his usual promptness, Carson took the trail which was followed without trouble over the snow. The Blackfeet had reason to fear some such demonstration, and they hurried off with such speed that they were not overtaken until fifty miles from camp.

The situation was a novel one. The Indians had come to a halt, and the horses were grazing on the side of a hill where the wind had blown away the snow. The Blackfeet had on snowshoes, which gave them an advantage over the trappers. The latter galloped in the direction of their horses, the moment they caught sight of them. The Blackfeet fired at the trappers, who returned a scattering volley, but no one was hurt on either side. Then followed skirmishing and maneuvering for several minutes, without either party gaining advantage. Finally, the Blackfeet asked for a parley, to which the trappers assented.

In accordance with the usual custom, one of the Indians advanced to a point midway between the two parties and halted. At the same time, one of the trappers went forward, the rest of the men keeping their distance and watching them.

The Blackfoot opened business by what might be termed an apology, which was no more genuine than many made by his civilized brethren under somewhat similar circumstances. He expressed great surprise to learn that the horses belonged to their good friends, the trappers. They had supposed all along that they were the property of the Snake Indians, whom the Blackfeet considered it their duty to despoil on every suitable occasion.

This glaring misrepresentation did not deceive the man who was acting as spokesman for his side. By way of reply, he asked that, if such was the case, why had not the Blackfeet come forward on discovering their mistake, greeted their white brothers as friends, and returned their property to them?

The replies were evasive, and the hunters became convinced that the Indians were seeking to gain time for some sinister purpose, but a full parley having been agreed upon, both parties left their guns behind and advanced to where their representatives were holding their interview.

The Blackfeet still professed the most ardent friendship and, as an emphatic token of the same, produced the calumet and began smoking the pipe of peace. The tobacco having been lit, each took several whiffs and then passed it to his neighbor, who did the same until the round was completed. This solemn pledge of goodwill having been exchanged, the convention or peace congress was opened, as may be said, in due and ancient form.

Carson and his companions were distrustful from the start, though it was hard for them to decide the meaning of the prolonged negotiations, since no one could see what the Blackfeet were to gain by such a course. They may have hoped to deceive the hunters and throw them off their guard, but if such was the case, they failed.

First of all, the leading warriors indulged in several long speeches, which were without point, but what was said in reply could admit of no doubt as to its meaning. The trappers understood the Blackfoot tongue well enough to make their responses models in the way of brevity and force. They said that it was idle to talk of friendship or peace until the stolen property was returned to its owners. The Indians still attempted to postpone or evade, but the complainants were in no mood for trifling, and they repeated their declaration more positively than before.

The Blackfeet were much more numerous than the whites and, confident of their strength, began to bluster and to assert that whatever they did would be dictated by their own wishes and not by any fear of their visitors. Whether they desired to avoid a fight or not can only be conjectured, but they finally sent back to where the horses were tethered and caused five of the worst to be picked out and brought forward.

When the trappers inquired the meaning of this proceeding, the Indians said that it was the best they could do, and the hunters must be content.

This last insult was the spark which exploded the magazine. Instantly every white man ran for his gun, and the Blackfeet did the same. A few seconds after, they wheeled about, and the sanguinary fight began.

Kit Carson and a companion were the first to obtain their guns, and as a consequence they led the advance. Each selected a warrior who was partially hidden by the trunk of a tree. Carson was in the act of firing, when he observed that his friend was examining the lock of his gun all unmindful of the fact that one of the Blackfeet had leveled his weapon directly at his breast. On the instant, Kit changed his aim and shot the Blackfoot dead, thereby saving the life of his friend, who could not have escaped had the weapon of his adversary been discharged.

This act of chivalry on the part of Carson simply transferred the peril of his friend to himself, for the Indian whom he had selected for his target was carefully sighting at him, at the very moment the gun was discharged. Kit saw what was coming and bounded to one side in the hope of dodging the bullet. Quick as he was, however, he did not entirely succeed, though the act doubtless saved his life. The ball from the rifle of his adversary grazed his neck and buried itself in his shoulder, shattering the head of one of the bones.

Carson, though badly hurt, did not fall or retreat. On the contrary, he tried desperately to reload his gun but found it impossible to raise his arm. He was hors de combat beyond all question and bleeding so fast that his weakness compelled him to lie down on the ground while the conflict went on about him. The fight was very hot for a time, the result being what may be called a drawn battle, with the advantage inclining to the side of the Indians. The trappers fell back to the safest place that presented itself and went into camp. They dared not start a fire, for they knew it would bring an attack from the Indians, but wrapping their saddle blankets around them, they bore the intense cold as best they could.

The sufferings of Carson were great. His wounds continued bleeding and froze upon the dressings, which were of the most primitive character. And yet not once through those hours of anguish did he utter a word of complaint. Many a strong man would have cried out in his agony, but one might have sat within arm's length of the mountaineer without knowing he was hurt at all.

More than that, Carson took his part in the council which was held in the cold and darkness. The conclusion reached was that the party of trappers were not strong enough to pursue the Blackfeet, and the proper course to pursue was to rejoin the main body and report what had been done. It would then be time enough to decide upon their future action.

When this program was carried out, a larger party of hunters under the lead of an experienced mountaineer resumed the pursuit, but nothing could be found of the Blackfeet. They had utilized the grace allowed them so well that it was impossible to overtake or trace them, and the indignant trappers were obliged to submit to their loss.

The severe cold moderated, and as spring was close at hand, the hunters pushed their trapping operations along the Green and Snake Rivers, meeting with unbounded success. They gathered more peltries than they had dared to hope for and, when warm weather approached, went into quarters, where they remained until the following fall, a party of traders having brought them all the supplies they needed.

The rugged constitution of Carson and his temperate habits caused him speedily to recover from his severe wound. He again became the active, vigilant, keen-witted guide and hunter who was looked up to by all as the most consummate master of woodcraft that had ever been known in the west.

Such a large party as were gathered at the summer rendezvous was certain to include many varieties of people. The frank, brave,

and open-hearted; the sly and treacherous; the considerate and cour-
teous; the quarrelsome and overbearing—indeed the temperaments
of the individuals composing the company were as varied as it is
possible to imagine.

Among them was a powerful Frenchman known as Captain Shunan. He had won his title by hard fighting, possessed a magnificent
physique, was brave and skilled in the use of arms, and was the most
quarrelsome individual in camp. It is impossible to picture a more iras-
cible and disagreeable personage than Captain Shunan, who appeared
to spend all his spare time in trying to provoke quarrels with those
around him. Sometimes he succeeded, but more often his insolence
was submitted to by men as brave as he but who wished to avoid trouble with him.

The activity and strength of the Frenchman were so great that a
skillful pugilist would have found difficulty in handling him. The only
ground upon which he could be met with anything like fairness was
where firearms were used.

On one of these occasions, the bully became unbearable in his
behavior. He knocked down several weak and inoffensive persons
and swaggered back and forth through camp, boasting that he could
trounce any one there. In the midst of his bluster, Carson walked up
in front of him and said in a voice loud enough to be heard by those
around, "Captain Shunan, there are plenty here who can easily chas-
tise you, but they prefer to submit to your impudence for the sake of
peace; however, we have had enough, and now I notify you to stop at
once, or I shall kill you!"

These were astounding words, and as may be supposed, when
uttered by a man six inches shorter and many pounds lighter than the
blustering captain, they fairly took away his breath. Carson spoke in

his quiet, soft voice as though there was not the least cause for excitement, but those who knew him noted the flash of his clear, gray eye and understood his deadly earnestness.

Captain Shunan was infuriated by the words of Carson. As soon as he could recover himself, he turned about, and without speaking a word, walked to his quarters. Kit did not need be told what that meant. He did the same, walking to his own lodge, from which he speedily emerged holding a single-barrel pistol. He was so anxious to be on the ground in time that he caught up the first weapon that presented itself.

Almost at the same moment, Captain Shunan appeared with his rifle. Carson observed him, and though he could have secured without difficulty a similar weapon, he did not do so. He was willing to give his burly antagonist the advantage, if it should prove such. The other trappers, as may be supposed, watched the actions of the two men with breathless interest. The quarrel had taken such a course that they were convinced that one or the other of the combatants would be killed. Captain Shunan had been so loud in his boasts that he did not dare swallow the insult put on him by the fragile Kit Carson. Had he done so, he would have been hooted out of camp and probably lynched.

As for Kit, his courage was beyond suspicion. He feared no man and was sure to acquit himself creditably no matter in what circumstances he was placed. He was the most popular member of the large company, while his antagonist was the most detested, but the love of fair play was such that no one would interfere, no matter how great the need for doing so.

The duelists, as they may be called, mounted each his horse and, circling about the plain, speedily headed toward each other and dashed forward on a dead run. As they approached, they reined up and halted face to face within arm's length.

Looking his antagonist straight in the eye, Carson demanded, "Are you looking for me? Have you any business with me?"

"No," growled the savage Frenchman but, while the words were in his mouth, brought his rifle to his shoulder and, pointing it at the breast of Carson, pulled the trigger; but Kit expected some such treacherous act, and before the gun could be fired, he threw up his pistol and discharged it, as may be said, across the barrel of the leveled weapon.

The ball broke the forearm of Captain Shunan at the very moment he discharged his gun. The shock diverted the aim so that the bullet grazed his scalp, inflicting a trifling wound, but the combatants were so close that the powder of the rifle scorched the face of the mountaineer.

Captain Shunan had been badly worsted and was disabled for weeks afterward. He accepted his fate without complaint and was effectually cured of his overbearing manner toward his associates.

12

RUNNING THE BLOCKADE
The *Banshee*'s First Battle

BY THOMAS E. TAYLOR

It was nearly impossible to get through the tight net set up by the ships of the Union Navy. Their blockade of southern ports was strangling the Confederacy, slowly and as surely as the battles on land. There was little hope unless rebel ships could somehow get through.

Wilmington was the first port I attempted; in fact, with the exception of one run to Galveston, it was always our destination. It had many advantages. Though farthest from Nassau, it was nearest to headquarters at Richmond and from its situation was very difficult to watch effectively. It was here, moreover, that my firm had established its agency as soon as they had resolved to take up the blockade-running business. The town itself lies some sixteen miles up the

Cape Fear River, which falls into the ocean at a point where the coast forms the sharp salient angle from which the river takes its name. Off its mouth lies a delta, known as Smith's Island, which not only emphasizes the obnoxious formation of the coast but also divides the approach to the port into two widely separated channels, so that in order to guard the approach to it, a blockading force is compelled to divide into two squadrons.

At one entrance of the river lies Fort Fisher, a work so powerful that the blockaders, instead of lying in the estuary, were obliged to form roughly a semicircle out of range of its guns, and the falling away of the coast on either side of the entrance further increased the extent of ground they had to cover. The system they adopted in order to meet the difficulty was extremely well conceived, and did we not know to the contrary, it would have appeared complete enough to ensure the capture of every vessel so foolhardy as to attempt to enter or come out.

Across either entrance an inshore squadron was stationed at close intervals. In the daytime the steamers composing this squadron anchored, but at night they got underway and patrolled in touch with the flagship, which, as a rule, remained at anchor. Farther out there was a cordon of cruisers, and outside these again, detached gunboats keeping at such a distance from the coast as they calculated a runner coming out would traverse between the time of high water on Wilmington bar and sunrise, so that, if any blockade-runner coming out got through the two inner lines in the dark, she had every chance of being snapped up at daybreak by one of the third division.

Besides these special precautions for Wilmington, there must not be forgotten the ships engaged in the general service of the blockade, consisting, in addition to those detailed to watch Nassau and other bases, of free cruisers that patrolled the Gulf Stream. From this it will be seen readily that, from the moment the *Banshee* left Nassau harbor till she had passed the protecting forts at the mouth of Cape Fear River, she and those onboard her could never be safe from danger or free for a single hour from anxiety. But, although at this time the system was already fairly well developed, the Northerners had not yet enough ships at work to make it as effective as it afterward became.

The *Banshee*'s engines proved so unsatisfactory that under ordinary conditions nine or ten knots was all we could get out of her; she was therefore not permitted to run any avoidable risks, and to this I attribute her extraordinary success where better boats failed. As long as daylight lasted, a man was never out of the cross trees, and the moment a sail was seen, the *Banshee*'s stern was turned to it till it was dropped below the horizon. The lookout man, to quicken his eyes, had a dollar for every sail he sighted, and if it were seen from the deck first, he was fined five. This may appear excessive, but the importance in blockade running of seeing before you are seen is too great for any chance to be neglected, and it must be remembered that the pay of ordinary seamen for each round-trip in and out was from £50 to £60.

Following these tactics we crept noiselessly along the shores of the Bahamas, invisible in the darkness, and ran on unmolested for the first two days out, though our course was often interfered with by the necessity of avoiding hostile vessels; then came the anxious moment on the third, when, her position having been taken at noon to see if she was near enough to run under the guns of Fort Fisher before the following daybreak, it was found there was just time but none to spare for accidents or delay. Still, the danger of lying out another day so close to the blockaded port was very great, and rather than risk it, we resolved to keep straight on our course and chance being overtaken by daylight before we were under the fort.

Now the real excitement began, and nothing I have ever experienced can compare with it. Hunting, pigsticking, steeplechasing, big-game shooting, polo—I have done a little of each—all have their thrilling moments, but none can approach "running a blockade," and perhaps my readers can sympathize with my enthusiasm when they consider the dangers to be encountered, after three days of constant anxiety and little sleep, in threading our way through a swarm of blockaders and the accuracy required to hit in the nick of time the mouth of a river only half a mile wide, without lights and with a coastline so low and featureless that as a rule the first intimation we had of its nearness was the dim white line of the surf.

There were, of course, many different plans of getting in, but at this time the favorite dodge was to run up some fifteen or twenty miles to the north of Cape Fear, so as to round the northernmost of the blockaders instead of dashing right through the inner squadron, then to creep down close to the surf till the river was reached, and this was the course the Banshee intended to adopt.

We steamed cautiously on until nightfall; the night proved dark but dangerously clear and calm. No lights were allowed—not even a cigar; the engine-room hatchways were covered with tarpaulins at the risk of suffocating the unfortunate engineers and stokers in the almost insufferable atmosphere below. But it was absolutely imperative that not a glimmer of light should appear. Even the binnacle was covered, and the steersman had to see as much of the compass as he could through a conical aperture carried almost up to his eyes.

With everything thus in readiness, we steamed on in silence except for the stroke of the engines and the beat of the paddle floats, which in the calm of the night seemed distressingly loud; all hands were on deck, crouching behind the bulwarks; and we on the bridge, namely, the captain, the pilot, and I, were straining our eyes into the darkness. Presently, Burroughs made an uneasy movement—"Better get a cast of the lead, Captain," I heard him whisper. A muttered order down the engine-room tube was Steele's reply, and the *Banshee* slowed and then stopped. It was an anxious moment, while a dim figure stole into the forechains, for there is always a danger of steam blowing off when engines are unexpectedly stopped, and that would have been enough to betray our presence for miles around. In a minute or two came back the report, "Sixteen fathoms—sandy bottom with black specks." "We are not as far in as I thought, Captain," said Burroughs, "and we are too far to the southward. Port two points and go a little faster." As he explained, we must be well to the northward of the speckled bottom before it was safe to head for the shore, and away we went again. In about an hour, Burroughs quietly asked for another sounding. Again she was gently stopped, and this time he was satisfied. "Starboard and go ahead easy," was the order now, and as we crept in, not a sound was heard but that of the regular beat of the paddle floats still dangerously loud in spite of our snail's pace. Suddenly Burroughs gripped my arm—

"There's one of them, Mr. Taylor," he whispered, "on the starboard bow."

In vain I strained my eyes to where he pointed; not a thing could I see, but presently I heard Steele say beneath his breath, "All right, Burroughs, I see her. Starboard a little, steady!" was the order passed aft.

A moment afterward I could make out a long, low, black object on our starboard side, lying perfectly still. Would she see us? That was the question, but no, though we passed within a hundred yards of her, we were not discovered, and I breathed again. Not very long after we had dropped her, Burroughs whispered, "Steamer on the port bow."

And another cruiser was made out close to us.

"Hard-a-port," said Steele, and round she swung, bringing our friend upon our beam. Still unobserved, we crept quietly on, when all at once a third cruiser shaped herself out of the gloom right ahead and steaming slowly across our bows.

"Stop her," said Steele in a moment, and as we lay like dead, our enemy went on and disappeared in the darkness. It was clear there was a false reckoning somewhere and that, instead of rounding the head of the blockading line, we were passing through the very center of it. However, Burroughs was now of opinion that we must be inside the squadron and advocated making the land. So "slow ahead" we went again, until the low-lying coast and the surf line became dimly visible. Still we could not tell where we were, and as time was getting on alarmingly near dawn, the only thing to do was to creep down along the surf as close in and as fast as we dared. It was a great relief when we suddenly heard Burroughs say, "It's all right. I see the 'Big Hill'!"

The "Big Hill" was a hillock about as high as a full-grown oak tree, but it was the most prominent feature for miles on that dreary coast and served to tell us exactly how far we were from Fort Fisher. And fortunate it was for us, we were so near. Daylight was already breaking, and before we were opposite the fort, we could make out six or seven gunboats, which steamed rapidly toward us and angrily opened fire. Their shots were soon dropping close around us, an unpleasant sensation when you know you have several tons of gunpowder under your feet. To make matters worse, the North Breaker shoal now compelled us to haul off the shore and steam farther out. It began to look ugly for us, when all at once there was a flash from the shore, followed by a sound that came like music to our ears—that of a shell whirring over our heads. It was Fort Fisher, wide awake and warning the gunboats to keep their distance. With a parting broadside, they steamed sulkily out of range, and in half an hour, we were safely over the bar. A boat put off from the fort and then—well, it was the days of champagne cocktails, not whiskies and sodas—and one did not run a blockade every day. For my part, I was mightily proud of my first attempt and my baptism of fire. Blockade running seemed the pleasantest and most exhilarating of pastimes. I did not know then what a very serious business it could be.

13

DANIEL BOONE, CAPTIVE

BY FRANCIS L. HAWKS

Daniel Boone was an observant man. After all, he could survive by him-self for weeks on end in the thick forests and mountains of the young America. What he saw as a prisoner of Native Americans changed the way he viewed their culture forever.

Let me tell you of some of the curious customs which Boone noticed among the Indians during his captivity. He had a fine opportunity for observation, and I think these strange customs will interest you.

It is not wonderful that Indian men and women are so hardy; they are trained to it from their youth, and Boone tells us how they are trained. When a child is only eight years old, this training commences; he is then made to fast frequently half a day; when he is twelve, he is made to fast a whole day. During the time of this fast, the child is left alone, and his face is always blacked. This mode of hardening them is kept up with girls until they are fourteen—with boys until they are eighteen. At length, when a boy has reached the age of eighteen, his parents tell him that his education is completed and that he is old enough to be a man! His face is now to be blacked for the last time. He is taken to a solitary cabin far away from the village; his face is blacked, and then his father makes to him a speech of this kind: "My son, the Great Spirit has allowed you to live to see this day. We have all noticed your conduct since I first began to black your face. All people will understand whether you have followed your father's advice, and they will treat you accordingly. You must now remain here until I come after you."

The lad is then left alone. His father then goes off hunting, as though nothing had happened, and leaves his boy to bear his hunger as long it is possible for him to starve and live. At length he prepares a great feast, gathers his friends together, and then returns. The lad is then brought home, his face is washed in cold water, his hair is shaved, leaving nothing but the scalp-lock; they all commence eating, but the food of the lad is placed before him in a separate dish. This being over, a looking glass and a bag of paint are then presented to him. Then they all praise him for his firmness and tell him that he is a man.

Strange as it may seem, a boy is hardly ever known to break his fast when he is blacked this way for the last time. It is looked upon as something base, and they have a dread that the Great Spirit will punish them if they are disobedient to their parents.

Another curious habit which surprised Boone was that of continually changing names. A white man carries the same name from the cradle to the grave, but among these people it was very different. Their principal arms, as you know, are the tomahawk and scalping knife, and he who can take the greatest number of scalps is the greatest man. From time to time, as warriors would return from an attack upon some enemy, these new names would begin to be known. Each man would count the number of scalps he had taken, and a certain number entitled him to a new name in token of his bravery. It is not wonderful that they were revengeful, when they were stimulated by this sort of ambition. Besides this, they believed that he who took the scalp of a brave man received at once all his courage and other good qualities, and this made them more eager in their thirst for scalps. In this way, names of warriors were sometimes changed three or four times in a year.

Marriages in this tribe were conducted very decently. When a young warrior desired to marry, he assembled all his friends and named the woman whom he wished for his wife. His relations then received his present and took it to the parents of the young woman. If they were pleased with the proposal, they would dress the young woman in her gayest clothes and take her, with bundles of presents, to the friends of the warrior; then, if she pleased, she was to be married. There was no compulsion in the matter. If she was not satisfied, she had only to return his present to the young warrior, and this was considered a refusal.

Their mode of burying their dead was very much like that of all the Indians. The dead body was sometimes placed in a pen made of sticks and covered over with bark; sometimes it was placed in a grave and covered first with bark and then with dirt; and sometimes, especially in the case of the young, it was placed in a rude coffin and suspended from the top of a tree. This last was a common mode of infant burial, and the mother of the child would often be found, long after, standing under the tree and singing songs to her babe.

Boone witnessed, too, the mode in which war parties start off for war. The budget, or medicine bag, is first made up. This bag contains something belonging to each man of the party—something usually representing some animal, such as the skin of a snake, the tail of a buffalo, the horns of a buck, or the feathers of a bird. It is always regarded as a very sacred thing. The leader of the party goes before with this; the rest follow in single file. When they come to a stand, the budget is laid down in front, and no man may pass it without permission.

To keep their thoughts upon the enterprise in which they are engaged, no man is allowed to talk of women or his home. At night, when they encamp, the heart of whatever animal has been killed during the day is cut into small pieces and then burnt. During the burning no man is allowed to step across the fire but must always walk around it in the direction of the sun. When they spy the enemy and the attack is to be made, the war budget is opened. Each man takes out his budget, or totem, and fastens it to his body. After the fight, each man again returns his totem to the leader. They are all again tied up and given to the man who has taken the first scalp. He then leads the party in triumph home.

Boone had not long been a prisoner among them when a successful war party returned home and celebrated their victory. When the party came within a day's march of the village, a messenger was sent in to tell of their success. An order was instantly issued that every cabin should be swept clean, and the women as quickly commenced the work. When they had finished, the cabins were all inspected to see if they were in proper order.

Next day the party approached the village. They were all frightfully painted, and each man had a bunch of white feathers on his head. They were marching in single file, the chief of the party leading the way, bearing in one hand a branch of cedar laden with the scalps they had taken, and all chanting their war song.

As they entered the village, the chief led the way to the war pole, which stood in front of the council house. In this house the council fire was then burning. The waiter, or Etissu of the leader, then fixed two blocks of wood near the war pole and placed upon them a kind of ark, which was regarded by them as one of their most sacred things. The chief now ordered that all should sit down. He then inquired whether his cabin was prepared and everything made ready according to the custom of his fathers. They then rose up and commenced the war whoop, as they marched round the war pole. The ark was then taken and carried with great solemnity into the council house, and here the whole party remained three days and nights, separate from the rest of the people.

Their first business now was to wash themselves clean and sprinkle themselves with a mixture of bitter herbs. While they were thus in the house, all their female relatives, after having bathed and dressed themselves in their finest clothes, placed themselves in two lines facing each other on each side of the door. Here they continued singing a slow monotonous song all day and night; the song was kept up steadily for one minute, with intervals of ten minutes of dead silence between. About once in three hours, the chief would march out at the head of his warriors, raise the war whoop, and pass around the war pole, bearing his branch of cedar.

This was all that was done for the whole three days and nights. At length the purification was ended, and upon each of their cabins was placed a twig of the cedar with a fragment of the scalps fastened to it to satisfy the ghosts of their departed friends. All were now quiet as usual, except the leader of the party and his waiter, who kept up the purification three days and nights longer. When he had finished, the budget was hung up before his door for thirty or forty days, and from time to time, Indians of the party would be seen singing and dancing before it. When Boone asked the meaning of all this strange ceremony, they answered him by a word which he says meant holy.

As this party had brought in no prisoners, he did not now witness their horrible mode of torture. Before he left them, however, he saw enough of their awful cruelty in this way. Sometimes the poor prisoner would be tied to a stake, a pile of green wood placed around him, fire applied, and the poor wretch left to his horrible fate, while, amid shouts and yells, the Indians departed.

Sometimes he would be forced to run the gauntlet between two rows of Indians, each one striking at him with a club until he fell dead. Others would be fastened between two stakes, their arms and legs stretched to each of them, and then quickly burnt by a blazing fire. A common mode was to pinion the arms of the prisoner and then tie one end of a grapevine around his neck, while the other was fastened to the stake. A fire was then kindled, and the poor wretch would walk the circle; this gave the savages the comfort of seeing the poor creature literally roasting, while his agony was prolonged.

Perhaps this was the most popular mode, too, because all the women and children could join in it. They were there, with their bundles of dry sticks to keep the fire blazing and their long switches to beat the prisoner. Fearful that their victim might die too soon and thus escape their cruelty, the women would knead cakes of clay and put them on the skull of the poor sufferer, that the fire might not reach his brain and instantly kill him. As the poor frantic wretch would run round the circle, they would yell, dance, and sing and beat him with their switches, until he fell exhausted.

At other times, a poor prisoner would be tied and then scalding water would be poured upon him from time to time till he died. It was amazing, too, to see how the warriors would sometimes bear these tortures. Tied to the stake, they would chant their war songs, threaten their captors with the awful vengeance of their tribe, boast of how many of their nation they had scalped, and tell their tormentors how they might increase their torture. In the midst of the fire, they would stand unflinching and die without changing a muscle. It was their glory to die in this way; they felt that they disappointed their enemies in their last triumph.

~~~~~~

While Boone was with them, a noted warrior of one of the western tribes, with which the Shawanese were at war, was brought in as a captive. He was at once condemned, stripped, fastened to the stake, and the fire kindled. After suffering without flinching for a long time, he laughed at his captors and told them they did not know how to make an enemy eat fire. He called for a pipe and tobacco. Excited by his bravery, they gave it to him. He sat down on the burning coals and commenced smoking with the utmost composure; not a muscle of his countenance moved. Seeing this, one of his captors sprang forward and cried out that he was a true warrior. Though he had murdered many of their tribe, yet he should live, if the fire had not spoiled him. The fire had, however, well nigh done its work. With that, he declared that he was too brave a man to suffer any longer. He seized a toma-hawk and raised it over the head of the prisoner; still a muscle did not move. He did not even change his posture. The blow was given, and the brave warrior fell dead.

While among them, Boone also witnessed the mode in which the Shawanese make a treaty of peace. The warriors of both tribes between which the treaty was to be made met together first, ate and smoked in a friendly way, and then pledged themselves in a sacred drink called cussena. The Shawanese then waved large fans made of eagles' tails and danced. The other party, after this, chose six of their finest young men, painted them with white clay, and adorned their heads with swans' feathers; their leader was then placed on what was called the "consecrated seat." After this they all commenced dancing and singing their song of peace. They danced first in a bending posture; then stood upright, still dancing and bearing in their right hands their fans, while in their left they carried a calabash tied to a stick about a foot long and with this continually beat their breasts. During all this, some added to the noise by rattling pebbles in a gourd. This being over, the peace was concluded. It was an act of great solemnity, and no warrior was considered as well trained who did not know how to join in every part of it.

Many other strange things were seen by Boone among these people, but these are enough to show you that he was among a strange people, with habits very unlike his own. It is not wonderful that he sighed to escape, when he looked upon their horrid tortures. Independently of his love for Boonesborough, he did not know but that such tortures might be his at any moment when they became excited. Fortunately, as we have seen, he did escape, and we will now go on with his story.

14

FROZEN

BY A. W. GREELY

Unforgiving ice, unfathomable temperatures, and an unwelcoming Artic often killed anyone rash enough to try to pass through the Bering Sea. The chances of survival for a crew of an unlucky ship caught in the ice were slim to none. Rescue from afar was impossible when travel was perilous, and sometimes a good day over the ice was measured in yards, not miles.

After a long and dangerous besetment in the polar ice to the north of Bering Strait, the American whaling ship *Navrach* was abandoned August 14, 1897. Twenty-one of her seamen perished on the moving ice pack of the Arctic Ocean in their efforts to reach land across the drifting ice. Captain Whitesides with his brave wife and six of the crew entrusted their fortunes to the sea and almost miraculously escaped by using a canvas boat, which was alternately hauled across the floes and launched where open water was reached.

On landing at Copper Island, off the coast of Asia, the party was in danger of death through starvation when rescued by the United States revenue cutter *Bear*, which chanced to touch at that point. The news of the loss of the *Navrach* and the reports of very bad ice conditions in the Arctic Ocean created great alarm in the United States, owing to the fact that no less than eight whaleships with crews of 265 men were missing that autumn. Appeals for prompt aid were made to the president of the United States by the members of the chamber of commerce of San Francisco and by other interested persons.

Refitting in three weeks' time, the United States revenue cutter *Bear*, manned by volunteers under Captain Francis Tuttle, R.C.S., sailed from Seattle on November 27, 1897, and wintered at Unalaska. The story of the relief of the whalers, happily and heroically accomplished by this expedition, forms the substance of this sketch.

From the character of the duties of the revenue-cutter service, its officers and men are not favored with such frequent opportunities for adventurous deeds as are those of the army and of the navy, but whenever occasion has arisen, they have ever shown those qualities of courage, self-sacrifice, and devotion which go far to inspire heroic action.

As the period of navigation had already passed for the northern seas, the *Bear* was to winter at Dutch Harbor, Unalaska, communicating with the distressed seamen by an overland expedition, which should aid and encourage them until the spring navigation should make their rescue possible. If practicable the land party was to be set ashore on the north side of Norton Sound, near Cape Nome, which would require some eight hundred miles of sledge travel at the least.

From the eager volunteers for this arduous and novel service, Captain Tuttle approved of Lieutenant D. H. Jarvis, commanding; Lieutenant E. P. Bertholf; and Dr. S. J. McCall, with a reindeer driver, Koltchoff.

With dauntless courage and skill, Captain Tuttle skirted the growing ice fields of the Bering Sea, seeking in vain a lead through which he could reach Norton Sound, but it was finally clear that the ship could not be put north of Nunavak Island without danger of her loss as well as sealing the fate of the whalers. The winter darkness, storm conditions, an uncharted coast, and drifting ice forced him to land the party as far north of Kuskowim Bay as could be safely reached. Fortunately, on December 16, a wild, stormy day, the shore ice drifted far enough seaward to enable a hasty landing to be made near Cape Vancouver.

There were forebodings of evil in attempting this winter journey now stretched out to fifteen hundred miles, under conditions which increased its perils. But with the splendid confidence and magnificent vitality of youth, the fearless revenue officers hailed with satisfaction the beginning of their arduous journey of mercy and relief.

South of the landing was a deserted village, but fortunately a few miles to the north, near Cape Vancouver, was the still-occupied Eskimo settlement of Tunanak. Ashore, Jarvis found himself in difficulty, for the snow-free rocky beach was impassable for his sledges, while he was without boats. Here, as elsewhere on this journey, the native aid was obtained on which he had counted from the knowledge of the kindly feelings of these children of the ice that he had gained in his past cruises in the Bering Sea region.

As there was now an ice-free channel along the coast, the Eskimo sea hunters deftly lashed together in pairs their kayaks (skin canoes), catamaran fashion, and piled thereon helter-skelter the various supplies. Jarvis and Bertholf watched this cargo stowing with great anxiety, not unmingled with doubt as to the outcome of the voyage. Following the progress of the kayaks and shouting advice and encouragement from the seashore, they were dismayed to see now and then a breaking wave threaten to overwhelm the boats and to find that the short sea trip had ruined much of the precious flour and indispensable hard bread.

Overhauling his cumbersome, heavy sledges and inspecting his few unsuitable dogs, he knew that they could never do all the work required. Fortunately he found a half-breed trader, Alexis, who agreed to furnish dogs, sledges, and serve as a guide to the party as far as the army post at Saint Michael. As the half-breed knew the short shore route and was familiar with the location and supplies of the succession of native villages, this enabled them to drop much of their heavy baggage and travel light. Their outfit was carefully selected, consisting of sleeping bags, changes of clothing, camp stoves, rifles, ammunition, axes, and a small supply of food.

Their three native sledges were open box frames, ten feet by two in size and eighteen inches high, resting on wooden runners a foot high. Tough, pliant lashings of walrus hide bound together with the utmost tightness the frame and the runners. This method of construction, in which not a bit of iron enters, avoids rigidity and thus gives a flexibility and life to the sledge, which enables it to withstand shocks and endure hard usage, which would soon break a solid frame into pieces. A cargo cover of light canvas not only closely fits the bottom and sides of the box frame but overlaps the top. When the cargo cover is neatly hauled taut and is properly lashed to the sides of the sledge the load, if it has been snugly packed, it is secure from accidents. Its compact mass is equally safe from thievish dogs, from the penetrating drift of the fierce blizzards, and from dangers of loss through jolts or capsizings.

Of a single piece for each dog, the harness used by the natives is of sealskin; the half-breeds often make it of light canvas, not only as better suited to the work but especially for its quality of noneatableness, which is a vital factor during days of dog famine on long journeys. The harness is collar-shaped with three long bands; the collar slips over the dog's head and one band extends to the rear over the animal's back. The other bands pass downward between the dog's legs and, triced up on each side, are fastened permanently to the back band, where there is also attached a drag thong or pulling trace about two feet long. In harnessing, the three loops described are slipped respectively over the head and legs of the dog.

The animals are secured in pairs to the long draught rope of the sledge by the Alaskan pioneers, who much prefer this method to the old plan of the natives, whereby the dogs were strung out in single file. With the dogs in couples, the draught line is shorter, so that the better-controlled animals will haul a larger load.

In the first day's journey, they crossed a mountain range two thousand feet high, and in making the descent of the precipitous northern slope, Jarvis records a sledging expedient almost unique in sledge travel. The four Eskimo drivers detached the dogs from the sledge and, winding around the runners small chains so as to sink in the deep snow and impede their progress, prepared to coast down the mountain. Two men secured themselves firmly on each sledge, and when once started, the descent was so steep that the sledges attained a fearful speed, which brought them almost breathless to the bottom of the range in ten minutes.

Jarvis describes in graphic language the trying task of feeding the always-famished, wolflike dogs:

They are ever hungry, and when one appears with an armful of dried fish, in their eagerness to get a stray mouthful the dogs crowd around in a fighting, jumping mass, which makes it difficult to keep one's balance. After throwing a fish to each dog, it takes all of us with clubs to keep off the larger fellows and to see that the weaker ones keep and eat their share. When being fed they are like wild animals—snarl, bite, and fight continually until everything is eaten.

As the dogs, worn out by the hard journey, could not be replaced by fresh ones at the Eskimo colony of Ki-yi-lieng, Bertholf and Koltchoff waited there to bring them up later, while Jarvis and McCall pushed on, marching across the Yukon delta in temperatures below zero daily. They found the natives of this alluvial region wretchedly poor and illy protected against the bitter cold. To the eye they were a motley crowd, as they had levied tribute for clothing on the birds of the air, the beasts of the tundra, the fish of the river, and the game of the sea. There were trousers and heavy boots from the seal, inner jackets of the breasts of the wild geese, fur ornamentation of the arctic fox, and the poorer Eskimos even made boots, when seal were lacking, from the tanned skin of the Yukon salmon.

With all their dire poverty, they were not unmindful of their duty to strangers and always offered the shelter of the *khazeem* (a hut built for general use by the unmarried men, from which women are rigidly excluded). His sense of fastidiousness had not yet left Jarvis, who surprised the Eskimos by tenting in the midwinter cold rather than endure the tortures of the stifling khazeem, which to the natives was a place of comfort and pleasure. Of this half-underground hut, Jarvis says in part,

The sides are of driftwood filled in with brush. The roof is ingeniously made by laying logs along the sides and lashing them thereto with walrus thongs. Two logs notched on the ends to fit securely are then laid across the first logs on opposite sides but a little farther in toward the center. This method is repeated until a sort of arch is formed, which is filled in with earth-covered brush, leaving a small hole in the center of the roof. Other drift-wood, split in rough slabs, forms the floor, leaving an entrance space about two feet square. From this hole in the floor, which is always several feet below the level of the surrounding ground, an entrance passage has been dug out large enough for a man to crawl through it into the main earth-floored room. Over the entrance opening is hung a skin to keep out the air, while the roof opening is covered with the thin, translucent, dried intes-tines of the seal or walrus, which gives faint light during the day.

In the khazeem the animal heat from the bodies of the natives, with that from seal-oil lamps, raises the temperature so high that the men sit around with the upper part of the body entirely naked. The only ventilation is through a small hole in the roof, invariably closed at night in cold weather. The con-dition of the air can be better imagined than described, with fifteen or twenty natives sleeping inside the small room.

The culmination of danger and suffering on the march in the delta journey was at Pikmiktellik, when they strayed from the trail and nearly perished in a violent storm. Almost as by miracle, they stag-gered by chance into the village long after dark, so exhausted that, without strength to put up their tent, they gladly occupied the dreaded khazeem.

Twelve days brought them to Saint Michael, where they were given cordial and humane aid from Colonel (now General) George M. Randall, United States Army, and the agents of the Alaska Com-mercial and North American Trading Companies. Without such help Jarvis must have failed. The feet of his dogs were worn bare by rapid, rough travel of 375 miles, the rubber-covered, goatskin sleeping bags were cold and heavy, which in bitterer weather would be actually dangerous. Deerskin clothing and fresh dogs were necessary for rapid travel, with light loads on which final success depended.

Leaving orders for Bertholf, yet far behind, to bring up relief supplies from Unalaklik to Cape Blossom by crossing the divide at the head of Norton Bay, Jarvis and McCall pushed ahead on January 1, 1898. The third day out, they met a native woman traveling south on snowshoes, who told them that she was with her husband and Mate Tilton of the Belvedere; the two parties had passed each other, unseen, on trails three hundred feet apart. Tilton brought news even worse than had been expected. Three ships had been crushed by the ice pack, two losing all their provisions, while five other ships were frozen up in the ocean ice. As the worn-out mate went south, Jarvis pushed on with new energy, realizing the great need ahead.

Severe storms and deep snow made travel very slow, and at times the runners sank so deep that the body of the sledge dragged, while the dogs were almost buried in their efforts to struggle on. They soon realized that actual arctic travel is far from being like the usual pictures of dog sledging. Instead of frisky dogs with tails curled over their backs, with drivers comfortably seated on the sledge, cracking a whip at the flying team, snarling dogs and worn-out men tramped slowly and silently through the unbroken snow.

It very rarely occurs that there is either a beaten or a marked trail, so the lead is taken by a man who keeps in advance, picking out the best road, while his comrades are hard at work lifting the sledge over bad places or keeping it from capsizing. The king dogs, who lead the way and set the pace, never stray from the broken path, save in rare instances of sighting tempting game, but follow exactly the trail breaker. One day Jarvis came to fresh, deep snow, where it took all four men to break a way for the sledge, and when they themselves were worn out, they had the misery of seeing their utterly exhausted dogs lie down on the trail, indifferent equally to the urging voice or the cutting whip. That wretched night the party had to make its camp in the open instead of at one of the native huts, which were always in view.

The dog teams were sent back from the Swedish mission, Golovin Bay, where reindeer were available. Of this new and unusual method of travel, Jarvis, who drove a single-deer sledge, says,

All hands must be ready at the same time when starting a deer train. As soon as the other animals see the head team start, they are off with a jump, and for a short time, they keep up a very high rate of speed. If one is not quick in jumping and in holding onto his sledge, he is likely either to lose his team or be dragged bodily along.

The deer is harnessed with a well-fitting collar of two flat pieces of wood, from which short traces go back to a breast-plate or single-tree under the body. From this a single trace, protected by soft fur to prevent chafing, runs back to the sledge. A single line made fast to the halter is used for guiding and, kept slack, is only pulled to guide or stop the deer. A hard pull brings the weight of the sledge on the head of the deer and generally brings him to a stop. No whip is used, for the timid deer becomes easily frightened and then is hard to control and quiet down. The low, wide sledges with broad runners are hard to pack so as to secure and protect the load.

As the dogs naturally attack the deer, it was henceforth necessary to stop outside the Eskimo villages, unharness the animals, and send them to pasture on the nearest beds of reindeer moss.

Jarvis thus relates his straying during a violent blizzard:

Soon after dark my deer wandered from the trail, became entan-
gled in driftwood on the beach, and finally wound up by running
the sledge full speed against a stump, breaking the harness, dragging the line from my hand, and disappearing in the darkness and
flying snow. It was impossible to see ten yards ahead, and it would
be reckless to start off alone, for the others were in advance, and
I might wander about all night, become exhausted, and perhaps
freeze. I had nothing to eat, but righting the sledge I got out my
sleeping bag in its lee and made myself as comfortable as possible.

His comrades were greatly alarmed as a reindeer dashed by them and,
fearing disaster, hastened back on the trail, which, although followed
with difficulty on account of the blinding snow, brought them to the
lieutenant still unharmed.

If the relief expedition was to be of use to the shipwrecked men, it
was important that food should be carried north. As this was impossible by sledge, it was evident that the sole method was to carry meat
on the hoof. The sole sources of supply consisted of two herds of
reindeer, at Teller and at Cape Prince of Wales. If these herds could
be purchased and if the services of skilled herders could be obtained
and the herd could be driven such a long distance, then the whalers
could be saved. To these three problems, Jarvis now bent his powers
of persuasion and of administrative ability, feeling that lives depended
on the outcome and that he must not fail.

The reindeer belonged in part to an Eskimo, Artisarlook, and in
part to the American Missionary Society, under the control and man-
agement of Mr. H. W. Lopp. Without the assent and active aid of these
two men, the proposed action would be impossible. Would he be able

to persuade these men to give him their entire plant and leave themselves destitute for men whom they had never seen and knew of only to hold them in fear? Would they consider the plan practicable, and would they leave their families and go on the arctic trail in the midst of an Alaskan winter? If they thought it a bounden duty, what was to happen to their families during their absence? Day after day these questions rose in the lieutenant's mind to his great disquietude.

With Jarvis and Bertholf, there was the stimulus of the esprit de corps, the honor of the service, always acting as a spur to their heroic labors, while in the case of Dr. McCall, there was also that sense of personal devotion to the relief of suffering that inspires the medical profession as a whole.

On January 19 Jarvis reached the house of Artisarlook, when he "almost shrank from the task." From this untaught, semicivilized native, wrestling for a bare subsistence with harsh, forbidding nature, what favor could be expected? The starving men were of an alien race and of that class from which too often his own people had reaped degradation, suffered outrage, and endured wrongs too grievous to be ignored or forgotten. To relieve these men, Artisarlook must voluntarily loan his entire herd of reindeer without certainty of replacement. He must leave behind him his wife, unprotected and subject to the vicissitudes of an arctic environment. He must also endure the hardships and sufferings incident to a midwinter drive, in the coldest month of the year, of reindeer across a country unknown to him—a desperate venture that might cost him his life. Altruistic souls of the civilized world might make such sacrifices, but would this Alaskan Eskimo?

Of the crisis Jarvis writes,

I almost shrank from the task. He and his wife were old friends, but how to induce them to give up their deer—their absolute property—and how to convince them that the government would return an equal number at some future time was quite another matter. Besides, he and the natives gathered about him were dependent on the herd for food and clothing. If I took the deer and Artisarlook away, these people were likely to starve unless some other arrangements were made for their living.

I explained carefully what the deer were wanted for, that he must let me have the deer of his own free will and trust to the government for an ample reward and the return of an equal number of deer.

Artisarlook and his wife, Mary, held a long and solemn consultation and finally explained their situation. They were sorry for the white men at Point Barrow, and they were glad to be able to help them. They would let me have their deer, 133 in number, which represented their all, if I would be directly responsible for them.

I had dreaded this interview for fear that Artisarlook might refuse, but his nobility of character could have no better exposition than the fact that he was willing to give up his property, leave his family, and go eight hundred miles to help white men in distress, under a simple promise that his property should be returned to him.

Has there ever been a finer instance of the full faith of man in brother man than is shown in this simple pact, by word of mouth, under the dark, gloomy sky of an Alaskan midwinter? Far from the business marts of crowded cities, in the free open of broad expanses of country, there are often similar instances of man's trusting generosity and of personal self-sacrifice but more often between those of kindred race than between the civilized man and the aborigine.

Giving written orders on the traders to tide over the winter for the natives, Jarvis pushed on, leaving Artisarlook and his herders to follow with the deer. Meantime the lieutenant had adopted the native garb, saying, "I had determined to do as the people who lived in the country did—to dress, travel, and live as they did and if necessary to eat the same food. I found the only way to get along was to conform to the customs of those who had solved many of the problems of existence in the arctic climate." His clothing consisted of close-fitting deerskin trousers and socks, with hair next to the skin; deerskin boots, hair out, with heavy sealskin soles; two deerskin shirts, one with hair out and the other with hair toward the skin; close hoods, with fringing wolfskin; and mittens, the whole weighing only about ten pounds. In stormy weather he wore an outer shirt and overalls of drilling, which kept the drifting snow from filling up and freezing in a mass the hair of the deerskins.

The five days' travel to the Teller reindeer station, near Cape Prince of Wales, were filled with most bitter experiences. The temperature fell to seventy-two degrees below freezing; the sea ice over which they traveled became of almost incredible roughness, while fearful blizzards sprang up. With increasing northing the days became shorter, and the exhausted reindeer had to be replaced by dogs. Much of the travel was in darkness, with resultant capsizings of sledges, frequent falls, and many bodily bruises. Of one critical situation, he reports,

The heavy sledge was continually capsizing in the rough ice. About eight o'clock at night, I was completely played out and quite willing to camp. But Artisarlook said, "No!" that it was too cold to camp without wood (they depended on driftwood for their fires) and that the ice-foot along the land was in danger of breaking off the shore at any minute. In the darkness I stepped through an ice crack, and my leg to the knee was immediately one mass of ice. Urging the dogs, we dragged along till midnight to a hut that Artisarlook had before mentioned. A horrible place, no palace could have been more welcome. Fifteen people were already sleeping in the hut, the most filthy I saw in Alaska, only ten by twelve feet in size and five feet high. Too tired to care for the filth, too tired even to eat, I was satisfied to take off my wet clothing, crawl into my bag, and to sleep.

Failure to find the house and to have his frozen clothing dried would have cost the lieutenant his life.

On arriving at Teller station, he had a new problem to solve—to win over the agent. He had high hopes, for although this representative of a missionary society was living on the outer edge of the world, yet he had become familiar with the vicissitudes of the frontier and, from vocation and through his associations, was readily moved to acts of humanity. Jarvis set forth the situation to Mr. W. T. Lopp, the superintendent, adding that he considered Lopp's personal services to be indispensable, as he knew the country, was familiar with the customs and characteristics of the natives, and was expert in handling deer. Lopp replied that "the reindeer had been builded on by his people as their wealth and support and to lose them would make a break in the work that could not be repaired. Still, in the interests of humanity, he would give them all, explain the case to the Eskimos, and induce them to give their deer also [aggregating about three hundred]." Lopp also gave his own knowledge, influence, and personal service, his wife, with a noble disregard for her own comfort and safety at being left alone with the natives, "urging him to go, believing it to be his duty."

It is needless to recite in detail the trials and troubles that daily arose in driving across trackless tundras (the swampy, moss-covered plains), in the darkness of midwinter, this great herd of more than four hundred timid, intractable reindeer. Throughout the eight hundred miles of travel, the reindeer drivers had to carefully avoid the immediate neighborhood of Eskimo villages for fear of the ravenous, attacking dogs, who, however, on one occasion succeeded in stampeding the whole herd. For days at a time, the herders were at their wits' ends to guard the deer against gaunt packs of ravenous wolves, who kept on their trail and, despite their utmost vigilance, succeeded in killing and maiming several deer. A triumphal but venturesome feat of Lopp's was the driving of the herd across the sea floes of the broad expanse of Kotzebue Sound, thus saving 150 miles of land travel and two weeks of valuable time.

While there were eight skilled herders, Lapps and Eskimos, the most effective work was that done by a little Lapp deer dog, who circled around the herd when on the march to prevent the deer from straying. If a deer started from the main herd, the dog was at once on his trail, snapping at his heels and turning him toward the others. Very few deer strayed or were lost, and 362 were brought to Barrow in good condition.

Traveling in advance, following the shoreline by dog sledge, Jarvis and McCall were welcomed with warm generosity, even by the most forlorn and wretched Eskimos, who asked them into their huts, cared for their dogs, dried their clothes, and did all possible for their safety and comfort. The relief party, however, suffered much from the begging demands of almost-starving natives, from the loss of straying dogs and the desertion of several unreliable native employees. They were quite at the end of their food when they reached, at Cape Krusenstern, their depot. This had been brought up across country from Unalaklik through the great energy and indomitable courage of Bertholf, whose journey and sufferings were no less striking than those of his comrades.

Inexpressible was the joy of the party when, fifty miles south of Point Barrow, the masts of the *Belvedere*, a whaleship fast in the ice, were sighted. Four days later they were at the point, their marvelous journey of 1,800 miles ended and their coming welcomed as a providential relief.

They found conditions frightful as regards the shelter, health, and sanitation of the shipwrecked whalers. Three ships had been lost, and another was ice-beset beyond power of saving. The captains of the wrecked ships had abandoned the care and control of their men as to quarters, clothing, food, and general welfare. Provisions were very short, and the seamen were depending on their safety through successful hunting among the caribou herds in the neighborhood of Point Barrow, which were rapidly disappearing.

Jarvis at once took charge of the situation. Dr. McCall found the seamen's quarters in a most horrible condition, its single window giving but a feeble glimmer of light at midday and its ventilation confined to the few air draughts through cracks in the walls. Eighty seamen occupied for sleeping, shelter, and cooking a single room twenty by fifty feet in size, wherein they were so badly crowded that there was scarcely room for all to stand when out of their bunks together. Moisture was continually dropping from the inner ceiling and walls, which were covered with frost. Their bedding was never dry, sooty grease was coated over all things, and no place was free from great accumulations of filth and its accompaniments. The whalers were "scarcely recognizable as white men," and large numbers of them would without doubt have perished of disease but for the opportune arrival of the relief party.

Order, cleanliness, decency, and discipline were instituted; the men were distributed in light, airy rooms; their clothing was washed and renovated and intercourse with the natives prohibited. By inspection, precept, and command, the general health greatly improved. At every opportunity individual men were sent south by occasional sledge parties. Hunting was systematized, but it failed to produce enough food for the suffering whalers. Recourse was then had to the herds driven north by Lopp and Artisarlook, and with the slaughter of nearly two hundred reindeer, suitable quantities of fresh meat were issued. Out of 275 whalers, only 1 died of disease. Captain Tuttle by daring seamanship reached Icy Cape July 22, 1898, and took onboard the *Bear* about a hundred men whose ships were lost.

With generous feeling Jarvis gives credit in his report to the whaling agent, A. C. Brower, and to "the goodness and help of the natives [Eskimos], who denied themselves to save the white people," subordinating with true heroic modesty his work to all others.

Gold and commerce have peopled the barren Alaskan wastes, which were the scenes of this adventurous journey, with its unique equipment and its cosmopolitan personnel of Eskimo, Lapp, and American.

While these men worked not for fame but for the lives of brother men, yet in Alaskan annals should stand forever recorded the heroic deeds and unselfish acts of Jarvis and McCall, of Bertholf and Lopp, and of that man among men—Eskimo Artisarlook.

15

HORROR IN GALVESTON

BY JOHN COULTER

The damage and destruction of the hurricane that virtually erased the growing and prosperous young city of Galveston from the map brought the attention of the entire country to the Texas coast. What happened next kept it there.

The frightful West Indian hurricane which descended upon the beautiful, prosperous, and progressive but ill-fated city of Galveston on Saturday, September 8, 1900, causing the loss of many thousands of lives and the destruction of millions of dollars' worth of property, and then ravaged central and western Texas, killing several hundred people and inflicting damage which cost millions to repair, has had no parallel in history.

When the gale approached the island upon which Galveston is situated, it lashed the waves of the Gulf of Mexico into a tremendous fury, causing them to rise to all but mountain height, and then it was that, combining their forces, the wind and water pounced upon their prey.

In the short space of four hours, the entire site of the city was covered by angry waters, while the gale blew at the rate of one hundred miles an hour; business houses, public buildings, churches, residences, charitable institutions, and all other structures gave way before the pressure of the wind and the fierce onslaught of the raging flood, and those which did not crumble altogether were so injured, in the majority of cases, that they were torn down.

Such a night of horror as the unfortunate inhabitants were compelled to pass has fallen to the lot of few since the records of history were first opened. In the early evening, when the water first began to invade Galveston Island, the people residing along the beach and near it fled in fear from their homes and sought the highest points in the city as places of refuge, taking nothing but the smaller articles in their houses with them. On and on crawled the flood, until darkness had set in and then, as though possessed of a fiendish vindictiveness, hastened its speed and poured over the surface of the town, completely submerging it—covering the most elevated ground to a depth of five feet and the lower portions ten and twelve feet.

The hurricane was equally malignant, if not more fiendish and cruel, and tore great buildings and beautiful homes to pieces with evident delight, scattering the debris far and wide; telegraph and telephone lines were thrown down; railway tracks and bridges—the latter connecting the island and city with the mainland—torn up; and the mighty, tangled mass of wires, bricks, sections of roofs, sidewalks, fences, and other things hurled into the main thoroughfares and cross streets, rendering it impossible for pedestrians to make their way along for many days after the waters and gale had subsided.

Forty thousand people—men, women, and children—cowered in terror for eight long hours, the intense blackness of the night; the swishing and lapping of the waves; the demoniac howling and shrieking of the wind; and the indescribable and awful crashing, tearing, and rending, as the houses, hundreds at a time, were wrecked and shattered, ever sounding in their ears. Often, too, the friendly shelter where families had taken refuge would be swept away, plunging scores and scores of helpless ones into the mad current which flowed through every street of the town, and fathers and mothers were compelled to undergo the agony of seeing their children drown, with no possibility of rescue; husbands lost their wives and wives their husbands, and the elements were only merciful when they destroyed an entire family at once.

All during that fearful night of Saturday until the gray and gloomy dawn of Sunday broke upon the sorrow-stricken city, the entire population of Galveston stood face to face with grim death in its most horrible shapes; they could not hope for anything more than the vengeance of the hurricane, and as they realized that with every passing moment souls were being hurried into eternity, is it at all wonderful that, after the strain was over and all danger gone, reason should finally be unseated and men and women break into the unmeaning gaiety of the maniac?

Not one inhabitant of Galveston old enough to realize the situation had any idea other than that death was to be the fate of all before another day appeared, and when this long and weary suspense, to which was added the chill of the night and the growing pangs of hunger, was at last broken by the first gleams of the light of the Sabbath morn, the latter was not entirely welcome, for the face of the sun was hidden by morose and ugly clouds, from which dripped, at dreary intervals, cold and gusty showers.

Thousands were swallowed up during the darkness and their bodies either mangled and mutilated by the wreckage which had been tossed everywhere, left to decompose in the slimy ooze deposited by the flood, or forced to follow the waves in their sullen retirement to the waters of the gulf.

Dejection and despondency succeeded fright; the majority of the businessmen of the city had suffered such losses that they were overcome by apathy; nearly all the homes of the people were in ruins; the streets were impassable, and the dead lay thickly on every side; all telegraph and telephone wires were down, and as miles and miles of railroad track had disappeared and the bridges carried away, there was absolutely no means of communication with the outer world, except by boat. The strange spectacle was then presented of the richest city of its size in the richest country in the world lying prostrate, helpless and hopeless, a prey to ghouls, vultures, harpies, thieves, thugs, and outlaws of every sort; its people starving, and the putrid bodies of its dead breeding pestilence.

The city of Galveston is situated on the extreme east end of the island of Galveston. It is six square miles in area, its present limits being the limits of the original corporation and the boundaries of the land purchased from the republic of Texas by Colonel Menard in 1838 for the sum of $50,000. Colonel Menard associated with himself several others, who formed a town site company with a capital of $1,000,000. The city of Galveston was platted on April 20, 1838, and seven days later the lots were put on the market. The streets of Galveston are numbered from one to fifty-seven across the island from north to south, and the avenues are known by the letters of the alphabet, extending east and west lengthwise of the island.

The founders of the city donated to the public every tenth block through the center of the city from east to west for public parks. They also gave three sites for public markets and set aside one entire block for a college, three blocks for a girls' seminary, and gave to every Christian denomination a valuable site for a church.

The growth of the city in population was slow until after the war of the rebellion. It is a remarkable fact that for the population Galveston does double the amount of business of any city in America. The population in 1890 was 30,000, showing an increase of over 400 percent in thirty years. At the time of the disaster, the population was estimated at 40,000.

Galveston has over two miles of completed wharfs along the bay front and others under construction, all of which are equipped with modern appliances. The Galveston Wharf Company, which owns practically all the wharfage, has expended millions during the last five years for improvements in the way of elevators and facilities for handling grain and cotton. During the cotton season, September 1 to March 31 inclusive, large oceangoing craft line the wharves, often thirty or more steamers and as many large sailing vessels being accommodated at one time, besides the numerous smaller vessels and sailing craft doing a coastwise trade.

Manufacturing is one of the chief supports of the city. In this branch of industry, Galveston leads any city in the state of Texas by 50 percent in number and more than 100 percent in capital employed and product turned out. Of factories the city has 306, employing a capital aggregating $10,886,900, with an output of $12,000,000 a year.

The jetty construction forms one of the chief features of its commercial advantages. The construction began in 1885, progressing slowly for five years, when the desire of the citizens for a first-class harbor led to the formation of a permanent committee, which succeeded in getting a bill through Congress authorizing an expenditure of $6,200,000 on the harbor. The bill provided that there should be two parallel stone jetties extending nearly six miles out into the gulf, one from the east point of Galveston Island, the other from the west point of Bolivar Peninsula. The jetties are fifty feet wide at the bottom and slope gradually to five feet above mean low tide and are thirty-five feet wide at the top, with a railroad track running their entire length, which railroad is the property of the federal government. The immediate effect of early construction of the jetties was to remove the inner bar, which formerly had thirteen feet of water over it, and which now has over twenty-one feet of water.

The principal business street of Galveston is the Strand, which is of made land 150 feet from the water of the bay, in the extreme northern end of the city. Besides being the principal port of Texas, Galveston is the financial center of the state, and some of the largest business houses in Texas have their offices in the Strand.

Concisely put and with no waste of words, the following facts comprise the history of the unfortunate city:

1. It is the richest city of its size in the United States.
2. Is the largest and most extensively commercial city of Texas.
3. Is the gateway of an enormous trade, situated as it is between the great west granaries and Europe.
4. Lies two miles from the northeast corner of the island of Galveston.
5. Is a port of entry and the principal seaport of the state.
6. Its harbor is the best, not only on the coastline of Texas but also on the entire gulf coast from the mouth of the Mississippi to the Rio Grande.
7. Is the nearest and most accessible first-class seaport for the states of Texas, Kansas, New Mexico, and Colorado; the Indian

Territory and the territory of Arizona; and parts of the states and territories adjoining those just mentioned.

8. Is today the gulf terminus of most of the great railway systems entering Texas.
9. Ranks third among the cotton ports of the United States.
10. Its port charges are as low as or lower than any other port in the United States.
11. Is the only seaport on the gulf coast west of the Mississippi into which a vessel drawing more than ten feet of water can enter.
12. Has steamship lines to Liverpool, New York, New Orleans, and the ports of Texas as far as the Mexican boundary.
13. Has harbor area of 24 feet depth and over 1,300 acres; of 30 feet depth and over 463 acres (the next-largest harbor on the Texas coast has only 100 acres of 24 feet depth of water).
14. Has the lowest maximum temperature of any city in Texas.
15. Has the finest beach in America and is a famous summer and winter resort.
16. Has public free school system unexcelled in the United States.
17. Has never been visited by any epidemic disease since the yellow fever scourge of 1867.
18. Has forty miles of street railways in operation.
19. Has electric lights throughout the city (plant owned by city).
20. It has millions invested in docks, warehouses, grain elevators, flouring mills, marine ways, manufactories, and mercantile houses.

"Galveston was the most promising town in the South, so far as shipping is concerned," said Thomas B. Bryan, the founder of North Galveston, the day after the disaster occurred.

There has been persistent opposition to it on the part of a railroad that wished the transportation of cotton and other produce farther east, but finally the geographical position of Galveston triumphed. Even Collis P. Huntington, the railroad magnate, succumbed, and later he inaugurated improvements in Galveston on the most colossal scale, involving an expenditure of many millions of dollars. One of the last announcements Mr. Huntington made before his death was that Galveston would become the greatest shipping port in America if money could accomplish it. At the time I was in Galveston, a few weeks ago, there was an army of workmen employed by the Southern Pacific Railroad, constructing great docks and wharves, which were to eclipse any on the globe.

Some conception of Galveston can be formed by supposing the business district of Chicago—say from Lake to Twenty-Second Street—were to extend out into the lake on a pier for a distance of three miles and at a height above the water varying from three to seven and possibly, in some places, nine feet. My own observation of Galveston induced my taking hold of the nearest eligible elevated locality for residences, which is North Galveston, sixteen miles from the city proper. It has an elevation above the water of fifteen to twenty feet more than Galveston and is free from inundation. No news has reached me from North Galveston, and though damage may have been done by wind, I am confident none can be done by water or waves.

Storms which move with the velocity of that which swept Galveston and which are common to the southern and southeastern coasts of the United States invariably originate, according to Weather Forecaster H. J. Cox of the United States Weather Bureau at Chicago, in "the doldrums," or that region in the ocean where calms abound. In this particular instance, the place was south of the West Indies and north of the equator. The region of the doldrums varies in breadth from sixty to several hundred miles and at different seasons shifts its extreme limits between five degrees south and fifteen degrees north. It is always overhung by a belt of clouds, which is gathered by opposing currents of the trade winds.

"The storm which swept Galveston and the surrounding country, I should say, originated at a considerable distance south of the West Indies, in this belt of calms," said Forecaster Cox the Monday night following the catastrophe.

It was caused by two strong currents meeting at an angle, and this caused the whirling motion which finally spent its force on the coast of Texas. It is seldom that a storm originating in the doldrums moves so far inland as did this one, but it is not, however, unprecedented. The reason this storm reached so far as Galveston was that the northwesterly wind moved about twice as fast as it usually does before reaching land. Usually the force of these winds are spent on the coast of Florida, and sometimes they reach as far north as North Carolina. When they strike the land at these points, they are given a northeasterly direction.

This storm missed the eastern coast of the United States and consequently was deflected to the west. Thunderstorms are prevailing in Kansas and all the district just north of the course of the storm, which is the natural result after such commotion of the elements. The conditions of the land are such about Galveston that, when the storm reached that far, it had no possible means of escape and hence the dire results. If there had been a chance for the wind to move further west along the coast, it would in all probability have passed Galveston, giving the place no more than a severe shaking up. In this event the worst effect would in all probability have been felt on the eastern coast of Mexico.

It was an absolute impossibility for anyone to form an idea of the extent and magnitude of the disaster within a week of its occurrence. The morning of Sunday, when the wind and the waves had subsided, the streets of the city were found clogged with debris of all sorts. The people of Galveston could not realize for several days what had happened. Four thousand houses had been entirely demolished, and hardly a building in the city was fit for habitation.

The people were apathetic; they wandered around the streets in an aimless sort of way, unable to do anything or make preparations to repair the great damage done. The Monday following the catastrophe, Galveston was practically in the hands of thieves, thugs, ghouls, vampires, and bandits, some of them women, who robbed the dead, mutilated the corpses which were lying everywhere, ransacked business houses and residences, and created a reign of terror, which lasted until the officers in command of the force of regulars stationed at the beach barracks sent a company of men to patrol the streets. The governor of the state ordered out all the regiments of the National Guard, and various associations of businessmen also supplied men, who assisted the soldiers in doing patrol duty in the city and suburbs.

The depredations of the lawless element were of an inconceivably brutal character. Unprotected women, whether found upon the streets or in their houses, were subjected to outrage or assault and robbed of their clothing and jewelry. Pedestrians were held up on the public thoroughfare in broad daylight and compelled to give up all valuables in their possession. The bodies of the dead were despoiled of everything, and in their haste to secure valuables, the ghouls would mutilate the corpses, cutting off fingers to obtain the rings thereon and amputating the ears of the women to get the earrings worn therein.

The majority of the thieves and vampires belonged in the city of Galveston and were reinforced by desperadoes from outside towns, like Houston, Austin, and New Orleans, who took advantage of the rush to the city immediately after the disaster, obtaining free transportation on the railroad and steamers upon a pretense that they were going to Galveston for the purpose of working with relief parties and the gangs assigned for burial of the dead. Their outrages became so flagrant and the people of the city became so terrified in consequence of their depredations that the city authorities, unable to cope with them, most of the officers of the police department having been victims of the flood, that an appeal was made to the governor to send state troops and procure the preservation of order. Captain Rafferty, commanding Battery O of the First Regiment of Artillery, USA, was also implored to lend his aid in putting down the lawless bands, and he accordingly sent all the men in his command who had not met death in the gale.

There was some delay in getting the state troops to Galveston because so many miles of railroad had been washed away, the adjutant general being compelled to notify some companies of militia by courier, but Captain Rafferty ordered his men on duty at once, with instructions to promptly shoot all persons found despoiling the dead.

The regulars were put on duty on Tuesday night and before morning had shot several of the thugs, who were executed on the spot when found in the act of robbery. In every instance the pockets of the harpies slain by the United States troops were found filled with jewelry and other valuables. On Wednesday evening the government troops came across a gang of fifty desperadoes, who were despoiling the bodies of the dead found enmeshed in the debris of a large apartment house. With commendable promptness the regulars put the ghouls under arrest and, finding the proceeds of their robberies in their possession, lined them up against a brick wall and without ceremony shot every one of them. In cases where the villains were not killed at the first fire, the sergeant administered coup de grace. Many of the thugs begged piteously for mercy, but no attention was paid to their feelings, and they suffered the same stern fate as the rest.

When the state troops arrived in the city, they took the same severe measures, and the result was that within forty-eight hours the city was as safe as it had ever been. The police arrested every suspicious character, and the jail and cells at the police station were filled to overflowing. These people were deported as soon as possible and notified that if they returned they would be shot without warning. The temper of the citizens of Galveston was such that they would not temporize in any case with those who were neither criminals or inclined to work. Every able-bodied man in town was impressed for duty in relief and burial parties, and whenever an individual refused to do the work required, he was promptly shot. By Thursday morning all the men required had been obtained, and relief and burial parties were filled to the quota deemed necessary, and the work of disposing of the bodies of the dead, administering to the wants of the wounded, and the clearing of the streets of the debris was proceeding satisfactorily.

The dead lay in the streets and vacant places in hundreds, and the heat of the sun began to have its natural effect. Decomposition set in, and the stench became unbearable. At first an effort was made to identify the corpses, but it was soon found that work could not be proceeded with, as any delay imperiled the living. Fears entertained in regard to pestilence were speedily verified, and the people of the city were taken ill by scores. It was difficult to obtain men to perform the duty of burying the bloated corpses of the victims of the catastrophe, and consequently the city authorities ordered that the dead be loaded on barges, taken a few miles out to sea, weighted, and thrown into the water. The ground had become so water-soaked that it was impossible to dig graves or trenches for the reception of the bodies, although in many instances people buried relatives and friends in their yards and the ground surrounding their residence. Along the beach hundreds of corpses were buried in the sand, but the majority of the burials were at sea. By Wednesday night 2,500 bodies had been cast into the water, while about 500 had been interred within the city limits. Precautions were taken, however, to mark the graves, and when the ground had dried sufficiently, the bodies were disinterred and taken to the various cemeteries, where, after burial, suitable memorials were erected to mark their last resting place. No attempts were made at identification after Wednesday, lists being simply made of the number of victims. The graves of those buried in the sand were marked by headboards with the inscriptions "White man, aged forty"; "White woman, aged twenty-five"; and "male" or "female" child, as the case might be.

So accustomed did the burial parties become to the handling of the dead that they treated the bodies as though they were merely carcasses of animals and not bodies of human beings, and they were dumped into the trenches prepared for their reception without ceremony of any kind. The excavations were then filled up as hurriedly as possible, the sand being packed down tightly. This might have seemed inhuman, unfeeling, and brutal, but the exigencies of the situation demanded that the corpses be put out of the way as speedily as possible. Great difficulty was experienced in securing men to transport bodies to the wharves where the barges lay.

Finally, however, patience ceased to be a virtue, and orders were given the guards to shoot any man who refused to do his duty under the circumstances. The result of this was that, the beginning of Wednesday, there was less delay in the matter of disposing of the dead. However, in spite of the activity of the burial parties, the work of clearing the streets of corpses was a most tedious one.

The forecast official of the United States Weather Bureau at Galveston made the following report, September 14, on the storm:

The local office of the United States Weather Bureau received the first message in regard to this storm at 4 p.m., September 4. It was then moving northward over Cuba. Each day thereafter, until the West India hurricane struck Galveston, bulletins were posted by the United States Weather Bureau officials giving the progressive movements of the disturbance.

September 6 the tropical storm had moved up over southern Florida; thence it changed its course and moved westward in the gulf and was central off the Louisiana coast the morning of the 7th, when northwest storm warnings were ordered up for Galveston. The morning of the 8th, the storm had increased in energy and was still moving westward, and at 10:10 a.m. the northwest storm warnings were changed to northeast. Then was when the entire island was in apparent danger. The telephone at the United States Weather Bureau office was busy until the wires went down; many could not get the use of the telephone on account of the line being busy. People came to the office in droves inquiring about the weather. About the same time the following information was given to all alike:

"The tropical storm is now in the gulf, south or southwest of us; the winds will shift to the northeast-east and probably to the southeast by morning, increasing in energy. If you reside in low parts of the city, move to higher grounds."

"Prepare for the worst, which is yet to come," were the only consoling words of the Weather Bureau officials at Galveston from morning until night of the 8th, when no information further could be given out.

The local forecast official and one observer stayed at the office throughout the entire storm, although the building was wrecked. The forecast official and one observer were out taking tide observations about 4 a.m., September 9. Another observer left after he had sent the last telegram which could be gotten off, it being filed at Houston over the telephone wires about 4 p.m. of the 8th. Over half the city was covered with tide water by 3 p.m. One of the observers left for home at about 4 p.m., after he had done all he could, as telephone wires were then going down. The entire city was then covered with water from one to five feet deep. On his way home, he saw hundreds of people, and he informed all he could that the worst was still to come, and people who could not hear his voice on account of the distance, he motioned them to go downtown.

The lowest barometer by observation was 28.53 inches at 8:10 p.m., September 8, but the barometer went slightly lower than this, according to the barograph. The tide at about 8 p.m. stood from six to fifteen feet deep throughout the city, with the wind blowing slightly over a hundred miles an hour. The highest wind velocity by the anemometer was ninety-six miles from the northeast at 5:15 p.m., and the extreme velocity was a hundred miles an hour at about that time. The anemometer blew down at this time, and the wind was still higher later, when it shifted to the east and southeast, when the observer estimated that it blew a gale of between 110 and 120 miles. There was an apparent tidal wave of from four to six feet about 8 p.m., when the wind shifted to the east and southeast and carried off many houses which had stood the tide up to that time.

The observer believed from the records he managed to save that the hurricane moved inland near Galveston, going up the Brazos Valley.

The warnings of the United States Weather Bureau were the means of thousands of lives being saved through the hurricane. It was so severe, however, that it was impossible to prepare for such destruction. The observer of the United States Weather Bureau at Galveston, to relieve apprehension, stated on September 14 that the barometer had gone up to about the normal, and there were no indications of another storm following.

The surviving people of Galveston did not awaken from sleep on Sunday morning, for they had not slept the night before. For many weary hours, they had stood face to face with death and knew that thousands had yielded up their lives and that millions of dollars' worth of property had been destroyed.

There was not a building in Galveston which was not either entirely destroyed or damaged, and the people of the city lived in the valley of the shadow of death, helpless and hopeless, deprived of all hope and ambition—merely waiting for the appearance of the official death roll.

Confusion and chaos reigned everywhere; death and desolation were on all sides; wreck and ruin were the only things visible wherever the eye might rest; and with business entirely suspended and no other occupation than the search for and burial of the dead, it was strange that the thoroughfares and residence streets were not filled with insane victims of the hurricane's frightful visit.

For days the people of Galveston knew there was danger ahead; they were warned repeatedly, but they laughed at all fears; business went on as usual; and, when the blow came, it found the city unprepared and without safeguards.

Owing to the stupefaction following the awful catastrophe, the people were in no condition, either physical or mental, to provide for themselves and therefore depended upon the outside world for food and clothing.

The inhabitants of Galveston needed immediate relief, but how they were to get it was a mystery, for Galveston was not yet in touch with the outside world by rail or sea. The city was sorely stricken and appealed to the country at large to send food, clothing, and water. The waterworks were in ruins and the cisterns all blown away, so that the lack of water was one of the most serious of the troubles.

Never did a storm work more cruelly. All the electric light and telegraph poles were prostrated, and the streets were littered with timbers, slate, glass, and every conceivable character of debris. There was hardly a habitable house in the entire city, and nearly every business house was either wrecked entirely or badly damaged.

On Monday there were deaths from hunger and exposure, and the list swelled rapidly. People were living as best they could—in the ruins of their homes, in hotels, in schoolhouses, in railway stations, in churches, in the streets by the side of their beloved dead.

So great was the desolation one could not imagine a more sorrowful place. Streetcars were not running; no trains could reach the town; only sad-eyed men and women walked about the streets; the dead and wounded monopolized the attention of those capable of doing anything whatever, and the city was at the mercy of thieves and ruffians. All the fine churches were in ruins. From Tremont to P Street, thence to the beach, not a vestige of a residence was to be seen.

In the business section of the city, the water was from three to ten feet deep in stores, and stocks of all kinds, including foodstuffs, were total losses. It was a common spectacle—that of inhabitants of the fated city wandering around in a forsaken and forlorn way, indifferent to everything around them and paying no attention to inquiries of friends and relatives.

God forbid that such scenes are enacted again in this country.

It was thought the vengeance of the fates had been visited in its most appalling shape upon the place which had unwittingly incurred its wrath.

It was fortunate after all, however, that those compelled to endure such trials were temporarily deprived of their understanding, were so stunned that they could not appreciate the enormity of the punishment.

The first loss of life reported was at Rietter's Saloon in the Strand, where three of the most prominent citizens of the town—Stanley G. Spencer, Charles Kellner, and Richard Lord—lost their lives and many others were maimed and imprisoned. These three were sitting at a table on the first floor Saturday night, making light of the danger, when the roof suddenly caved in and came down with a crash, killing them. Those in the lower part of the building escaped with their lives in a miraculous manner, as the falling roof and flooring caught on the bar, enabling the people standing near it to crawl under the debris. It required several hours of hard work to get them out.

Fully seven hundred people were congregated at the city hall, most of them more or less injured in various ways. One man from Lucas Terrace reported the loss of fifty lives in the building from which he escaped. He himself was severely injured about the head.

Passing along Tremont Street, out as far as Avenue P, climbing over the piles of lumber which had once been residences, four bodies were observed in one yard and seven in one room in another place, while as many as sixty corpses were seen lying singly and in groups in the space of one block. A majority of the drowned, however, were under the ruined houses. The body of Miss Sarah Summers was found near her home, corner of Tremont Street and Avenue F, her lips smiling, but her features set in death, her hands grasping her diamonds tightly. The remains of her sister, Mrs. Claude Fordtran, were never found.

The report from St. Mary's Infirmary showed that only eight persons escaped from that hospital. The number of patients and nurses was one hundred. Rosenberg Schoolhouse, chosen as a place of refuge by the people of that locality, collapsed. Few of those who had taken refuge there escaped—how many cannot be told and will never be known.

Never before had the Sabbath sun risen upon such a sight, and as though unable to endure it, the god of the day soon veiled his face behind dull and leaden clouds and refused to shine.

Surely it was enough to draw tears even from inanimate things.

At the Union Depot, Baggage Master Harding picked up the lifeless form of a baby girl within a few feet of the station. Its parents were among the lost. The station building was selected as a place of refuge by hundreds of people, and although all the windows and a portion of the south wall at the top were blown in and the occupants expected every moment to be their last, escape was impossible, for about the building the water was fully twelve feet deep. A couple of small shanties were floating about, but there was no means of making a raft or getting a boat.

Every available building in the city was used as a hospital. As for the dead, they were being put away anywhere. In one large grocery store on Tremont Street, all the space that could be cleared was occupied by the wounded.

It was nothing strange to see the dead and crippled everywhere, and the living were so fascinated by the dead they could hardly be dragged away from the spots where the corpses were piled. There were dead by the score, by the hundreds, and by the thousands. It was a city of the dead, a vast battlefield, the slain being victims of flood and gale. The dead were at rest, but the living had to suffer, for no aid was at hand.

In the business portion of the town, the damage could not be even approximately estimated. The wholesale houses along the Strand had about seven feet of water on their ground floors, and all window panes and glass protectors of all kinds were demolished.

On Mechanic Street the water was almost as deep as on the Strand. All provisions in the wholesale groceries and goods on the lower floors were saturated and rendered valueless.

In clearing away the ruins of the Catholic Orphans' Home, heart-rending evidence of the heroism and love of the sisters was discovered. Bodies of the little folks were found which indicated by their position that heroic measures were taken to keep them together so that all might be saved. The sisters had tied them together in bunches of eight and then tied the cords around their own waists. In this way they probably hoped to quiet the children's fears and lead them to safety. The storm struck the home with such terrific force that the structure fell, carrying the inmates with it and burying them under tons of debris. Two crowds of children, tied and attached to sisters, have been found. In one heap the children were piled on the sisters, and the arms of one little girl were clasped around a sister's neck. In the wreck of the home, over ninety children and sisters were killed. It was first believed that they had been washed out to sea, but the discovery of the little groups in the ruins indicates that all were killed and buried under the wreckage.

Sunday and Monday were days of the greatest suffering, although the population had hardly sufficiently recovered from the shock of the mighty calamity to realize that they were hungry and cold. On Monday all relief trains sent from other cities toward Galveston were forced to turn back, the tracks being washed away. On Tuesday Mayor Jones of Galveston sent out the following appeal to the country:

It is my opinion, based on personal information, that five thousand people have lost their lives here. Approximately one-third of the residence portion of the city has been swept away. There are several thousand people who are homeless and destitute—how many there is no way of finding out. Arrangements are now being made to have the women and children sent to Houston and other places, but the means of transportation are limited. Thousands are still to be cared for here. We appeal to you for immediate aid.

WALTER J. JONES,
Mayor of Galveston

Some relief had been sent in, the railroad to Texas City, six miles away, having been repaired, boats taking the supplies from that point into Galveston.

Food and women's clothing were the things most needed just then. While the men could get along with the clothes they had on and what they had secured since Sunday, the women suffered considerably, and there was much sickness among them in consequence. It was noticeable, however, that the women of the city had, by their example, been instrumental in reviving the drooping spirits of the men. There was a better feeling prevalent Tuesday among the inhabitants, as news had been received that, within a few days, the acute distress would be over, except in the matter of shelter. Every house standing was damp and unhealthy, and some of the wounded were not getting along as well as hoped. Many of the injured had been sent out of town to Texas City, Houston, and other places, but hundreds still remained. It would have endangered their lives to move them.

The following order was posted on the streets at noon of Tuesday:

To the Public: The city of Galveston being under martial law and all good citizens being now enrolled in some branch of the public service, it becomes necessary, to preserve the peace, that all arms in this city be placed in the hands of the military. All good citizens are forbidden to carry arms, except by written permission from the mayor or chief of police or the major commanding. All good citizens are hereby commanded to deliver all arms and ammunition to the city and take Major Faylings's receipt.

WALTER C. JONES, Mayor

Starting as soon as the water began to recede Sunday morning, a relief party began the work of rescuing the wounded and dying from the ruins of their homes. The scenes presented were almost beyond description. Screaming women, bruised and bleeding, some of them bearing the lifeless forms of children in their arms; men, broken-hearted and sobbing, bewailing the loss of their wives and children; streets filled with floating rubbish, among which there were many bodies of the victims of the storm, constituted part of the awful picture. In every direction, as far as the eye could reach, the scene of desolation and destruction continued.

It was certainly enough to cause the stoutest heart to quail and grow sick, and yet the searchers well knew they could not unveil one-hundredth part of the misery the destructive elements had brought about. They knew, also, that the full import and heaviness of the blow could not be realized for days to come.

Although those in the relief party were prepared to see the natural evidences following upon the heels of the mighty storm, they did not anticipate such frightful revelations. It was a butchery without precedent, a gathering of victims that was so ghastly as to be beyond the power of any man to picture.

As the party went on, the members met others who made reports of things that had come under their notice. There were fifty killed or drowned in one section of town, one hundred in another, five hundred in another. The list grew larger with each report.

It was a matter of wonder, and increasing wonder, too, that a single soul escaped to tell the tale. No one seemed entirely sane, for there was madness in the very air. All moved in an atmosphere of gloom; it was difficult to move and breathe with so much death on all sides. Yet no one could keep his eyes off of those horrible, fascinating corpses. They riveted the gaze. Life and death were often so closely intermingled they could not be told apart. It was the apotheosis of the frightful.

Those who had escaped the hurricane and flood were searching for missing dear ones in such a listless way as to irresistibly convey the idea that they did not care whether they found them or not. It was the languor of hopelessness and despair. Some of those who had lost their all were even merry, but it was the glee of insanity.

As Sunday morning dawned, the streets were lined with people, half-clad, crippled in every conceivable manner, hobbling as best they could to where they could receive attention of physicians for themselves and summon aid for friends and relatives who could not move.

Police Officer John Bowie, who had recently been awarded a prize as the most popular officer in the city, was in a pitiable condition; the toes on both of his feet were broken, two ribs caved in, and his head badly bruised, but his own condition, he said, was nothing. "My house, with wife and children, is in the gulf. I have not a thing on earth for which to live."

The houses of all prominent citizens which escaped destruction were turned into hospitals, as were also the leading hotels. There was scarcely one of the houses left standing which did not contain one or more of the dead as well as many injured.

The rain began to pour down in torrents, and the party went back down Tremont Street toward the city. The misery of the poor people, all mangled and hurt, pressing to the city for medical attention, was greatly augmented by this rain. Stopping at a small grocery store to avoid the rain, the party found it packed with injured. The provisions in the store had been ruined, and there was nothing for the numerous customers who came hungry and tired. The place was a hospital, no longer a store.

Farther down the street a restaurant, which had been submerged by water, was serving out soggy crackers and cheese to the hungry crowd. That was all that was left. The food was soaked full of water, and the people who were fortunate enough to get those sandwiches were hungry and made no complaint.

It was hard to determine what section of the city suffered the greatest damage and loss of life. Information from both the extreme eastern and extreme western portions of the city was difficult to obtain at that time. In fact, it was nearly impossible, but the reports received indicated that those two sections had suffered the same fate as the rest of the city and to a greater degree. Thus the relief party wended its way through streets which, but a few hours before, were teeming with life. Now they were the thoroughfares of death. It did not seem as if they could ever resound to the throb of quickened vitality again. It seemed as though it would take years to even remove the wreckage. As to rebuilding, it appeared as the work of ages. Annihilation was everywhere.

As marked out on the charts of the United States Weather Bureau at Washington, the storm which struck Galveston had a peculiar course. It was first definitely located south by east of San Domingo, and the last day of August, the center of the disturbance was approximately at a point fixed at 14 degrees north latitude and 68 degrees west longitude. From there it made a course almost due northeast, passing through Kingston, Jamaica, and if it had continued on this same line, it would have struck Galveston just the same but somewhat earlier than it did. The storm apparently was headed for Galveston all the time, but on Tuesday of last week, when almost due south of Cienfuegos, Cuba, it changed its course so as to go almost due north, across the island of Cuba, through the toe of the Florida peninsula, and up the coast to the vicinity of Tampa. Here the storm made another sharp turn to the westward and headed again almost straight for Galveston.

It was this sharp turn to the westward which could not be anticipated, so the Weather Bureau sent out its hurricane signals both for the Atlantic and the gulf coast, well understanding that the prediction as to one of these coasts would certainly fail. As soon as the storm turned westward from below Tampa, the Weather Bureau knew the Atlantic coast was safe and turned its attention toward the gulf.

The people of Galveston had abundant warning of the coming of the hurricane but, of course, could not anticipate the destructive energy it would gain on the way across the Gulf of Mexico.

The Weather Bureau was informed that the first sign of the disturbance was noticed on August 30 near the Windward Islands. On August 31 it still was in the same neighborhood. The storm did not develop any hurricane features during its slow passage through the Caribbean Sea and across Cuba but was accompanied by tremendous rains. During the first twelve hours of September 3, in Santiago, Cuba, 10.50 inches of rain fell, and 2.80 inches fell in the next twelve. On September 4 the rainfall during twelve hours in Santiago was 4.44 inches, or a total fall in thirty-six hours of 17.20 inches. There were some high winds in Cuba the night of September 4.

By the morning of the 6th, the storm center was a short distance northwest of Key West, Florida, and the high winds had commenced over southern Florida, forty-eight miles an hour from the east being reported from Jupiter and forty miles from the northeast from Key West. During the 6th barometric conditions over the eastern portion of the United States so far changed as to prevent the movement of the storm along the Atlantic coast, and it, therefore, continued northwest over the Gulf of Mexico.

On the morning of the 7th, it apparently was central south of the Louisiana coast, about longitude 89, latitude 28. At this time storm signals were ordered up on the north Texas coast and during the day were extended along the entire coast. On the morning of the 8th, the storm was nearing the Texas coast and was apparently central at about latitude 28, longitude 94.

Galveston's disastrous storm was predicted with startling accuracy by the weather prophet, Prof. Andrew Jackson DeVoe. In the *Ladies' Birthday Almanac*, issued from Chattanooga, Tennessee, in January, 1900, Prof. DeVoe forecasts the weather for the following month of September as follows:

This will be a hot dry month over the northern states but plenty of rain over the Atlantic coast states. First and second days hot and sultry. Third and fourth heavy storms over the extreme northwestern states, causing thunderstorms over the Missouri Valley and showery, rainy weather over the whole country from 5th to 8th.

On the 9th a great cyclone will form over the Gulf of Mexico and move up the Atlantic coast, causing very heavy rains from Florida to Maine from 10th to 12th.

Houston was the great rendezvous for supplies sent to Galveston, and they poured in there by the carload, beginning with Tuesday. The response to the appeal for aid by the people of Galveston, on the part of the United States and, in fact, every country in the world, was prompt and generous.

That relief was an absolute necessity was made apparent from the appearance of the refugees who began to flock into Houston as soon as the boats began to run to Galveston after the catastrophe. In addition to these, thousands of strangers arrived also, and the Houston authorities were at a loss as to what to do with them. Some of these visitors were from points far distant, who had relatives in the storm-stricken district and had come to learn the worst regarding them; others there were who had come to volunteer their services in the relief work, but the greatest number consisted of curious sightseers, almost frantic in their efforts to get to the stricken city and feed their eyes on the sickening, repulsive, and disease-breeding scenes. In addition there were hundreds of the sufferers themselves, who had been brought out of their misery to be cared for here.

The question of caring for these crowds came up at a mass meeting of the Houston general relief committee held Monday. Every incoming train brought scores more of people, and immediate action was necessary. It was decided finally to pitch tents in Emancipation Park, and there as many of the strangers as possible were cared for. The hotels could not accommodate one-tenth of them.

First attention, naturally, was given the survivors of the storm. Mayor Brashear sent word to Mayor Jones of Galveston that all persons, no matter who they were, rich or poor, ill or well, should be sent to Houston as soon as possible. They would be well provided for, he said. The urgency of his message for the depopulation of Galveston, he explained, was that, until sanitation could be restored in the wrecked city, everybody possible should be sent away.

It was estimated that nearly one thousand of the unfortunate survivors were sent to Houston on Tuesday from Galveston in response to

Mayor Brashear's request. Every building in Houston at all habitable was opened to them, and all the seriously ill comfortably housed. The others were made as comfortable as possible, but it was not only food and clothing that was wanted; the only relief some of them sought could not be furnished. They were grieving for lost ones left behind—fathers, mothers, sisters, wives, and children. Nearly everybody had some relative missing, but few of them were certain whether they were dead or alive. All, however, were satisfied that they were dead.

Men, bareheaded and barefooted, with sunken cheeks and hollow eyes; women and children with tattered clothing and bruised arms and faces; and mere infants with bare feet bruised and swollen were among the crowds seen on the streets of Houston. Women of wealth and refinement, with hatless heads and gowns of rich material torn into shreds, were among the refugees. At times a man and his wife, and sometimes with one or two children, could be seen together, but such sights were infrequent, for nearly all who went to Houston had suffered the loss of one or more of their loved ones.

But with all this suffering, there was a marvelous amount of heroism shown. A week before most of these people had happy homes, and their families were around them. The Tuesday following the disaster, they were homeless, penniless, and with nothing to look forward to. Yet there was scarcely any whimpering or complaining. They walked about the streets as if in a trance; they accepted the assistance offered them with heartfelt thanks and apparently were greatly relieved at being away from the scenes of sorrow and woe at home. They were all made to feel at home in Houston, that they were welcome, and that everything in the power of the people of Houston would be done for their comfort and welfare, and yet they seemed not to understand half that was said to them.

John J. Moody, a member of the committee sent from Houston to take charge of the relief station at Texas City, reported to the mayor of Houston on Tuesday as follows:

To the Mayor—Sir: On arriving at Lamarque this morning, I was informed that the largest number of bodies was along the coast of Texas City. Fifty-six were buried yesterday and today within less than two miles, extending opposite this place and toward Virginia City. It is yet six miles farther to Virginia City, and the bodies are thicker where we are now than where they have been buried. A citizen inspecting in the opposite direction reports dead bodies thick for twenty miles.

The residents of this place have lost all—not a habitable building left, and they have been too busy disposing of the dead to look after personal affairs. Those who have anything left are giving it to the others, and yet there is real suffering. I have given away nearly all the bread I brought for our own use to hungry children.

A number of helpless women and beggared children were landed here from Galveston this afternoon and no place to go and not a bite to eat. Tomorrow others are expected from the same place. Every ten feet along the wreck-lined coast tells of acts of vandalism; not a trunk, valise, or tool chest but what has been rifled. We buried a woman this afternoon whose finger bore the mark of a recently removed ring.

The United States government furnished several thousand tents for the Houston camp, which was under the supervision of the United States Marine Hospital authorities.

General McKibbin, who was sent to Galveston by the War Department to investigate the conditions prevailing there, made the following official report on Wednesday, September 12:

Houston, Texas, September 12, 1900—Adjutant General, Washington—Arrived at Galveston at 6 p.m., having been ferried across bay in a yawl boat. It is impossible to adequately describe the condition existing. The storm began about 9 a.m. Saturday and continued with constantly increasing violence until after midnight. The island was inundated; the height of the tide was from eleven to thirteen feet. The wind was a cyclone. With few exceptions, every building in the city is injured. Hundreds are entirely destroyed.

All the fortifications except the rapid-fire battery at San Jacinto are practically destroyed. At San Jacinto every building except the quarantine station has been swept away. Battery O, First Artillery, United States Army, lost twenty-eight men. The officers and their families were all saved. Three members of the hospital corps lost. Names will be sent as soon as possible. Loss of life on the island is possibly more than one thousand. All bridges are gone, waterworks destroyed, and all telegraph lines are down.

Colonel Roberts was in the city and made every effort to get telegrams through. City under control of committee of citizens and perfectly quiet.

Every article of equipment or property pertaining to Battery O was lost. Not a record of any kind is left. The men saved had nothing but the clothing on their persons. Nearly all are without shoes or clothing other than their shirts and trousers. Clothing necessary has been purchased and temporary arrangements made for food and shelter. There are probably five thousand citizens homeless and absolutely destitute who must be clothed, sheltered, and fed. Have ordered 20,000 rations and tents for 1,000 people from Sam Houston. Have wired commissary general to ship 30,000 rations by express. Lieutenant Perry will make his way back to Houston and send this telegram.

McKIBBIN

Captain Charles S. Riche, USA, corps of engineers, when seen after he had completed a tour of inspection of the government works around Galveston, made the following statement:

The jetties are sunk nearly to mean low tide level but not seriously breached. The channel is as good as before, perhaps better, twenty-five feet certainly.

Fort Crockett, fifteen-pounder implacements, concrete all right, standing on filling; water underneath. Battery for eight mortars about like preceding, and mortars and carriages on hand unmounted and in good shape. Shoreline at Fort Crockett has moved back about six hundred feet. At Fort San Jacinto, the battery for eight twelve-inch mortars is badly wrecked, and magazines reported fallen in. The mortars are reported safe. No piling was under this battery. Some of the sand parapet is left. The battery for two ten-inch guns badly wrecked. Both gun platforms are down and guns leaning. The battery for two 4.7-inch rapid-fire guns, concrete standing upon piling, both guns apparently all right. The battery for two fifteen-pounder guns, concrete apparently all right, standing on piling.

Fort Travis, Bolivar Point—Battery for three fifteen-pounder guns, concrete intact, standing on piling. East gun down. Western gun probably all right. The shoreline has moved back about one thousand feet on the line of the rear of these batteries.

Under the engineers' corps are the fortifications, built at a considerable expense; also the harbor improvements, upon which more than $8,000,000 had been expended.

"I fear Galveston is destroyed beyond its ability to recover," is the manner in which Quartermaster Baxter concluded his report, made September 12, to the War Department at Washington. He recommended the continuance of his office only long enough to recover the office safes and close up accounts and declared all government works were wrecked so restoration was impossible.

This gloomy prophecy for the city's future was reflected in an official report to Governor Sayers of Texas by ex–state treasurer Wortham, who spent a day at Galveston, investigating the situation. His statement claimed that 75 percent of the city was demolished and gives little hope for rebuilding.

Mr. Wortham, who acted as aid to Adjutant General Scurry, Texas National Guard, during the inquiry, said in his report:

The situation at Galveston beggars description. I am convinced that the city is practically wrecked for all time to come.

Fully 75 percent of the business of the town is irreparably wrecked, and the same percent of damage is to be found in the residence district. Along the wharf front, great ocean steamers have bodily bumped themselves on the big piers and lie there, great masses of iron and wood, that even fire cannot totally destroy. The great warehouses along the waterfront are smashed in on one side, unroofed and gutted throughout their length, their contents either piled in heaps on the wharves or along the streets. Small tugs and sailboats have jammed themselves half into the buildings, where they were landed by the incoming waves and left by the receding waters. Houses are packed and jammed in great confusing masses in all of the streets.

Great piles of human bodies, dead animals, rotting vegetation, household furniture, and fragments of the houses themselves are piled in confused heaps right in the main streets of the city. Along the gulf front, human bodies are floating around like cordwood. Intermingled with them are to be found the carcasses of horses, chickens, dogs, and rotting vegetable matter. Above all arises the foulest stench that ever emanated from any cesspool, absolutely sickening in its intensity and most dangerous to health in its effects.

Along the Strand adjacent to the gulf front, where are located all the big wholesale warehouses and stores, the situation is even worse. Great stores of fresh vegetation have been invaded by the incoming waters and are now turned into garbage piles of most befouling odors. The gulf waters while on the land played at will with everything, smashing in doors of stores, depositing bodies of humans where they pleased, and then receded, leaving the wreckage to tell its own tale of how the work had been done. As a result, the great warehouses are tombs, wherein are to be found the dead bodies of human beings and carcasses, almost defying the efforts of relief parties.

In the pile of debris along the street, in the water, and scattered throughout the residence portion of the city are to be found masses of wreckage, and in these great piles are to be found more human bodies and household furniture of every description.

Handsome pictures are seen lying alongside of the ice-cream freezers and resting beside the nude figure of some man or woman. These great masses of debris are not confined to any one particular section of the city.

The waters of the gulf and the winds spared no one who was exposed. Whirling houses around in its grasp, the wind piled their shattered frames high in confusing masses and dumped their contents on top.

Men and women were thrown around like so many logs of wood and left to rot in the withering sun.

I believe that, with the best exertions of the men, it will require weeks to secure some semblance of physical order in the city, and it is doubtful even then if all the debris will be disposed of.

I never saw such a wreck in my life. From the gulf front to the center of the island, from the ocean back, the storm wave left death and destruction in its wake.

There is hardly a family on the island whose household is not short a member or more, and in some instances entire families have been washed away or killed. Hundreds who escaped from the waves did so only to become victims of a worse death by being crushed by falling buildings.

Down in the business portion of the city, the foundations of great buildings have given way, carrying towering structures to their ruin. These ruins, falling across the streets, formed barricades on which gathered all the floating debris and many human bodies. Many of these bodies were stripped of their clothing by the force of the water and the wind, and there was nothing to protect them from the scorching sun, the millions of flies, and the rapid invasion of decomposition that set in.

Many of the bodies have decayed so rapidly that they could not be handled for burial.

Some of the most conservative men on the island place the loss of human beings at not less than 7,500 and possibly 10,000, while others say it will not exceed 5,000.

Chief Willis L. Moore, of the United States Weather Bureau at Washington, being asked his opinion of the idea of rebuilding Galveston on some other site, replied as follows:

Weather Bureau, US, Washington, DC, September 13, 1900.

I should not advise the abandonment of the city of Galveston. It is true that tropical hurricanes sometimes move westward across the gulf and strike the Texas coast, but such movement is infrequent. Within the last thirty years, no storm of like severity has touched any part of the coast of the United States. There are many points on both the Atlantic and gulf coasts, some of them occupied by cities the size of Galveston, that are equally exposed to the force of both wind and water should a hurricane move in from the ocean or gulf and obtain the proper position relative to them. It would not be advisable to abandon these towns and cities merely because there is a remote probability that, at some future time, a hurricane may be the cause of great loss of life and property.

We have just passed through a summer that, for sustained high temperature, has no parallel within the last thirty years. Records of low temperature, torrential rains, and other meteorological phenomena that have stood for twenty and thirty years are not infrequently broken. There does not appear to be, so far as we know, any law governing the occurrence or recurrence of storms. The vortex of a hurricane is comparatively narrow, at most not more than twenty or thirty miles in width. It is only within the vortex that such a great calamity as has befallen Galveston can occur.

It would seem that, rather than abandon the city, means should be adopted at Galveston and other similarly exposed cities on the Atlantic and gulf coasts to erect buildings only on heavy stone foundations that should have solid interiors of masonry to a height of ten feet above mean sea level. Rigid building regulations should allow no other structures erected for habitations in the future in any city located at sea level and that is exposed to the direct sweep of the sea.

But Galveston should take heart, as the chances are that not once in a thousand years would she be so terribly stricken, and high, solid foundations would doubtless make her impregnable to loss of life by all future storms.

WILLIS L. MOORE,

Chief US Weather Bureau

The courage of Galveston's businessmen under the distressing conditions was shown by the utterances of Mr. Eustace Taylor, one of the best-known residents of that city, a cotton buyer known to the trade in all parts of the country. Mr. Taylor was asked on Thursday succeeding the flood for an opinion as to the future of Galveston.

"I think," he said

that what we have done here for the four days which have passed since the storm has been wonderful. It will take us two weeks before we can ascertain the actual commercial loss. But we are going to straighten out everything. We are going to stay here and work it out. We will have a temporary wharf within thirty days, and with that we can resume business and handle the traffic through Galveston.

I think that, within thirty or forty days, business will be carried on in no less volume than before. I am going to stand right up to Galveston.

If it costs me the last cent, I will stand up for Galveston. With our temporary wharf, we shall put from one thousand to two thousand men at work loading vessels, while we are waiting for the railroads to restore bridges and terminals on the island. We shall bring business by barges from Virginia Point and load in midstream. In this way we shall not only resume our commercial relations, but we shall be able to put the labor of the city at work.

This port holds the advantage over every other port of this country for accommodating ten million producers and will accommodate millions of tons, and in inviting these millions, as we have, to continue their business through this port, we must in our construction do it on the same lines employed by the communities of Boston, New York, Buffalo, and Chicago, the stability of which was plainly illustrated in some structures recently erected in our community.

The port is all right. The ever-alert engineers in charge of the harbor here have already taken their soundings. The fullest depth of water remains. The jetties, with slight repair, are intact, and because of these conditions, which exist nowhere else for the territory and people it serves, the restoration will be more rapid than may be thought, and the flow of commerce will be as great and, for the courage and fortitude and foresight to look beyond the unhappy events of today, as prosperous and secure as in any part of our prosperous country.

J. C. Stewart, a well-known grain elevator builder, arrived at Galveston on Thursday in response to a telegram from General Manager M. E. Bailey of the Galveston Wharf Company. He at once made an inspection of the grain elevators and their contents and then said not 2 percent of the elevators had been damaged. The spouts were intact, and elevator "A" would be ready to deliver grain to ships the following Sunday.

The wheat in elevator "A" was loaded into vessels just as rapidly as they arrived at the elevator to take it. As soon as the elevator was emptied of its grain, the wheat from elevator "Q" was transferred to it and loaded into ships. Very little of the wheat in elevator "B" had been injured, but the conveyors were swept away, and it was necessary to transfer the grain to elevator "A" in order to get it to the ships. Mr. Bailey put a large force of men to work clearing up each of the wharves, and the company was ready for new business all along the line within eight days.

Pestilence could only be avoided here by cremation. That was the order of the day. Human corpses, dead animals, and all debris were therefore to be submitted to the flames. On Thursday upward of four hundred bodies, mostly women and children, were cremated, and the work went rapidly on. They were gathered in heaps of twenty and forty bodies, saturated with kerosene, and the torch applied.

A conflict of authority, due to a misunderstanding, precipitated a temporary disorganization of the policing of the city of Galveston on Thursday. When General Scurry, adjutant general of the Texas National Guard, arrived at Galveston on Tuesday night with about two hundred militia from Houston, he at once conferred with the chief of police as to the plans for guarding property, protecting the lives of citizens, and preserving law and order. An order was then issued by the chief of police to the effect that the soldiers should arrest all persons found carrying arms, unless they showed a written order signed by the chief of police or mayor of the city giving them permission to go armed.

Sheriff Thomas had, meantime, appointed and sworn in 150 special deputy sheriffs. These deputies were supplied with a ribboned badge of authority but were not given any written or printed commission. Acting under the order issued by the chief of police, Major Hunt McCaleb of Galveston, who was appointed as aide to General Scurry, issued an order to the militia to arrest all persons carrying arms without the proper authority. The result was that about fifty citizens wearing deputy sheriff badges were taken into custody by the soldiers and taken to police headquarters. The soldiers had no way of knowing by what authority the men were acting with these badges and would listen to no excuses.

General Scurry and Sheriff Thomas, hearing of the wholesale arrests, called at police headquarters and consulted with Acting Chief Amundsen. The latter referred General Scurry to Mayor Jones. Then General Scurry and Sheriff Thomas held a conference at the city hall. These two officers soon arrived at an understanding, and an agreement was decided upon to the effect that all persons deputized as deputy sheriffs and all persons appointed as special officers should be permitted to carry arms and pass in and out of the guard lines. General Scurry suggested that the deputy sheriffs and special police—and the regular police, for that matter—guard the city during the daytime and that the militia take charge of the city at night.

General Scurry was acting for and by authority granted by Mayor Jones and promptly said he was there to work in harmony with the city and county authorities and that there would be no conflict. When General Scurry and Sheriff Thomas called upon the mayor, the mayor said that he knew that, if the adjutant general, the chief of police, and the sheriff would get together, they could take care of the police work.

It was known that people were coming to Galveston by the score, that many of them had no business there, and that the city had enough to do to watch the lawless element of Galveston without being burdened with the care of outsiders.

All deputy sheriffs wearing the badge issued by the sheriff carried arms thereafter and made arrests and were not interfered with in any way by the military guards.

On Thursday, September 13, trainload after trainload of provisions, clothing, disinfectants, and medicines were lined up at Texas City, six miles from Galveston, all sent to the suffering survivors of the storm-swept city. Across the bay were thousands of people, friends of the dead and living, waiting for news of the missing ones and an opportunity to help, but only a meager amount of relief had at that time reached the stricken town. Two telegraph wires had been put up and partial communication restored to let the outside world know that conditions there were far more horrible than was at first supposed. That was about all. It was not that which was needed; it was a more practicable connection with the mainland. True, more boats had been pressed into service to carry succor to the suffering and the suffering to succor, but they were few and small, and although working diligently night and day, the service was inadequate in the extreme. And the people were still suffering—the sick dying for want of medicine and care, the well growing desperate and in many cases gradually losing their reason.

While there were many who could not be provided for because the necessary articles for them could not be carried in, there were hundreds who were being benefited. Those supplies which had arrived had been of great assistance, but they were far from ample to provide for even a small percentage of the sufferers, estimated at thirty thousand. Even the rich were hungry. An effort was being made on the part of the authorities to provide for those in the greatest need, but this was found to be difficult work, so many were there in sad condition. A rigid system of issuing supplies was established, and the regular soldiers and a number of citizens were sworn in as policemen. These attended to the issuing of rations as soon as the boats arrived.

Every effort was put forth to reach the dying first, but all sorts of obstacles were encountered because many of them were so badly maimed and wounded that they were unable to apply to the relief committees, and the latter were so burdened by the great number of direct applications that they were unable to send out messengers.

The situation grew worse every minute; everything was needed for man and beast—disinfectants, prepared foods, hay, grain, and especially water and ice. Scores more of people died that day as a result of inattention, and many more were on the verge of dissolution, for at best it was to be many days before a train could be run into the city, and the only hope was the arrival of more boats to transport the goods.

The relief committee held a meeting and decided that armed men were needed to assist in burying the dead and clear the wreckage, and arrangements were made to fill this demand. There were plenty of volunteers for this work but an insufficiency of arms. The proposition of trying to pay for work was rejected by the committee, and it was decided to go ahead impressing men into service, issuing orders for rations only to those who worked or were unable to work.

Word was received that refugees would be carried from the city to Houston free of charge. An effort was made to induce all who are able to leave to go because the danger of pestilence was frightfully apparent.

There was any number willing to depart, and each outgoing boat, after having unloaded its provisions, was filled with people. The safety of the living was a paramount consideration, and the action of the railroads in offering to carry refugees free of charge greatly relieved the situation. The workers had their hands full in any event, and the nurses and physicians also, for neglect, although unavoidable, often resulted in the death of many.

It was estimated $2,500,000 would be needed for the relief work. The banks of Galveston subscribed $10,000, but personal losses of the citizens of Galveston had been so large that very few were able to subscribe anything. The confiscation of all foodstuffs held by wholesale grocers and others was decided upon early in the day by the relief committee. Starvation would inevitably ensue unless the supply was dealt out with great care. All kerosene oil was gone, and the gas works and electric lights were destroyed. The committee asked for a shipload of kerosene oil; a shipload of drinking water; and tons of disinfectants, such as lime and formaldehyde, for immediate use; and money and food next. Not a tallow candle could be bought for gold or light of any kind procured.

No baker was making bread, and milk was remembered as a past luxury only. What was there to do with? Everything was gone in the way of ovens and utensils.

It was absolutely necessary to let the outside world know the true state of things. The city was unable to help itself. In fact, a great part of the mighty, noble state of Texas was prostrate. Even the country at large was paralyzed at the sense of the magnitude of the disaster and was, for the time being, powerless to do anything. The entire world was thrilled with alarm, it being instinctively felt that the worst had not yet been made known. Twenty-five thousand people had to be clothed and fed for many weeks and many thousands supplied with household goods, as well. Much money was required to make their residences even fit to live in.

During the first few days after the disaster, it was almost beyond possibility to make any estimate of the amount of money necessary to even temporarily relieve the sufferings of the unfortunate people.

As a means of enlightenment, Major R. G. Lowe, business manager of the *Galveston News*, was asked to send out a statement to the Associated Press for dissemination throughout the globe, and he accordingly dispatched the following to Colonel Charles S. Diehl, general manager of the Associated Press at the headquarters in Chicago:

Galveston, Texas, September 12—Charles S. Diehl, general manager the Associated Press, Chicago: A summary of the conditions prevailing at Galveston is more than human intellect can master. Briefly stated, the damage to property is anywhere between $15,000,000 and $20,000,000. The loss of life cannot be computed. No lists could be kept, and all is simply guesswork. Those thrown out to sea and buried on the ground wherever found will reach the horrible total of at least three thousand souls.

My estimate of the loss on the island of the city of Galveston and the immediate surrounding district is between four thousand and five thousand deaths. I do not make this statement in fright or excitement. The whole story will never be told because it cannot be told. The necessities of those living are total. Not a single individual escaped property loss. The property on the island is wrecked, fully one-half totally swept out of existence. What our needs are can be computed by the world at large by the statement herewith submitted much better than I could possibly summarize them. The help must be immediate.

R. G. LOWE,

Manager, *Galveston News*

Thursday evening at the Tremont Hotel in Galveston occurred a wedding that was not attended with music and flowers and a gathering of merrymaking friends and relatives. On the contrary, it was peculiarly sad. Mrs. Brice Roberts expected some day to marry Earnest Mayo; the storm which desolated so many homes deprived her of almost everything on earth—father, mother, sister, and brother. She was left destitute. Her sweetheart, too, was a sufferer. He lost much of his possessions in Dickinson, but he stepped bravely forward and took his sweetheart to his home.

Galveston began, September 14, to emerge from the valley of the shadow of death into which she had been plunged for nearly a week, and on that day, for the first time, actual progress was made toward clearing up the city. The bodies of those killed and drowned in the storm had for the most part been disposed of. A large number was found when the debris was removed from wrecked buildings, but on that date there were no corpses to be seen, save those occasionally cast up by the sea. As far as sight at least was concerned, the city was cleared of its dead.

They had been burned, thrown into the water, buried—anything to get them quickly out of sight. The chief danger of pestilence was due almost entirely to the large number of unburied cattle lying upon the island, whose decomposing carcasses polluted the air to an almost unbearable extent. This, however, was not in the city proper but was a condition prevailing on the outskirts of Galveston. One great trouble heretofore had been the inability to organize gangs of laborers for the purpose of clearing the streets.

The situation in the stricken city on Wednesday, September 12, was horrible indeed. Men, women, and children were dying for want of food, and scores went insane from the terrible strain to which they had been subjected.

In his appeal to the country for aid, issued on Tuesday, September 11, Mayor Walter J. Jones said fully five thousand people had lost their lives during the hurricane, this estimate being based upon personal information. Captain Charles Clarke, a vessel owner of Galveston and a reliable man, said the death list would be even greater than that, and he was backed in his opinion by several other conservative men who had no desire to exaggerate the losses but felt that they are justified in letting the country know the full extent of the disaster in order that the necessary relief might be supplied. It was the general opinion that to hide any of the facts would be criminal.

Captain Clarke was not a sensationalist, but he well knew that the truth was what the people of the United States wanted at that time. If the people of the country at large felt they were being deceived in anything, they would be apt to close their pocketbooks and refuse to give anything. If told the truth, they would respond to the appeal for aid generously.

When relief finally began to pour in, it was remarkable how soon the women of the city plucked up courage and went to work with the men. They had suffered frightfully, but they refused to give up hope. Many called upon the mayor and offered their services as nurses. Others prepared bandages for the wounded and aided the physicians in procuring medicines for the sick. They went among the men who were engaged in burying and otherwise disposing of the dead and cheered them with bright faces and soothing words. They were everywhere, and their presence was as rays of sunshine after the black clouds of the storm.

A regular fleet of steamers and barges was plying between Galveston and Texas City, only six miles distant, and which had railway communication with all parts of the United States. As the railroad line to Texas City had been repaired, trains were sent in there as close together as possible, but this did not prevent many hundreds in Galveston from dying of starvation and lack of medical attendance.

A leading city official of Galveston gave the following version of the Reign of Terror, as the regime of the thugs and ghouls was called:

Galveston suffered in every conceivable way since the catastrophe of Saturday. Hurricane and flood came first, then famine, and then vandalism. Scores of reckless criminals flocked to the city by the first boats that landed there and were unchecked in their work of robbery of the helpless dead Monday and Tuesday.

Wednesday, however, Captain Rafferty, commanding the regulars at the beach barracks, sent seventy men of an artillery company there to do guard duty in the streets and, being ordered to promptly shoot all those found looting, carried out their instructions to the letter.

Over one hundred ghouls were shot Wednesday afternoon and evening, and no mercy was shown vandals. If they were not killed at the first volley, the troops—regulars of the United States Army and those of the Texas National Guard—saw that the coup de grace was administered.

Not only had these fiends robbed the dead, but they mutilated the bodies as well, in many instances fingers and ears of dead women being amputated in order to secure the jewelry. Some of the business organizations of the city also furnished guards to assist in patrolling the streets, and fully one thousand men are now on duty.

Wednesday evening the regulars shot forty-nine ghouls after they had been tried by court-martial, having found them in possession of large quantities of plunder. The vandals begged for mercy, but none was shown them, and they were speedily put out of the way. The bandits, as a rule, obtained transportation to the city by representing themselves as having been engaged to do relief work and to aid in burying the dead. Shortly after the first bunch of thieves was executed, another party of twenty was shot. The outlaws were afterward put out of the way by twos and threes, it being their habit to travel in gangs and never alone. In every instance the pockets of these bandits were found filled with plunder.

More than two thousand bodies had been thrown into the sea up to Wednesday night, this having been decided upon by the authorities as the only way of preventing a visitation of pestilence, which, they felt, should not be added to the horrors the city had already experienced. Tuesday evening, shortly before darkness set in, three barges containing seven hundred bodies were sent out to sea, the corpses being thrown into the water after being heavily weighted to prevent the possibility of their afterward coming to the surface. As there were few volunteers for this ghastly work, troops and police officers were sent out to impress men for the service, but while these unwilling laborers, after being filled with liquor, agreed to handle the bodies. Finally city firemen came forward and attended to the disposal of the corpses of the colored victims. These were badly decomposed, and it was absolutely necessary to get them out of the way to prevent infection.

No attempt had been made so far to gather up the dead at night because the gas and electric light plants were so badly damaged that they could furnish no illumination whatever. By Thursday night, however, some of the arc lights were ready for use. Since Wednesday morning no efforts at identification were made by the searchers after the dead, it being imperative that the bodies be disposed of as soon as possible. While the barges containing the bodies were on their way out to sea, lists were made, but that was the only care taken in regard to the victims, many of whom were among the most prominent people of the city. Of the hundreds buried at Virginia Point and other places along the coast, not 10 percent were identified, the stakes at the heads of the hastily dug graves simply being marked, "White woman, aged thirty," "White man, aged forty-five," or "Male" or "Female child."

Ninety-six bodies were buried at Texas City, all but eight of which floated to that place from Galveston. Some were identified, but the great majority were not. State troops were stationed at Texas City and Virginia Point to prevent those who could not give a satisfactory account of themselves from boarding boats bound for Galveston. In burying the dead along the shore of the gulf, no coffins were used, the supply being exhausted. There was no time to knock even an ordinary pine box together. Cases were known where people have buried their dead in their yards.

As soon as possible, the work of cremating the bodies of the dead began. Vast funeral pyres were erected and the corpses placed thereon, the incineration being under the supervision of the fire department. Matters had come to such a pass that even the casting of bodies into the sea was not only dangerous to those who handled them, but there was the utmost danger in carrying the decomposed, putrefying masses of human flesh through the streets to the barges on the beach. The cemeteries were not fit for burial purposes, and no attempt whatever was made to reach them until the ground was thoroughly dried out. Then the bodies of those buried in private grounds, yards, and in the sands along the beach, not only on Galveston Island, but at Virginia Point and Texas City, were removed to the public places of interment, where suitable memorials were set up to mark their last resting places. It might have been deemed unfeeling and even brutal, but the fact was that the bodies of the unidentified victims received small consideration, being handled roughly by the workmen and thrown into the temporary graves along the beach as though they were animals and not the remains of human beings. No prayers were uttered, save in isolated instances, and the poor mangled bodies were consigned to the trench as hurriedly as possible. The burying parties had no time for sentiment, and so accustomed had the workers in the "dead gangs," as they were named, become to their gruesome task that they even laughed and joked when laying away the corpses.

Special attention was given the wounded. Physicians were on duty all the time, some of them not having been to bed since Friday night longer than an hour at a time. Victims not badly hurt were put aside for those suffering and actually requiring the services of surgeons. There were thousands of them. There were few in Galveston who did not bear the marks of wounds of some sort.

SOURCES

Chute, Arthur Hunt. "The Last Pirate." In *Great Pirate Stories*, edited by Joseph Lewis French. New York: Tudor, 1922.

Collins, Daniel. "Beheaded." In *Narrative of the Shipwreck of the Brig* Betsey. Wiscasset, ME: John Dorr, 1825.

Cook, D. J. "A Lynching in Golden." In *Hands Up; or, Thirty-Five Years of Detective Life in the Mountains and on the Plains*, compiled by John W. Cook. Denver: W. F. Robinson Printing, 1897.

Coulter, John. "Horror in Galveston." In *The Complete Story of the Galveston Horror*. New York: United Publishers of America, 1900.

Ellis, Edward S. "Kit Carson on the Frontier." In *The Life of Kit Carson*. Philadelphia: J. Wannamaker, 1889.

Fox, Richard. "Deluge: Heroics in the Johnstown Flood." In *The Disaster Which Eclipsed History*. New York: Richard Fox, 1898.

Greely, A. W. "Frozen." In *True Tales of Arctic Heroism in the New World*. New York: Charles Scribner's Sons, 1912.

Hawks, Francis L. "Daniel Boone, Captive." In *The Adventures of Daniel Boone, The Kentucky Rifleman*. New York: D. Appleton, 1850.

Holland, Rupert S. "How the *Merrimac* Was Sunk in Cuba." In *Historic Adventures: Tales from American History*. Philadelphia: George W. Jacobs, 1913.

Huntington, George. "An Ill-Fated Robbery." In *Robber and Hero*. Northfield, MN: Christian Way, 1895.

LaGuardia-Kotite, Martha. "The Falls." In *So Others May Live: Coast Guard Rescue Swimmers, Saving Lives, Defying Death*. Guilford, CT: Lyons Press, 2006.

Leech, Samuel Vanderlip. "Eyewitness: The Raid at Harpers Ferry." In *The Raid of John Brown at Harpers Ferry*. Washington, DC: DeSoto, 1909.

McGlashan, C. F. *History of the Donner Party: A Tragedy of the Sierras*. Truckee, CA: Crowley and McGlashan, 1879.

Mills, Kathryn. "Superstorm: Inside Hurricane Sandy." In *Superstorm: Nine Days inside Hurricane Sandy*. New York: Dutton/Penguin, 2014.

Moran, Frank E. "The Tunnel at Libby Prison: A Civil War Escape." In *Famous Adventures and Prison Escapes of the Civil War*. New York: Century, 1913.

Taylor, Thomas E. "Running the Blockade: The *Banshee*'s First Battle." In *A Personal Narrative of Adventures, Risks, and Escapes during the American Civil War*. London: John Murray, 1896.

Young, Samuel Hall. "The Nome Stampede." In *Adventures in Alaska*. New York: Fleming H. Revell, 1919.